Top Tips
from Consumer Reports

Top Tips from Consumer Reports

How to Do Things Better, Faster, Cheaper

by the Editors of Consumer Reports Books

Little, Brown and Company • Boston • Toronto

This special Little, Brown edition of *Top Tips from Consumer Reports* has been published by permission of Consumers Union of United States, Inc.

RRD

Published simultaneously in Canada
by Little, Brown & Company (Canada) Limited

Printed in the United States of America

Library of Congress Catalog Card No. 83-080602

Top Tips from Consumer Reports is a Consumer Reports Book published by Consumers Union, the nonprofit organization that publishes Consumer Reports, the monthly magazine of test reports, product Ratings, and buying guidance. Established in 1936, Consumers Union is chartered under the Not-For-Profit Corporation Law of the State of New York.

The purposes of Consumers Union, as stated in its charter, are to provide consumers with information and counsel on consumer goods and services, to give information on all matters relating to the expenditure of the family income, and to initiate and to cooperate with individual and group efforts seeking to create and maintain decent living standards.

Consumers Union derives its income solely from the sale of Consumer Reports and other publications. In addition, expenses of occasional public service efforts may be met, in part, by noncommercial contributions, grants, and fees. Consumers Union accepts no advertising or product samples and is not beholden in any way to any commercial interest. Its Ratings and reports are solely for the use of the readers of its publications. Neither the Ratings nor the reports nor any Consumers Union publication, including this book, may be used in advertising or for any commercial purpose. Consumers Union will take all steps open to it to prevent such uses of its material, its name, or the name of Consumer Reports.

Top Tips

from Consumer Reports

Contents

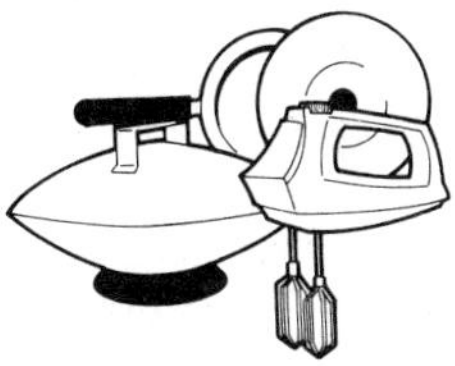

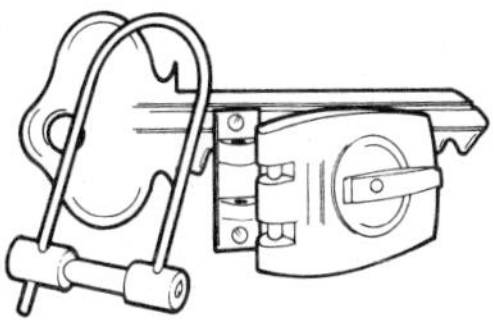

Introduction

Top Tips from Consumer Reports can help you shop for a car, decide whether to buy your own phone, bake a better cake, get rid of acne, bar burglars from your windows. It gives you advice on buying a variety of products for your home, for your health, and for your leisure time. With this book, you can find out how best to wash, clean, and polish a lot of things—and save money and time in the process. You'll also get tips on using your appliances efficiently, saving fuel when you drive, estimating your retirement income needs, painting your house, and making your own tape recordings.

If you know Consumer Reports Books, this title may strike you as different from others we've published. And you'd be right. *Top Tips from Consumer Reports* is a first for us.

Top Tips is not on a single subject such as *Consumer Reports Guide to Used Cars,* or on closely related topics such as *The Medicine Show*. Instead, this book covers eleven different categories. Check the table of contents for the categories, but scan the index to find out what the book is all about. You'll see there are more than 500 major entries for the eleven categories—a lot of information on a wide range of subjects.

Top Tips is a book you can use in several different ways. Read the entire book—or a complete section—from beginning to end, if you like. Or you can pick up the book and browse through it. We believe you'll find suggestions that intrigue you and ideas you'll want to try. Or go to the subjects that interest you—a recipe for dinner, advice on microwave ovens, help with foot problems. Look in the book if your car won't start. Turn immediately to batteries and then maybe to the clear directions for using booster cables to jump-start. (Need to buy booster cables? That's covered too.)

In *Top Tips,* we say everything we want to say on a particular topic in a page and a half or two pages, rarely requiring more space than that. Sometimes it takes only a few sentences to make our point. This is not a book that delves into a subject in depth. (If you want more information on something we cover, we refer you to Consumer Reports magazine.)

Preparing this book. Consumer Reports is the source for this book. In fact, if you were to read completely and carefully every issue of the magazine for the last several years you would in time find every topic that appears in *Top Tips*. But now you don't have to bother—we've done it for you. A great number of the top tips come from recent issues of Consumer Reports—but we think you get them better, faster, and cheaper in *Top Tips* than if you had to search through all those pages of the magazine.

Distilling tip-length topics from more extensive presentations in the pages of Consumer Reports magazine required the combined efforts of many Consumers Union staff members. Writing tips so they would be easy to read and simple to follow was a collaborative process among book editors, magazine editors, and CU's technical staff.

Engineers, chemists, food technologists, and other Technical Department specialists reviewed all items involving the testing of products, buying advice, and suggestions about using a product. Editors who prepare reports for the magazine in such areas as health and medicine, financial matters, and related kinds of consumer services reviewed the tips taken from their reports. As a result of this review procedure, before we went to press we made sure that every item included in the book reflects our current advice to consumers.

Using this book. To help make *Top Tips* easy to use, we asked our indexers to create the most complete and helpful index possible. And we ask you to turn to the index more than you may be accustomed to. You'll find there a good overview of the topics included in the book.

Also to help you locate information, we've grouped topics within the eleven categories alphabetically. At the bottom of each page you'll find the category title and the subject covered on that page. (There may be other subjects on the same page. That's why you need to refer to the index for the full scope of the book.)

We think you'll find *Top Tips from Consumer Reports* informative and easy to use. If you have any suggestions for the next edition, please send them to us at Consumer Reports Books, 256 Washington Street, Mount Vernon, New York 10550.

The Editors of Consumer Reports Books

Appliances

Choosing an air conditioner

Air conditioners are unquestionably effective appliances. They cool the air and dehumidify it. But they're also expensive to buy and run.

Energy efficiency. You can reduce the impact of an air conditioner on your electricity bill by choosing your unit with energy efficiency in mind.

Check the energy efficiency ratio of the unit. (The EER is a measure of how effectively an air conditioner uses electricity.) Choose a unit with an EER of 7.5 or higher.

Automatic setting. At an air conditioner's regular setting, the fan runs all the time to keep air moving through the unit. That way, the thermostat keeps in touch with changes in room temperature. Many models also have an "automatic" or "energy-saver" setting that turns the fan off whenever the air conditioner isn't actively cooling. But that doesn't mean performance must suffer with an automatic setting. In some models we tested, temperature variations were less on an automatic setting than on a regular setting.

■ Using an automatic setting can chop a few dollars off your electric bill over a cooling season.

■ The automatic setting should also help keep room humidity down. (Moving air would otherwise pick up moisture that had condensed on the cooling coils.)

Slide-out chassis. Most air conditioners are designed for double-hung windows. Some models have a slide-out chassis that eases the tasks of installation and maintenance. The slide-out model also allows through-the-wall installation.

Settings. "Hi-cool" and "lo-cool" settings merely change the fan's speed, with some effect on dehumidifying but not on actual cooling.

■ A high speed can provide a little extra breeze, while a low speed reduces noise and energy consumption.

■ A number of machines have "fan-only" settings that let you stir up room air a bit without cooling it. You can get the same effect on units that lack the setting by turning the thermostat to its warmest position.

Noise. Before you buy a unit, try to check the noise levels at both high and low settings. A raucous machine could be especially hard to live with in a bedroom or a study. Outdoors, an air conditioner's noise could be annoying near a patio or a neighboring bedroom.

Installing an air conditioner

If winters are cold where you live, you'll get plenty of practice installing your air conditioner—if you follow our advice. To keep heating costs down, we suggest that you remove your air conditioner each autumn, put up a storm window in its place, and then restore the unit in summer.

An air conditioner sitting in a window can cost you a lot of heat in winter. The mounting panels at the machine's sides are poor insulators and are apt to leak heat. Cold air can also blow right through the machine.

Here's what our engineers suggest about installing an air conditioner.

Get help. It would be wise to enlist the aid of a helper when you install—or remove—an air conditioner. Most of the models we tested were bulky awkward heavyweights.

Positioning. Mount the air conditioner so that it slopes slightly toward the outside. That will keep rain or condensate from dripping back into your room. A slope of ¼ inch per foot is about right. Most models have a leveling adjustment to help you establish the proper slope.

Electrical safety. It's important to mount—and use—an air conditioner with the following safety considerations in mind.

■ Be sure the circuit's wall outlet is grounded.

■ If you must use an extension cord, use only a heavy-duty one sold specifically for air conditioners.

■ Don't use a toaster, iron, or other high-current appliance on the same circuit while the air conditioner is running.

Using an air conditioner

Here are a few suggestions from our engineers about using your air conditioner.

Louvers. Air conditioners have several sets of louvers to control side-to-side and up-and-down airflow. With most of the models we tested, we got commendably even air distribution when we pointed one set of vertical louvers left and the other set right, and pointed the horizontal ones a bit upward.

Setting. Here's what to do to find the dial settings you like.

■ Set the dial at its coolest position.

■ When the room is cool enough, turn the dial until the compressor cycles off. That will be your setting for daytime use. If the unit is in a bedroom, you may want to repeat the process at night to find the right temperature for sleeping.

■ Once you've found the settings you prefer, note where they are on the dial. You can then shift between them readily.

Using an automatic setting. With most models that have an "automatic" or "energy-saver" setting, you may have to get used to dealing with a few extra problems.

■ All running noise stops when the fan cycles off. Sleepers may awaken when the fan goes on again.

■ In the morning, if the unit is silent, you may forget that it's on, leaving it to cool an empty room all day.

Exhaust/ventilate settings. All the units we tested could be set to "exhaust," or remove, room air. A few could also "ventilate," or draw in, air from outside.

■ Such provisions are only minimally effective, at best. They won't clear a room of cigarette smoke very fast, for example.

■ Don't use these settings when you need maximum cooling. The warm air they bring in imposes an extra load on the machine and your electricity bill.

Filter-cleaning. A plastic-foam filter inside the unit retains dust from air moving through the unit. The filter needs only a rinse now and then. To save a mess at the sink, you can use a vacuum cleaner instead.

On one model we tested, you could simply slide the filter out, making it especially easy to check and clean. Most other models make you open or remove the front panel to get at the filter.

An air conditioner that heats too

It's possible to buy an air conditioner that can be operated in "reverse" to heat your room. Should you consider buying a reverse-cycle air conditioner? Yes, if you live in an area where winters are mild (usually not below 35°F or so) and summers are hot enough to justify air conditioning. Ideally, use a reverse-cycle unit in a space that has no other heating and that you expect to cool in the summer.

How reverse-cycle units work. An air conditioner cools your room by heating the great outdoors—it extracts heat from air and pumps it outside. A reverse-cycle air conditioner can pump heat indoors as well as out.

If may be hard to think of chilly air as containing heat, but it does. That heat is a form of energy, there to be extracted by the air conditioner.

In its heating role, a reverse-cycle air conditioner is a space heater. Like any space heater, it allows you to lower the thermostat setting of a central heating system while keeping the room you're in at a comfortable level.

Cost of operating. As the outside temperature drops, it becomes harder for a reverse-cycle air conditioner to extract energy from the air. So its capacity and efficiency are reduced. Some manufacturers say their reverse-cycle units should not be run when outside air is colder than 45°F. The saving on your heating bill would be modest at best.

■ A typical electric space heater, when set at high, uses some 1,500 watts to produce about 5,000 British thermal units per hour. At the national average electricity rate of 6.75 cents per kilowatt-hour, the space heater would cost about $20 to operate to produce 1 million Btu. (That's about 200 hours of operation.)

■ The reverse-cycle unit we tested would give you the same amount of heat for a little more than $7, provided the outdoor temperature was no lower than 45°.

■ The reverse-cycle air conditioner would provide the greatest saving in homes with conventional electric heating. The $7 worth of heat provided by the unit would cost nearly $20 if supplied by the central heater.

■ Homes with oil heat would also see a saving. The furnace would use about $11 worth of oil (at $1.23 per gallon) to provide the same amount of heat that the reverse-cycle unit could supply for $7.

■ With gas heat, there would be little if any saving. Where gas is billed at 54.8 cents per therm, a gas furnace would use about $7 in fuel to provide the same amount of heat as the reverse-cycle air conditioner.

Maintaining an air conditioner

If you pay a little attention to maintenance of your air conditioner, it will repay you with longer life and more efficient operation.

■ The fan motor on some models requires oiling periodically, perhaps once a season. (If your unit has a slide-out chassis, the job will be easier to do.)

■ In some areas, the condenser fins that face outdoors may clog with dust and grime. Clean them each summer when you put the air conditioner back in the window. The dusting brush of a canister vacuum serves well. Use the vacuum as a blower for hard-to-reach spots.

Why buy a ceiling fan?

With their slow-moving blades, ceiling fans can do an effective job of stirring the air in a room. Some models can also add a certain amount of charm to a room.

Advantages. People who use a ceiling fan know that it isn't just for show. It's an effective way to make a room feel cooler. A fan can churn up a storm during the heat of the afternoon and stir up a gentle breeze in the quiet of the evening. And it cools safely, without sound and fury, at a reasonable operating cost.

■ Large blades allow a ceiling fan to move lots of air while running sedately and quietly.

■ A properly installed ceiling fan is out of reach—safer if children are around.

■ Operating costs for the fans we tested varied considerably. Even the most profligate model in our test group, however, would cost about 9.5 cents for eight hours of operation at the national average electricity rate of 6.75 cents per kilowatt-hour. At its lowest speed, the same model's operating costs would add up to a bit more than 2.5 cents for eight hours of use.

Limitations. A ceiling fan is not cheap. Nor can it substitute for a portable box fan or an air conditioner.

■ You'll probably pay dearly to get that look of Bourbon Street or Casablanca in your house. Most of the ceiling fans we tested were $250 and up. Only three were less than $200.

■ Unlike a portable fan, a ceiling fan can't bring cool outside air into a room. A ceiling fan can only circulate the air that's already there. You can't move a ceiling fan from room to room as you can a box fan. And you can't expect a fan—either one on the ceiling or one on the floor—to dehumidify. That's an air conditioner's job.

Choosing a ceiling fan

Based on our tests, you needn't be overly concerned about how powerful a ceiling fan is. Any one of the fans we tested would move enough air to keep you cool in a moderate-sized room in most parts of the country.

When you shop for a fan, you should consider these points.

Blade size. The size of a fan is defined by the diameter, or sweep, of its blades.

■ The most common size is 52 inches.

■ A 36- or 38-inch model would be best where space is tight—in a room up to about 10 by 10 feet or in an alcove.

Noise. Some models we tested were virtually silent when running at their lowest speed. Others made quite a bit of noise. Check a fan you're considering for noise levels at both low and high speeds.

■ A low-volume noise can be annoying in an otherwise quiet setting.

■ A fan that suffers from a particular type of noise at low speed may not sound worse—or even as bad—at high speed. The humming that some fans produce at low speed comes from the speed control components, which are essentially inactive at maximum speed. So a model that hums at low speed could be quiet at high speed.

Speed controls. All the fans we tested gave you a choice of at least two speeds. Some models also have a control that provides three speeds or infinitely variable speed.

■ If you want the look and feel of the old-fashioned ceiling fan and the lazy way in which its blades sweep by, look for a minimum speed of about 50 revolutions per minute or less.

■ Some models we tested had a screw that allowed you to adjust the lowest speed. When making that adjustment, don't set the speed too low or the fan may not start.

Optional light kits. These attach to the the fan's motor housing and are generally available with most ceiling fans. When we checked prices for the kits, they ranged from $10 to $75 extra.

Installing a ceiling fan

To go by the book, you should hire an electrician to install a ceiling fan. But the instructions that came with the fans we tested were obviously aimed at do-it-yourselfers.

Assembling. Ceiling fans are shipped disassembled. Putting one together isn't a difficult job—if you pay attention to detail.

■ Before you begin, make sure that the wooden blades aren't warped. If they are, they won't run true. Putting things right means replacement with a complete set of four matched blades (something your dealer should do at no charge).

■ Check the mounting holes on the blades. In our tests, two brands had blades with mislocated mounting holes. We had to enlarge some holes to attach the blades.

Installation. Here are two ways to install a ceiling fan.

■ One easy method is to put up the fan in place of an existing light fixture, which has the wiring already in place.

■ An alternative would be to use a decorative chain to camouflage a wire you draped along the ceiling and down to a wall outlet.

■ With either method, be sure that the mounting hardware holding the fan is secure. The hardware should be able to support at least 45 to 50 pounds.

Safe use of a ceiling fan

When installing and using a ceiling fan, you should keep in mind the following cautions.

■ Don't install a ceiling fan unless the ceiling is at least 8 feet high. For reasonably safe clearance, the blades of the fan should be at least 7 feet from the floor. If you use an optional light kit that attaches to the fan's motor housing, you reduce head clearance under the fan.

■ Even with 7 feet of head space, take special care if you install a fan in areas of the house where you might raise your arms while getting dressed or where you might playfully raise a child overhead.

■ Watch out for curtains that could get tangled in the blades.

Ceiling fan: An advantage in winter?

Many manufacturers claim that a ceiling fan can blow hot as well as cold—that it can save energy in wintertime. Based on our experience, we'd say that a ceiling fan isn't much of an advantage in the winter, under most circumstances.

Here's what we found when we tested fans for winter use in a large room with a 10-foot ceiling. No matter whether a fan was running in forward or reverse, and no matter what the room temperature was, we always felt cooler when the fan was running than when it was off.

A subsequent check of temperature at various levels showed why: The air temperature at the ceiling was only a few degrees warmer than at the floor. The cooling effect of the air movement outweighed any improvement in temperature distribution, even when the fan ran at low speed.

In a few very special situations, it's possible there might be a saving in a room with a very high ceiling or one with a localized heat source such as a wood stove.

Do you need a dehumidifier?

Before investing in a dehumidifier—and paying higher electricity bills—try to solve your problems by improving ventilation and taking other measures to remove moisture from the air.

■ Installing ventilating fans in the bathroom and kitchen can reduce humidity.

■ Adding a vent or louvered doors to storerooms or closets may help prevent mildew from growing in those areas.

■ A poorly vented clothes dryer is another source of excess humidity that's easily corrected.

■ One cause of a damp basement is condensation of warm humid air as it enters the relatively cool basement. Improving the basement's ventilation by installing a fan or by opening doors and windows can reduce condensation.

■ If dripping cold-water pipes are a problem, wrap them with insulation to stop them from sweating.

■ If moisture in the ground is a cause of dampness in the house, it's a condition that's not always easy to fix. If your house has a crawl space or basement with a dirt floor, covering it with plastic sheeting (or installing insulation with a vapor barrier) may help keep moisture out of the house.

■ Leaking or major seepage through basement walls calls for repairing the walls or improving the drainage around the house.

Choosing a dehumidifier

If you've found no way to prevent dampness, mildew, and other unpleasant symptoms of high humidity, you'll probably need to shop for a dehumidifier. Our advice, based on the tests we ran, is to buy a large dehumidifier, regardless of the size or the dampness of the room.

■ Our tests revealed that dehumidifiers with a capacity of 25 or 30 pints generally used significantly less electricity to extract a pint of water from the air than smaller models.

■ Even if a room is small and not very damp, a large dehumidifier would still be cheaper to operate than a smaller, less efficient model.

■ A large dehumidifier would reduce humidity in a room faster than a smaller model and would run less often to maintain the level of humidity.

■ Given a choice, select a 30-pint model over a 25-pint one. A 30-pint model would have to operate less to remove water from the air, thus making noise less often and putting less wear on the compressor. And the extra capacity of a 30-pint model often comes at no extra cost.

■ Many of the large, more efficient models cost no more to buy than the smaller, less efficient models.

■ If you can hold off until the end of the summer, which is the end of the dehumidifying season in most parts of the country, do your shopping then. You're likely to find the highest discounts at that time.

Choosing and using a dishwasher

Which features make sense on a built-in dishwasher? Based on the designs we tested, the guidelines below reflect the recommendations of our engineers.

A pots-and-pans cycle imposes extra costs for meager benefits. Such cycles don't make the washing action more vigorous; they merely extend wash time. (Some provide extra water or extra heat for the wash water, too.)

■ The regular cycle on the machines we tested handled the challenge of cleaning messy casseroles almost as well as the special cycle. Our conclusion: If a pot won't come clean in a regular cycle, it probably won't come clean at all.

■ Using a pots-and-pans cycle extends operating time by at least one-quarter to one-half hour. The corresponding increase in electricity consumption would range from about 0.2 to 1.0 kilowatt-hour. The machine's total electricity consumption could easily be twice that of a normal cycle.

■ Your wisest course might be to soak your pans first, then wash them along with the dishes. Select no-heat drying, which we recommend for saving energy with every load (see below). In this instance, it will also avoid baking on surviving residue.

A rinse-and-hold cycle rinses the dishes of the worst dirt, then holds them until you put in enough other dishes to justify running an entire wash cycle.

■ We doubt whether this feature is necssary to use, even for small families that accumulate dishes slowly.

■ Most of the machines we tested had little trouble with heavily soiled loads that had been left standing unrinsed overnight.

A china/crystal cycle on most machines is intended for fine or delicate items. It's usually only an unheated or shortened version of the normal cycle. Think twice about using even the gentlest of such cycles on delicate items you care about.

■ Glassware may topple and break.

■ Jiggle induced by the water's action may cause tiny scratches whose cumulative effect would be noticeable. Such scratches can also provide starting points for cracks.

■ The rather harsh chemicals in detergents used for machine washing may attack gold trim and similar decorative patterns.

Short wash lets you bypass the first one or two parts of the machine's regular cycle to handle loads that are only slightly soiled. You thereby make a small saving in time, water, electricity, and detergent.

No-heat drying can save you some energy, but your dishes may have to sit overnight to dry completely. If you want quicker results, open the door a bit after the last rinse. The load should then dry in an hour or two unless the weather is muggy.

On a regular cycle, with heated drying, most of the dishwashers we tested used 0.6 to 0.7 kilowatt-hour of electricity. No-heat drying typically cut that use by 0.2 to 0.3 kwh, or about one-third. Over the course of a year, that can save you some money.

Gas or electric dryer: Which to buy?

If natural gas is available to your home, it's generally in your interest to buy a gas dryer. But no matter which type you choose, don't buy a dryer with more features than you need.

Gas dryers tend to cost from $30 to $50 more than their electric counterparts (they're somewhat more complicated machines). But that difference in purchase price can easily be made up in energy saving in the first year of use.

The gas dryers we tested have been generally faster than the electric dryers, presumably because the gas models produced more heat. Most of the gas units we tested were rated at 22,000 British thermal units per hour. Electric units were typically rated at 5.5 kilowatts, the equivalent of almost 19,000 Btu/hr.

The higher energy cost of gas models, however, rarely exacts a penalty in higher operating cost. Because natural gas in most areas tends to be cheaper than electricity, a gas dryer usually costs less to run.

Even at a high natural gas rate of 70 cents per therm (approximately 100 cubic feet), operating costs for the gas dryers we tested ranged from $27 to $30 for 400 drying loads, about a year's worth of laundry. (That cost included the electricity a gas dryer uses to power the motor that drives the drum and exhaust fan.) The comparable range for electric models, at the high rate of 10 cents per kilowatt-hour, ranged from $92 to $104.

As a rule, gas and electric dryers cost the same to run when the cost per therm of gas is about twenty-five times the cost per kilowatt-hour. If the cost per therm is less than that, gas is cheaper; if it's more, electricity is cheaper.

Efficient use of a clothes dryer

You can contribute to the conservation of energy by the way you use a clothes dryer.

■ Always try to run the dryer as fully loaded as possible—but don't exceed its rated capacity.

■ If possible, sort the laundry by fabric type so you can dry all similar fabrics on the same cycle.

■ Clean the lint trap after each load.

■ Unless you're proficient in estimating the time needed for a particular load, use an automatic cycle. It will turn the dryer off when the clothes are dry.

Permanent-press in the dryer

Here are some pointers for drying permanent-press items in a clothes dryer.

■ Dryer manufacturers usually recommend a medium temperature setting on machines with three or four settings, a high temperature on machines with two settings.

■ Permanent-press items should be cooled as they're tumbling to prevent wrinkles from resetting. If your model has only two temperature settings, use the permanent-press cycle. It differs from the regular-load cycle only in the length of the cool-down period—ten minutes, typically, instead of five.

■ If your dryer provides a setting for added tumble time (up to 2½ hours on some models), the duration of the automatic cool-down period can be extended, if necessary. The extra no-heat tumbling ensures that clothes are thoroughly cooled and not resting rumpled in case you're not immediately ready to remove them from the drum. Models with long added tumble times don't keep the drum moving continuously; the drum turns for about ten seconds every five minutes. Even so, this is wasteful of energy and should not be used routinely.

Cotton in the dryer

Almost any dryer will do an adequate job with cotton—one of the most common, or "regular," fabrics.

Things made of cotton can generally be dried without problems in a dryer. They can tolerate high heat and are largely indifferent to the way they're brought back to room temperature. If after drying the texture seems harsh, it's probably due to the absence of a "softening" agent in the wash water. Adding a fabric softener when you wash cotton should take care of that.

Choosing a freezer: Chest or upright?

If you're buying a freezer, you have to choose between a chest and an upright model. The space you have available might well make that decision for you: Chest freezers take up considerably more floor space than uprights.

Chest freezers have some advantages, though they can be less convenient to use than uprights.

■ The chest freezers we tested proved to be slightly more energy-efficient than the uprights. The design of the chests help explain their slightly lower energy costs. When you open the lid of a chest freezer, cold air tends to stay put. But when you open the door of an upright, the colder air at the bottom spills out and warmer air moves in to take its place. The compressor in an upright has to run more often to keep the air cold.

■ Chest freezers can run for longer periods between defrostings than uprights.

■ Chest models provide fairly uniform cooling throughout the storage space.

■ Defrosting and draining a chest freezer can be a chore. An upright is fairly easy to defrost.

■ Searching through a chest full of frozen food to retrieve something can also be a chore. Food stored in a chest freezer does have a way of getting jumbled, in time. Shelves in an upright help keep food orderly, which makes it easier for you to get to the package you want.

■ The frost-free uprights we tested performed well, but they are the most expensive to buy and operate.

Setting up a new freezer

Here are a few simple steps you should take to get a new freezer ready for its first load of food.

■ Put the freezer in a dry, well-ventilated place that has a sturdy floor. Adjust the leveling legs on an upright so that it's slightly tilted—just enough to make the door close by itself. The corner pads of a chest freezer should sit squarely on the floor or on blocks of 2 × 4 lumber. Putting the freezer up on blocks will make it easier to drain the chest when you defrost it.

■ Check the door seal for tightness. The simplest check is to close the door over a dollar bill. If you don't feel some resistance when you pull out the bill, the seal isn't tight enough. Check for tightness at several points around the door. Correcting a loose seal on an upright is a job for a service technician. (These days, technicians may check a seal by putting a floodlight inside the freezer and watching for light leaks around the seal.)

■ You may be able to flex a chest freezer's lid enough to tighten the seal yourself. Push down on the corner near where the seal is loose while pushing up on the opposite corner.

■ Put a thermometer inside the freezer, in the middle of the freezer space. Leave it in place for at least a day before adjusting the freezer's thermostat.

■ When you load the freezer, you may have to allow an extra few inches at the back, top, or sides so that heat can dissipate from the freezer's condenser.

Defrosting a freezer

You'll need to defrost a manual-defrost freezer about twice a year—more often than that if you live in an especially warm and humid area or if you open the freezer often. Other things being equal, an upright will need defrosting more often than a chest.

■ Generally, when the frost is ¼- to ½-inch thick, it's time to defrost. A thick layer of ice increases operating costs, for the ice acts as insulation.

■ Defrost when your frozen-food supply is low. If you work quickly, you may be able to keep the food in the refrigerator temporarily (or outdoors on a cold winter day). Otherwise, pack the food in dry ice (see below).

■ Get rid of the frost by opening the freezer door and placing pans of hot water inside to thaw the frost. Keep the freezer door closed during defrosting.

■ Don't use knives or ice picks to hack away at the ice build-up. Models with an interior of plastic, painted aluminum, or porcelain-on-steel are more resistant to chipping and rusting than those with a painted steel interior.

When a freezer's not working

If you expect your freezer to be out of commission for more than half a day, do what you can to keep the food frozen.

■ Use dry ice if you can find it. Cover the food with cardboard, then don gloves and put chunks of dry ice on top of the cardboard.

■ If you can't get dry ice, leave the freezer closed and hope for the best.

If food thaws. Don't refreeze food that has thawed. It loses both in flavor and in texture. More important, food could spoil once it's thawed.

Most freezer manufacturers include a warranty that will pay about $100 to $200 for food lost if the freezer breaks down and causes the food to thaw.

Pros and cons of a microwave oven

A microwave oven can be an expensive purchase: Its price puts it into the major appliance category. Before you buy a microwave oven, you should carefully weigh the pros and cons of adding this costly appliance to your kitchen counter top. (See below for our comments on safety.)

Fixing food. As we note in more detail below, there are some foods that the microwave oven prepares quite well. With others, the quality is less successful.

■ Microwave ovens really don't do justice to meat, for example. And making full-course meals from scratch requires a good deal of effort.

■ If you plan to use the oven for convenience foods or for quick workday meals, you'll probably be happy with it.

Frozen food. In some ways a microwave oven teams well with frozen food.

■ Frozen breads and cakes defrost in just a minute or two.

■ Some frozen foods can be tricky to cook in a microwave oven. Results were not always perfect with moist frozen foods, such as casseroles and stews. Instructions say to break up these foods with a spoon a number of times during the defrost cycle. Though we tried that, the exterior portion of a deep bowl of stew, for example, began to cook while the interior remained frozen solid. Freezing stews and casseroles in shallow containers would make the defrosting chore easier and faster.

Saving energy. If you buy a microwave oven to save energy, you could be disappointed. How much energy you'll really save depends on how often you use the oven and on how you use it.

■ Because a microwave oven cooks foods faster and more directly than your conventional oven, it does save some energy in cooking. But the cost of the energy you use for cooking is only a small part of your total energy bill.

■ What's more, defrosting in the microwave oven uses energy that isn't used in ordinary defrosting in the refrigerator.

Saving on cleanup. If kitchen cleanup is the bane of your existence, a microwave oven will suit you. Cleaning any part of a microwave oven is easy compared with cleaning a conventional oven. Food splatter doesn't bake on, for instance.

■ You can cook pudding in a glass bowl that goes right into the refrigerator. No gooey pan to clean and no sticky bottom.

■ Fixing a cup of tea in a microwave oven is the ultimate in convenience. You heat, brew, and drink with the same cup. (Just don't use a cup with gold trim.)

■ You can heat dinner right on your dinner plate, if you like. (But don't use a plate with metal trim.)

Making the adjustment. Microwave cooking is quite different from conventional cooking. Learning how to get the most out of a microwave oven is no small accomplishment.

■ Some dishes don't make sense to prepare in a microwave oven. For example, the moist foods that require constant stirring when cooked in a microwave are best done on the range top. One recipe for microwaved hollandaise sauce requires stirring every fifteen seconds. That's a lot of door opening and a lot of inconvenience.

■ It's a rare dish that you can simply place in a microwave oven and then forget about until it's evenly and perfectly cooked. Many dishes need stirring. Some need to be repositioned or rotated as they cook. Plastic wrap often has to be put on, or taken off.

■ Even in quick-defrosting by microwave there are some foods that require the same kind of attention as with conventional cooking. You can't break up pork chops, for example, to hasten their defrosting. You have to turn such foods over now and then as they cook.

Learning how. Consumer Reports readers who responded to our questionnaire on microwave ovens spoke strongly in favor of taking cooking lessons to learn how to use a microwave oven.

■ Adult education programs and country extension services usually offer such courses for a modest fee.

■ Manufacturers offer courses, too. Their lessons are generally free.

Microwaved food: Dishes we disliked

No matter how fast or how convenient microwave cooking is, speed and ease are meaningless if you don't like the food. So we cooked some typical foods in microwave ovens and judged the results. We found that some dishes would have tasted better or been easier to prepare with a conventional oven.

Foods that don't brown. Overall, we'd say that the biggest drawback to microwave cooking is the lack of browning.

■ We microwaved several rolled roasts, striving for rare. They came out juicy and tender, but the lack of a crisp dark-brown outside was a disappointment. And we were unable to make a rich brown gravy out of the drippings. In our opinion, microwave cooking is no way to treat a $15 roast—cook it in a conventional oven instead.

■ If you like chicken with crisp brown skin, roast your bird in a conventional oven. The unstuffed roasters we microwaved all tasted very good. The meat was tender and juicy. But the yellowy cooked fat was most unappetizing.

■ Our microwaved hamburgers were a failure. They emerged from the oven gray-brown and oozing. We missed the crisp brown outside, and we didn't like the steam-table taste.

■ The microwaved quiche we prepared looked pale and wan. But its flavor and texture were good.

Combination dishes. Not all one-dish meals can be cooked to perfection in a microwave oven.

■ When we tried to do justice to a TV dinner, the results were disappointing. The vegetables cooked before the meat. We think you can do much better with a regular oven.

■ Leftover dinners of meat, potatoes, and vegetables, all cooked together, were judged fair in our tests. One part of the dinner heated before the others. Putting each part in the oven in order of their heating requirements is a bother, but it would work better.

Cooking entire meals. Microwave cookbooks give directions for cooking entire meals, all at once. We tried it. It didn't work too well.

■ All the foods had to be fully assembled before cooking began. That required about an hour.

■ Cooking took less than an hour, but that didn't mean there was a minute to sit back and relax or even start setting the dinner table. The food in the oven required constant attention for the entire cooking period.

■ We think there's less wear and tear on the cook if the food is done separately and sequentially.

Microwaved food: Dishes we liked

You've heard the claims. A microwave oven is great for fast meals. Our tests showed that certain dishes do very well indeed in a microwave oven.

■ Microwaved vegetables came out most successfully of all the dishes we tried. Best of those we prepared were brussels sprouts; they were a bright appetizing green—flavorful, too. Corn on the cob cooked in the husk tasted cornier than usual. But the kernels weren't as crunchy as they would be if the corn had been boiled.

■ A baked potato can cook in record time in a microwave oven. But microwave-baked potatoes may not be the kind you're accustomed to. With those we cooked, the texture of the skin was softer than that of a regular baked potato—more like the skin on a potato that has been baked in foil.

■ Stew is a main dish that comes out nicely in a microwave oven. Our recipe didn't require braising the meat. All we had to do was put meat, tomatoes, and seasoning into a casserole dish and cook it for forty-five minutes. Then the vegetables went in. Naturally, the meat wasn't a braised brown—but in our stew that was acceptable. The tomatoes gave some color. All the ingredients cooked to an appropriate degree of doneness, and the flavors blended nicely.

■ Microwaves work well with liquids. If you're making a pudding or warming some soup, the results should be fine—though you have to stir a thick liquid several times during cooking so it heats uniformly. We stirred a batch of vanilla pudding twice during its six-minute cooking time. It came out smooth, creamy, and tasty.

Choosing and using a microwave oven

Based on tests of microwave ovens, our engineers suggest the following points to consider in buying a microwave oven and using it effectively once installed.

What features? Very few frills are necessary to do the things a microwave oven does well.

■ Because most foods are cooked on a full-power setting, having a choice of ten settings may just complicate things. In fact, as we see it, a microwave oven can operate quite satisfactorily with only four settings: full power, three-quarter power, half power, and a low setting mostly for defrosting.

■ Because a microwave oven doesn't prepare meats to their best advantage, you may not want to cook large cuts of meat in it. So you may not need a microwave oven that comes with a temperature probe.

■ If you plan to cook roasts in a microwave oven, however, and have a unit with a probe, you should be wary of overcooking a roast. Set the probe's desired temperature 10 to 20 degrees lower than you would if you were cooking in a conventional oven. (The temperature of a microwaved roast will rise an extra 10, 20, or even 30 degrees during several minutes of standing.) When the oven signals that the roast is done, take the roast out and insert a meat thermometer. When the meat reaches the desired temperature, carve.

■ The ovens with a turntable were the best in our tests (and Consumer Reports readers who responded to our survey liked them best). But even they did only a fair job of cooking evenly. To obtain an evenly cooked casserole, say, it would still be wise to stir the food during cooking.

■ A start button is a good idea on a microwave oven. It means you must make some effort to operate the oven. Without the button, accidental operation is more likely to occur. Running an empty oven can damage it. Some manufacturers, in fact, recommend leaving a glass of water in the oven at all times to prevent that.

Installation and maintenance. As counter-top appliances go, microwave ovens are large. How best to install them needs careful consideration.

■ Some can be built in, with a special kit. A convenient place in many kitchens would be above the conventional built-in range. But some of our readers have reported breakdowns that, according to their service technicians, were related to heat and humidity generated by the regular oven below the microwave.

■ Whether built in or not, a microwave oven must be positioned so the vents on the bottom, top, or back aren't blocked. A blower ventilates the oven and cools the working parts during use. If not properly cooled, the parts might fail prematurely.

■ Most manufacturers say that a microwave oven should have its own 15-amp circuit. If you have to run a light or two off the same circuit, choose a model with wattage on the low side. Don't try to use a microwave oven and a toaster at the same time. That will trip the circuit breaker or blow the fuse.

■ The door on most ovens opens to the left (a few have a swing-down door). Think about that when you're deciding where to put the oven.

■ We agree that it's a good idea to keep receipts for all servicing required after installation—even service covered by the warranty. If a problem is chronic or isn't satisfactorily resolved, the manufacturer may take that record into account after the warranty expires.

Microwave cookware: What to use

If you invest in a microwave oven, does that mean you'll have to buy an expensive array of cookware for your new kitchen appliance? Not necessarily. Our tests showed that you could manage quite nicely with equipment you may have on hand for conventional cooking.

Use what you have. You no doubt already have several items suitable for microwave cooking.

■ You probably own glass casseroles and baking dishes that you use in your conventional oven. These utensils can also be used in a microwave oven, unless they have a decorative metal trim.

■ Foods in plastic freezer containers can be defrosted in a microwave oven right in the container. Just remove the lid and make sure the food doesn't get too hot.

■ Paper towels are good for cooking bacon in a microwave oven. You can even heat food in straw serving baskets.

What not to use. If you really get into microwave cooking, you'll find yourself changing a lot of old habits. One of them is what you cook in.

■ Because metal reflects the microwave energy, metal pots and pans—and dishes with metal trim—don't work in a microwave oven. If you use a metal pot in a microwave oven, you'll have, at best, a mostly cold meal. At worst, you'll have a damaged oven.

■ Many ceramic dishes can be used successfully in a microwave oven, but be wary. Some ceramic dishes have metal in the glaze or impurities in the clay. Oven manufacturers usually describe a procedure you can follow to check the suitability of your particular dishware.

■ Don't use your good china in a microwave oven. Even though you can heat dinner directly in the dish in which it's served, it doesn't make sense to risk using fine china in this way.

Microwave cookware: What to buy

If you add a microwave oven to your kitchen equipment, will you need to buy additional cookware? Perhaps, if you do a lot of microwave cooking.Does that mean you should buy cookware marketed specifically for use in microwave ovens? It depends on the type of cooking you'll do in your new oven.

Cookware for roasting. Our survey of microwave oven owners indicated that many didn't like roasts made in microwave ovens. We didn't, either. If you come to the same conclusion, you won't have much use for a roasting rack.

■ If you want to try to roast occasionally, you can improvise a roasting rack with a dish and an inverted saucer or casserole lid.

■ If you decide to buy a roasting rack, select the biggest one that you can use in your oven. And, since you're spending the money, try to get a rack that also functions as a baking tray.

Cookware for browning. We don't advise buying cookware made specifically to brown food in a microwave oven.

■ A browning dish requires preheating in the microwave so it becomes hot enough to brown the food placed in it. Even so, we found the dishes beiged—not browned—foods such as pork chops.

■ Foods cooked on a browning dish need a lot of attention—turning and rotating—to cook evenly. Cooking something on a browning dish can take twice as long as cooking it in a plain dish. Hamburgers can actually take more time to cook on a browning dish than on a range.

■ Because of the bother involved in cooking with a browning dish and the mediocre results, we think it's a waste to buy one. Your range may still be best for cooking pork chops, hamburgers, fried eggs, and the like.

Other cookware. Some utensils made just for microwave use are silly. Don't buy a bacon rack, for instance. Use paper towels instead. They work fine.

■ If you need to supplement your supply of casseroles and baking dishes, go to hardware and variety stores. They still sell the same sort of glass cookware they've sold for years—for quite a bit less money than for many of the dishes specifically designed for microwave use. In one of those stores, you might find an "old-fashioned" glass dish—along the lines of the $3 *Pyrex* baking dish we found—that suits your needs as well as a more expensive microwave utensil.

■ If you do buy special cookware for your microwave oven, try to find utensils that will do double duty. Cookware that you can also use with a conventional oven and range is a better investment than cookware usable only in the microwave oven. Read instructions carefully before you buy.

Are microwave ovens safe?

Are microwave ovens safe? There's no way to answer that question with complete certainty. Safety is a matter of degree, however, and our engineers and medical consultants believe that microwave ovens can be operated with a minimum of risk from radiation if the following cautions are observed.

■ There are only a few tenuous findings suggesting that exposure to low-level microwave radiation (which might occur very close to an oven) may be harmful. And those studies have usually involved prolonged continuous exposure of small animals. If there is any hazard to people, it would help minimize the exposure if frequent approaches to the oven were avoided.

■ There's virtually no evidence to suggest that exposures for brief periods at a distance of about 4 feet could be harmful to health. Accordingly, keeping at least 4 feet from a working oven would be a sensible precaution (when not actually cooking or processing food in the oven).

Leakage. Try to operate and maintain the oven in a way that will minimize leakage.

■ It's particularly important that the oven door closes properly and that no damage occurs to the hinges, latches, sealing surfaces, or the door itself. If the door is a swing-down type, for example, don't use it as a loading shelf.

■ Make sure that no soil or food residue accumulates around the door seal.

■ Avoid placing any objects between the sealing surfaces.

■ Have the oven tested for leakage every few years. We suggest that any checking be done by an expert. The manufacturer's authorized service center should have testing equipment or may be able to advise you about whom to contact.

Safe cooking of pork requires special care. Uneven cooking—a characteristic of microwave ovens—might leave parts of a pork chop or roast insufficiently cooked. Although trichinosis is rarely encountered in the U.S. today, the U.S. Department of Agriculture recommends these precautions for cooking pork in a microwave oven.

■ Rotate the dish for more even cooking.

■ Allow the pork to stand in aluminum foil several minutes after cooking to ensure thorough heating.

■ Use a meat thermometer to make sure the pork has reached 170°F throughout.

Buy a microwave/convection oven?

Are microwave/convection ovens "the best of both worlds," as their manufacturers claim? It's true the combination ovens let you cook with microwaves, cook via convection, or combine the two methods. But these units may not be the answer to everyone's oven needs.

If you own a microwave oven, you can manage quite nicely without the combination oven. There's no reason for you to feel compelled to upgrade.

■ For the things a microwave oven does well—defrosting, warming, cooking vegetables—an ordinary microwave oven with a few power levels is all you need.

■ You already have a good adjunct to the conventional range oven and so there's no need to invest in the combination oven.

If you want to replace a range, don't buy a microwave/convection oven and expect it to equal the cooking performance of an ordinary range oven. The conventional oven is still a better all-around baker, a more even roaster, and a crisper broiler than the combination unit.

If you want to buy a microwave oven, carefully consider the pros and cons of the combination ovens first.

■ The things a microwave does poorly—browning and crisping, for example—are done better with the combination oven. And all the combinations we tested produced rich brown juices for gravy—something you could never achieve with an ordinary microwave oven.

■ When we used the ovens in the combination mode, cooking was slower than with straight microwave cooking. Still, the ovens were faster than a conventional oven for many tasks. We baked meatloaves in the tested ovens in one-half to two-thirds the time it took to bake them in the conventional electric range oven. But for some things, regular cooking was faster. It took less time to broil hamburgers in the conventional oven, for instance, than it did to cook them in the combination ovens.

■ A combination oven takes up lots of space—even more than an ordinary microwave—not only because it's large, but because it needs room at the top and back so the vents can work properly. Otherwise, some parts of the oven could overheat.

■ With combination ovens, you'll get the mess of a conventional oven because convection heat bakes on grease. We think it's best to clean combination ovens often with a soapy sponge so grease doesn't build up.

■ As with ordinary microwave ovens, the combinations are not big energy savers. It's unlikely that you could save enough energy with a microwave oven to justify its cost. The same is true of combination ovens. In fact, they sometimes use more electricity than a conventional oven.

Why buy a portable fan?

Portable box fans aren't glamorous, but they can ventilate a room effectively or whip up a breeze. They're easily carried to the kitchen by day and to the bedroom by night. While box fans can't cool on the grand scale as an air conditioner can, they're about the cheapest appliance around for summer cooling.

Ventilation. With a box fan, air movement can be used to ventilate.

■ Put a fan in or near a window to exhaust warm indoor air while drawing in cool air from outside through another window.

■ Used this way, a box fan can do the job of a window fan, pushing warm air from a room to make way for cool air from outdoors.

Circulation. Air movement can be used to circulate. Put a fan on a table or the floor to stir up the air and speed up evaporation from your skin.

Choosing a portable fan

Most portable fans offer few variations in controls and features. Legs, a handle, and a speed selector switch are all that most have—or need. That leaves only a few points to consider when shopping for a fan.

Size. The 20-inch model—that's measured by the sweep of the blade—is the most popular size portable fan. Any of the 20-inch fans we tested could handle ventilation or air circulation in a modest-sized room. Some of the fans were powerful enough to ventilate one floor of an average-sized house. Others could handle a small or medium-sized apartment.

Noise. At their speediest, when displacing the most air, all the fans we tested produced about the same mild roar.

At the lowest speed, when moving much less air, most fans were quiet. A few of the fans in our test group, however, were judged noisy even at their low speed.

Reversible motor. One fan we tested had a reversible motor, which allows you to shift from intake to exhaust without turning the entire fan around.

A reversible motor could be handy in a fan that's usually window-mounted, but it's not much of an advantage with a free-standing box fan.

Safe use of a portable fan

A portable fan can be hazardous—especially in a home with young children.

The whirling blades of a fan can be dangerous, but all fans have a grille that provides reasonable protection against accidental contact with the blades. No fan, however, can be considered safe for a small child's fingers. A fan set on a table or windowsill is likely to be less accessible to a small child than a fan set on the floor.

Danger when it's raining. We don't recommend operating a fan in or even near an open window when it's raining.

■ Current leakage and short circuits could result if rain gets into the motor of a window-mounted fan.

■ Some manufacturers take an even stricter line. Their instructions specifically warn against using the fan in a window, and some models are labeled or marked to that effect. Such a warning, in a readily visible location, is required for any fan that carries an Underwriters Laboratories listing without having met UL requirements for rain resistance.

Overload protection. A fan equipped with an automatically resetting overload protector can cope with a short-lived problem—temporary blockage of the airflow, say. But if the protector trips for no apparent reason, it's a sign that something is amiss internally.

■ At that point, have the fan repaired or replaced.

■ Always disconnect a fan before trying to clean or service it.

From portable to window fan

Some manufacturers of box fans provide inexpensive mounting kits to convert a portable fan into a relatively permanent window fan. Making that conversion would be a wise move if you're planning to use a box fan only for ventilation. As a window fan, the unit would be off the table or floor and out of the way. And the draft-tight seal provided by the mounting panels would permit good air intake.

Using a range

No matter whether you cook with electricity or gas, you can minimize energy use with a conventional oven by heeding some very simple reminders from our engineers.

■ Try to leave the oven alone while it's on. Money flies out the oven door whenever a curious cook opens it for a peek.

■ Keep the drip bowls on your stove as clean and brightly polished as possible. That will allow radiant energy to be reflected back for cooking.

■ With an electric model, match the size of your pots as exactly as possible to the element you're cooking on. The range performs best when cooking utensils are centered on the heat sources.

■ With an electric model, use flat-bottomed utensils on the cooktop. That way pots can make as complete contact as possible with the heating elements.

Cleaning an oven with heat

When you choose a range, you would do well to get one that has a "self-cleaning" feature. We're in favor of self-cleaning—a proven convenient process that might, in the long run, save you some money in fuel bills and expense for oven-cleaning products.

Because self-cleaning ranges are made to rid their ovens of slops and spills through the application of high heat, they usually have their broil and bake elements in a single heavily insulated chamber. It is the extra insulation that raises the possibility of long-term energy savings.

All the self-cleaners we tested—both gas and electric—heated to the level required to incinerate oven soil. And all reduced a test soil consisting of a tough baked-on coating of lard and processed cheese squares to an ashy residue that was easily wiped away. (However, cleaning by hand was needed around the oven door seals.)

We look with far less favor on "continuous-clean" ranges, which come with a special oven finish that, it's claimed, purge ranges of dirt during ordinary cooking. They have a porous interior finish that's supposed to let soils dissipate at normal baking temperatures.

■ We found that the special finish tends to absorb and hide soil rather than get rid of it.

■ Worse, that already dull finish can't be scoured or treated with chemical oven cleaners. So the remnants of bad spills may linger on for the life of the oven.

Which type of refrigerator/freezer?

Refrigerator/freezers come in various configurations. The most popular type by far is the top-freezer, but some do come with the freezer on the bottom and some with the freezer on the side.

Is either of these less-popular types a better bet than a top-freezer model? We think not. The cost factors make a top-freezer your best choice.

Where the other types shine. To be sure, the variant models do have their advantages.

■ Side-by-sides usually provide more freezer space than top freezers, as well as multiple freezer shelves arranged for orderly storage and easy access.

■ Bottom-freezers put the frequently used refrigerator section at eye level and the less-used freezer below—accessible but out of the way. Bottom-freezer models also offer a bit more freezer space in proportion to refrigerator space than do top-freezer models.

Where the other types falter. To get the advantages of a bottom model or a side-by-side, however, you pay and pay.

■ Both side-by-sides and bottom-freezers command a premium price.

■ What's more, side-by-sides have been less reliable than top freezers, according to past surveys of Consumer Reports readers.

■ Finally, you're not likely to find a bottom-freezer or a side-by-side that's highly energy-efficient. So the premium you pay for such models continues to grow from month to month as your electric bills come in.

Temperatures in a refrigerator/freezer

Temperatures within a refrigerator/freezer always represent a compromise.

■ We recommend setting the freezer compartment at 0°F because at that temperature food keeps its quality about twice as long as at 5°. Below 0°, the benefits are slight in relation to the extra energy used. You'll need to get a refrigerator/freezer thermometer to make accurate settings.

■ In the refrigerator compartment, we advise shooting for 37°F. That's close enough to the near-freezing temperatures at which fresh meats and some fruit and vegetables keep best. And it's not too cool to damage foods that do better above 40°.

Which type of vacuum should you buy?

Any vacuum should be able to tidy a carpet of dog hairs, the contents of a spilled bowl of peanuts, and the like. But not every type of vacuum is an equally effective choice for your home. Unfortunately, you're not likely to find one perfect vacuum. Here's why.

■ Uprights do well on carpets but are ungainly and ineffectual on bare floors and for above-the-floor cleaning. If your home has expanses of carpeting, an upright would be a wise choice.

■ Canisters that clean by suction alone excel at cleaning bare surfaces but do poorly with carpets. If your decor tends toward bare floors, you might prefer a suction-only canister.

■ Canisters with a "power nozzle" attempt to combine the best features of the other two designs. But mainly because a power-nozzle canister sacrifices convenience, it is not the perfect solution to all vacuuming needs.

■ Our engineers suggest that if you're considering getting an inexpensive power-nozzle model, you might do better to buy instead both an upright and a canister. You could purchase the two for very little more than what you'd have to pay for the power-nozzle alone.

Using a vacuum cleaner

A vacuum cleaner is a relatively convenient and safe appliance. But our engineers offer a few cautions.

■ In our tests, some power-nozzle canisters drew as much as 12 amps. Uprights and suction-only canisters drew moderate electric current, from 3 to 9 amps. Thus, with power nozzles, it's wise to turn off as many electrical devices as possible on the circuit powering the vacuum before beginning to clean.

■ Avoid using light-duty extension cords with any type of vacuum cleaner.

■ Don't use a vacuum cleaner outdoors.

■ Don't use a vacuum cleaner on wet surfaces.

Vacuum cleaner bags

In testing vacuum cleaners, our engineers noted that, by and large, the useful bag capacity of the uprights was a good deal greater than that of the canisters.

The uprights proved to be generally low in suction. But that fact did not affect performance on their primary job of carpet cleaning.

The suction created by a typical upright was scarcely affected by dirt buildup. With many of the canisters in our test group, however, suction started to drop rapidly after the bag had become about a quarter full. The decline in suction soon set a limit to the usable capacity of the bag.

Choosing a washing machine

Buying a new washing machine? Our engineers suggest a few guidelines for you to consider.

■ No need to go all out for features when buying a washing machine. Our view is that higher-priced machines are more complicated but not much more useful than machines in the moderate-priced range.

■ If you presoak a lot of things, a soak cycle is a help. Most soak cycles consist of a fill period, one or two brief periods of agitation (each followed by a soak period), then a short spin period. Of course, you can soak laundry in any machine. But in washers without a soak cycle, you have to shut off the machine manually.

Using a washing machine

Here are some suggestions from our engineers for using a washing machine effectively.

■ Heating water is the most expensive part of doing laundry, so it makes sense to use as little hot water as possible. Unless you have a load of unusually dirty or greasy clothes, don't use a hot wash. You can save about half of your water-heating cost by using a warm wash instead of hot. Using a cold wash is the ultimate saving, of course.

■ Always use a cold rinse. Warm water doesn't rinse any better, and it may wrinkle permanent-press fabrics.

■ You can save water, energy, and detergent by adjusting the water level to the size of the load. But washing a few large loads is more economical than washing several small loads.

■ Add bleach after the tub has filled and the clothes are submerged, preferably in the last five minutes or so of the wash period. That avoids bleach damage. It also gives the detergent's brightening agents a chance to work. They're most effective before the bleach goes in.

■ Don't misuse the controls. While the washer is running, never crank the timer through one or two cycles to get the one you want. The likely result will be a startling sequence of clanks, bangs, and hisses—and needless wear and tear. Never turn a washer's timer backward. (If you succeed in turning it backward, you may have already broken it.) Don't try to change speeds while the machine is running. With some models, changing from "normal" to "gentle" speed during operation may bend a part of the drive mechanism and leave the machine with only one speed. (That's easily repaired, but at the cost of a house call.)

Choosing the right whole-house fan

The key to getting the best from a whole-house fan is to choose one of the right air-moving capacity for your house. With a fan of the right capacity, the air indoors would be replaced with outdoor air every minute or two. So rooms in the house would cool off almost as fast as the garden.

Your house's volume. The formula for finding the proper capacity for your house is simple enough to work out.

■ Multiply length by width by height of each room, hallway, and stairwell to be ventilated. Don't figure in closets, storage rooms, or the attic itself.

■ Add the results. Your answer (in cubic feet) will bear a relationship to desired fan capacity (expressed in cubic feet per minute, or cfm).

■ If you live in a region where summers are typically long and hot, the relationship should be about one to one. A house with 6,000 cubic feet of living space, for example, would warrant a fan capable of moving 6,000 cubic feet of air a minute. If you live where typical summer temperatures aren't extreme, divide the volume of your house by two to find the proper fan capacity—3,000 cfm for a 6,000-cubic-foot house.

The fan's capacity. A fan usually has two ratings for its air delivery. The second rating will be the more useful of the two.

■ Most of the fans we tested carried a manufacturer's rating of 10,000 cfm or so. That number represents "free air delivery," or performance when nothing restricts airflow. Such ratings aren't very helpful because something usually does restrict the air. A house's size and layout and the fan's location all contribute to the restriction. So do the fan shutters that are generally installed in the attic.

■ Accordingly, you'll usually find a second rating on these fans, representing performance when airflow is not totally free. The second rating is derived from the amount of air that can be delivered by a fan working against a standard air pressure load. That rating may not give an absolute yardstick, but it will help you choose a fan of the right capacity for your house.

■ Your calculation shouldn't necessarily rule out some fans whose capacity may be greater than you need. In the case of one- or two-speed fans, you'll want a fairly close match between house volume and fan capacity at maximum speed. But if a variable-speed model has somewhat more capacity than your house warrants, you can always turn it down to a speed that suits your needs.

Using a whole-house fan

A house that's fan-ventilated at night can retain some of the cooling effect by day—at least for a while.

■ After you turn off the fan in the morning, close windows, and draw shades.

■ When the house grows uncomfortably warm later in the day, it's time to open things up and run the fan. The breeze should make you feel more comfortable despite the heat. Also, by helping to keep attic temperature down, the fan can cool off the house quicker again in the evening.

Automobiles

Should you join an auto club?

Does it pay to join an auto club? According to a survey of Consumer Reports readers, it's likely to depend on where you live and your lifestyle. You probably don't really need an auto club if you live outside the freeze-and-snow belt and don't do much traveling.

In any case, many auto insurance companies offer optional coverage of emergency road-service costs for less than $10 a year. At the time we surveyed our readers, an individual membership in an auto club ran from $23 to $45.

Membership in an auto club, however, may be worth it to you because of the reassurance it provides—along with some services that may not be readily available otherwise. In addition to road maps and advice about routes, some clubs offer members a range of travel-planning services.

If you decide you want to join, you'll have a choice between a full-service club and a limited-service club.

■ The advantage of a full-service club is that it usually provides no-cost road service—you don't have to pay for service and then apply for reimbursement. An affiliated garage or service station will try to get your car back into operation on the spot or will tow it to the garage if necessary. The club picks up the bill for that basic service, though you'd have to pay for parts and any extensive repairs.

■ The advantage of a limited-service club is that you're free to choose any garage you want. If your car won't start when you want to leave home, for example, you can call your local service station for help even if the station isn't affiliated with your club. The limited-service club will reimburse you, up to a preset limit, after you've made your own arrangements for service.

Help your battery last longer

Here are ten ways to help your battery last longer.

1. Keep the battery firmly secured so it can't bounce around. Vibration and shock can damage it. But don't overtighten the hold-down hardware, or you may crack the battery case.

2. Use a special cable puller when removing stubborn cables from a battery whose terminals are on top. Excessive force applied to the battery terminals can cause internal battery damage. Don't overtighten the screws on a side-terminal battery or you may strip the threads.

3. Be careful when using tools in the engine compartment. A wrench laid carelessly across both terminals, or between the positive terminal and a metal component in the car, could short-circuit the battery and cause internal plates to buckle and break.

4. The gases produced by a battery being charged are highly explosive. Keep open flames, cigarettes, and sources of sparks away from the battery while it's charging.

5. Be sure all electrical connections are clean and tight. Wash off corrosive deposits, using a tablespoon of baking soda dissolved in a cup of water. (Don't let any of the solution get into the battery cells.) Wipe the battery clean with a rag or a paper towel. Clean the terminals and clamps with a wire brush or a special tool. Replace cables, clamps, and clamping screws that have suffered obvious damage.

6. Check the level of the acid in each cell regularly (in batteries with removable cell caps) and add water—never acid—when necessary. Distilled water is best, but naturally soft tap water is satisfactory. If you must add water often, the battery is probably being overcharged or is going bad. Have the car's charging system checked. (Be very careful if acid splashes or overflows from the battery. It can burn your skin and eat through clothing or metal.)

7. In freezing weather, add water to the battery only if you're going to drive the car immediately. Otherwise, the water won't mix with the acid. If the water should freeze, it could damage the battery.

8. Check the condition and tension of the alternator belt regularly. If you're not sure which belt is which, ask a mechanic to show you. Replace a cut, cracked, or frayed belt. When pressed moderately hard (with about a 10-pound force) midway between pulleys, the belt should deflect about a half inch. A belt that is loose may slip.

9. If your car stands idle for an extended time, particularly in cold weather, recharge the battery occasionally with a plug-in battery charger.

10. Don't use chemical additives in the battery. We don't know of any that has been proved worthwhile. Such chemicals may also void your battery warranty.

Need a new battery? Maybe not

If the engine fails to start, it may not be the battery. To find out, here are five simple things to try.

1. If the starter motor cranks normally but the engine won't start, the engine may need a tuneup or repairs.

2. If the starter motor won't crank or cranks weakly, check the battery's electrical connections. Be sure that the terminal clamps are tight. Clean the terminals and wiring clamps, wash off corrosive deposits, and check for necessary replacements (as described in Step 5, above).

3. If everything seems all right so far, check the condition of the battery tester, or hydrometer. (On a "sealed" battery—one without cell caps—there may be an indicator eye that shows the state of charge.) If the hydrometer shows all the battery cells at or near full charge, the battery and the charging system are probably all right. An old battery, however, may show a full charge even though it can't provide adequate current under heavy load, as during winter starting. A load test, done by a mechanic, can diagnose that condition. If the battery passes the load test but the starter motor won't crank, the problem may lie in the starter motor, the solenoid switch, the ignition switch, or the wiring.

4. A discharged battery may still be serviceable if its case isn't cracked. Try to recharge the battery with a plug-in charger, or have it recharged by a service station. If the battery accepts and holds the charge, and if it passes a mechanic's load test, don't replace it. Have the car's charging system checked.

5. When hydrometer readings from any two cells differ by much more than about 0.025 (or, with a ball-type hydrometer, when they differ consistently by one ball or more), recharge the battery and check again with the hydrometer. If there's still a similar difference, replace the battery.

Shopping for a battery

Don't replace your old battery until you've performed all the tests we've described above. But once you're sure you're in the market for a battery, take these guidelines into account when you shop.

Warranty. If you plan to keep your car a long time, we suggest that you get the battery offering the longest and best warranty for the money.

■ The batteries with the longest warranties generally have the greatest electrical capacities. And that means the batteries will probably last the longest and provide the most reliable starting under severe conditions.

■ If you plan to keep your car only a short time, however, you might be better off choosing by price rather than by warranty.

■ A good warranty need not mean a premium-priced model. Some batteries may carry nonprorated warranties for as long as you own your car.

Type. If your car's original battery was a maintenance-free model, you should replace it with another of that type. But if the original battery was a conventional model, you have a choice to make.

■ If, like many motorists, you tend to neglect inspecting the fluid level in your car battery for weeks and months at a time, you would probably be wise to buy a maintenance-free model.

■ But if you don't mind checking and topping off your battery regularly, a conventional battery might be an attractive choice, particularly at a good price.

Size. If your car has spare length in its battery tray, you may be able to install a battery of the next larger size. Such a battery would have greater electrical capacity—sometimes for the same price.

Performance. To get a reliable idea of a battery's performance, check two specifications commonly quoted by battery makers: cold-cranking capacity and reserve capacity.

■ Cold-cranking capacity tells you how much current, in amperes, the battery can deliver for thirty seconds at 0°F without dropping below a specified voltage. The higher the number, the greater the battery's starting power. Cold-cranking capacity is especially important in areas where temperatures drop to well below freezing. As a rule, allow at least one ampere of cold-cranking capacity per cubic inch of engine displacement. A 350-cubic-inch V8, say, should have a battery with a cold-cranking capacity of at least 350 amps.

■ Reserve capacity is the time, in minutes, during which the battery can deliver a 25-amp current at 80° without dropping below a specified voltage. That figure indicates the battery's ability to keep the engine and essential electrical accessories operating if the car's charging system fails. The higher the number, the longer your car can limp along until you get the charging system repaired.

Shopping for booster cables

With battery booster cables and the help of another car, you can probably "jump-start" your car if your battery fails on the road. Here's what to look for when buying a pair of booster cables.

Length. Booster cables come in lengths of 8 to 20 feet or more. We think that 12- or 16-foot cables are sensible choices. It could be difficult to get two cars close enough to each other to use 8-foot cables.

Cable construction. Most of the booster cables we tested were "tangle-resistant." That means the two cables were joined along most of their length, like lamp cord, to minimize tangling. (But separated cables can be joined with electrical tape at regular intervals.)

Clamps. Some clamps are plastic with metal inserts. In cars with little clearance around the battery's positive terminal, plastic clamps can help prevent accidental metal-to-metal contact and a short circuit.

How to use booster cables safely

It can be dangerous to connect booster cables carelessly. A car battery emits combustible gases, and connecting a booster cable incorrectly could produce a spark that could cause an explosion. A battery explosion is especially dangerous because the acid inside the battery could spatter on your skin or into your eyes.

To be safe, observe the following precautions.

■ Make sure the two cars do not touch. Shift the transmission in each car into neutral or park, and set the parking brake. Switch off the ignition, lights, and all electrical accessories in each car. Check to be sure that both cars have batteries of the same voltage. (Almost all cars on the road today have a 12-volt battery.)

■ Never connect booster cables to a frozen battery. Check the cells for ice. If you can see ice, stop. Otherwise, add water to any cell whose level is low. If the dead battery is "sealed," look for a built-in indicator dot. If it's yellow or clear, don't try to jump-start the car. Instead, charge the battery with an off-car charger for at least twenty-four hours.

(continued on next page)

■ Use one of the cables to connect the positive terminals of the two batteries to each other (Steps 1 and 2 on the diagram). The positive terminal is usually marked "+" or "POS" and is sometimes painted red.

■ Connect one end of the second cable to the negative terminal of the healthy battery (Step 3). The negative terminal is usually marked "−" or "NEG."

■ Connect the other end of the second cable to any unpainted part of the engine block in the disabled car (Step 4). It's important that you do Step 4 last. If the final connection should produce a spark, as it often does, at least the spark will be well away from the battery.

■ Be sure you don't cross-connect the cables. Mixing up the positive and negative terminals could damage both batteries, as well as the cars' alternators. Check to see that the cables aren't close to the fans or belts. Don't smoke or hold an open flame near a battery.

■ In some cars, clearance around the battery terminals is a problem. The booster cable clamp could easily touch some nearby sheet metal and short out. You may have to place a dry rag or newspaper between the clamp and the sheet

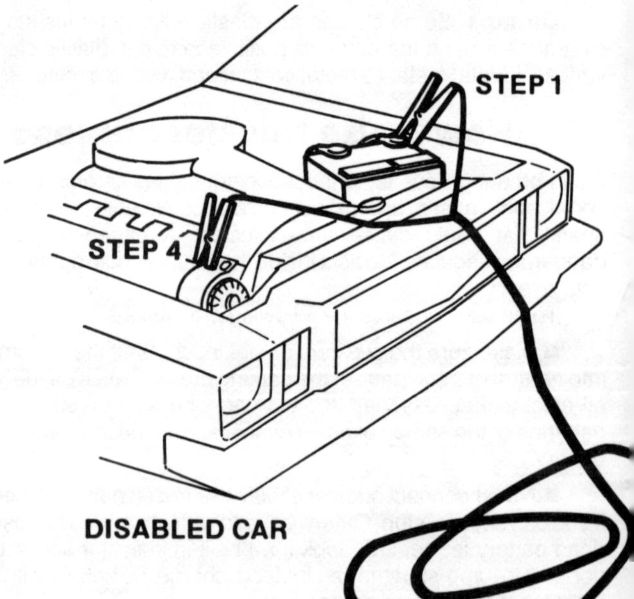

metal to prevent accidental contact. The air conditioning lines in some General Motors cars with side-terminal batteries also present a shorting hazard, but you can gently bend those lines away. (Another problem with these side-terminal batteries: They have small screws instead of conventional terminals and the clamps on booster cables can't get a firm grip on the screws. Get special adapters, which are available for such batteries.)

■ After you hook up the cables, start the engine of the car with the healthy battery and run the engine at fast idle for a few minutes. That will charge the dead battery a bit and reduce the load on the booster cables.

■ Finally, start the disabled car's engine.

■ Disconnect the booster cables in reverse order. Begin with Step 4: Undo the connection to the disabled car's engine block first.

■ Caution: These instructions apply only to cars with negative-grounded electrical systems. All American cars made since 1958 (and foreign cars since 1971) are so equipped. If your car is positive-grounded, refer to the owner's manual for instructions on jump-starting.

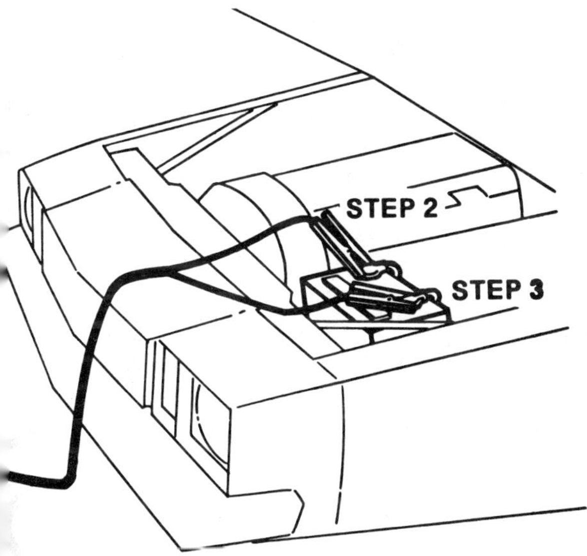

HEALTHY CAR

Choosing a child safety seat

Although all child safety seats may meet minimum federal safety requirements, they are not equally easy to install, equally convenient to use, or equally comfortable. In choosing among the restraint systems used in convertible and toddler-only safety seats, you should try to select a model that is convenient enough for you to use regularly and comfortable enough for your child to stay put once placed in the seat. In any case, be sure the model you select can be properly installed—and returned if it won't work in your car. (See below for our comments on installation.)

Five-point harness. Usually quite comfortable for children, a five-point harness allows them to move their arms and hands freely.

This design requires some patience on the part of the parents, however. The straps tangle easily, and can get trapped beneath children as they climb into the seat. It takes time to adjust the five straps.

If you shop for a five-point harness, look for the following features:

■ A short crotch strap. The crotch strap should be as short as possible to hold the lap straps in their proper position, low and flat across a child's thighs.

■ A separately adjustable crotch strap. That's an advantage because it's easier to pull the crotch strap short if it can be adjusted independently of the shoulder straps.

■ Ease of fastening and adjusting. Try out the straps to make sure they are reasonably convenient to use.

Full-shield. Toddlers are likely to be least comfortable in this type of seat because there's no place for the arms. The shield is too high to be a comfortable resting place, and there's no room at the sides or on the lap for the arms.

The full-shield design, however, is easy on parents, because there's nothing to adjust or buckle.

If you decide on a full-shield design, take extra care when you use the seat. Tests with some models have shown that the rather heavy shield can fall from its upraised position during the fuss of seating a child—and that can hurt.

Harness/partial shield. These safety seats can be a convenient compromise between the five-point harness, with its adjustment difficulties, and the uncomfortable full-shield design.

Our auto engineers warn that with all models of this design that they examined the shield must fit rather tightly against the child's midsection. That could cause some pressure or heat discomfort in warm weather.

If you decide on the harness/partial shield combination, choose a model that will be comfortable for your child. Some harness/partial shield seats restrict arm movement in front. Some can be especially objectionable to a child because the shield also inhibits side movement.

Front or back. The decision whether to place a safety seat in the front or back of a car may vary with the age of the child and to some extent with the type of car you drive.

■ Infant seats, which face rearward, can safely travel in the front seat. Convertible seats, when used for an infant, also travel in the rear-facing semi-reclined position—the safest position for infants *and* toddlers.

■ Eventually, though, toddlers demand to face the front of the car. That's when you turn a convertible seat around and make other adjustments to convert the seat from an infant carrier to a toddler seat.

■ At this stage, it's wise to move the convertible seat to the back of the car, if possible, or to shop for a model to be used in the rear. It's desirable to assign toddlers to the car's rear seat, away from the instrument panel and windshield.

Cloth or vinyl. Except for a few models, child safety seats are sold with a choice of cloth or vinyl upholstery. Choose cloth upholstery. Children get hot and sweaty in vinyl seats. In a car that has been parked in the sun, metal can get hot enough to burn a child. Feel the seat and hardware before setting your child down. On hot days, keep an unoccupied seat covered with a light-colored cloth.

Using a booster seat

A booster seat for an older bigger child is usually safe when anchored in the front seat by the car's own lap/shoulder belts, which also restrain the child. Safe use of a booster seat in the rear requires a crucial additional step—installation of a tether.

A booster seat lets a child sit high enough to see out of the car. In the front seat, the car's safety belt passes under the handles of the booster seat, preventing the seat from slipping out from under the child in a crash. The handles also keep the car's lap belt over the child's thighs, and route the shoulder belt so it fits comfortably.

If you want to use a booster seat in the rear, you must first install a separate harness attached to a tether that must be anchored to the car somewhere behind the safety seat. This arrangement serves as a substitute for the front-seat shoulder belt.

The tether can be bolted to the window ledge of a sedan or to the floor of a hatchback or station wagon. But the job can require some doing. You usually have to drill a hole through sheet metal. New car dealers are strangely reluctant to perform this task, in our experience.

Because the tether may be difficult to install, there's a temptation to use a booster in the rear with a lap belt alone. Don't do that. It would severely compromise the safe use of the booster seat.

Installing and using a child seat

A child's car seat is hardly a safety device if it's not properly secured in the car. If you have trouble installing a seat, return it and try another model.

Here are some of the problems you can run into when trying to install seats properly.

Threading through the frame. Typically, you install a seat for a toddler by weaving the car's belt in and out of the seat frame or through slots in the shell.

■ Check the belt paths. If they are very narrow, installation can be difficult.

■ The rear safety belts in some cars present a problem. Rear-seat belts on some Japanese imports have such bulky buckles housing the belt's retracting mechanism that they may not fit through the safety seat's frame or shell.

Tightening the belt. Once the safety belt is threaded through the frame, it must be pulled very tight. That's best done by holding the seat down with a knee to create some slack while tugging at the belt. Sometimes, after the car's belt has been threaded through the frame, the buckle lands in an awkward position on the frame, making the belt difficult or impossible to tighten. In that case, return the seat for a different model.

The car's belt system. Should you want to install a safety seat in the front of the car, you may need to take extra precautions if you own an imported car. Most imports have belts that consist of a continuous loop of webbing and a free-sliding latch plate. Although they would restrain the seat in a crash, these belts may not secure a child safety seat during the stops and turns of normal driving.

With some models, you may be able to adapt the belt system by buying a special locking clip to lock the latch plate and secure the seat. The clips are sold in the parts department of some car dealerships and by safety seat manufacturers. (Some Japanese imports, however, have front lap/shoulder belts that can't be tightened around a safety seat even with a locking clip.)

Special problems. Certain cars and certain child safety seats present additional problems.

■ Some safety belts are too short to use with a safety seat.

■ In some cars, particularly small ones, a safety seat with a pop-up partial shield or armrest, when the seat is unoccupied, could block the driver's rear view. In that case, the shield or armrest must be buckled down even when not in use.

■ If the safety seat you choose requires a tether, be sure to install it properly. Without a properly fastened tether, the seat will provide less crash protection than a nontethered seat.

■ If a tethered safety seat is used in a car's front seat, the tether can be hooked to the rear safety belt in the seat behind. But you sacrifice a passenger seat to the tether. And if the car has high-backed bucket seats in front, a tether will probably slip off.

Child seats: Summary of recommendations

To help you decide which type of child safety seat to buy, here in summary are the recommendations of our auto engineers.

A convertible safety seat is probably the most practical of the various child safety seats. It will grow with the child.

■ Look for a model that you find easy to use and that also seems comfortable for a child.

■ Make sure the model you select fits your car.

An infant seat is what you may prefer for a baby.

■ It's easy to carry in and out of the car, and it will work well as a baby seat outside the car.

■ You'll probably find that a model with buckled straps is a lot easier to use than one with a fixed harness.

■ Make sure the seat isn't so upright that the infant's head flops forward.

A toddler seat is appropriate for an older child. Choose a model that is easy to use in the rear seat—the safest place for a toddler.

■ Look for a safety seat that, unlike the boosters, can be used in a car's rear without a tether.

■ Look for a model that can be "permanently" strapped in.

■ It should be big enough for an older larger child. (The main drawback will probably be that it may not contain a child who has a mind to climb out.)

Pros and cons of a tethered seat. A convertible or booster seat that requires a tether can be difficult to install properly. When properly installed, however, a tethered safety seat does have some advantages.

■ In a severe crash, a properly tethered seat will provide more head restraint than a nontethered one. Additional head restraint might be especially important in a small car.

■ A tether will also cure the problem that may crop up if you can't tighten a seat belt enough to keep a child seat securely in place.

■ If you buy a seat without a tether and later decide you want one, contact the seat manufacturer. Most should be able to supply one.

In case of accident

In choosing a child safety seat, what features would work best in case of an accident? A Consumer Reports reader asked:

"How easy is it to get a child out of a seat in case of an accident?"

Our auto engineers replied that, as a general rule, seats that are convenient to get a child into are also the easiest to get a child out of. After an accident, however, it's probably best to unbuckle the safety belt holding the seat in place and then remove child and seat together.

How long are child seats needed?

By what age can a child safely use the car's lap belt or lap/shoulder belt?

We urge that children use a child safety seat until they have outgrown a booster seat. However, safety belts can be used safely under the following conditions.

- In the rear seat—if no safety seat is available and if state law doesn't set an age limit of its own—a child over the age of one year should be able to use existing lap belts.

- Belts in the front seat are best used when the child is tall enough so that the shoulder strap goes across the child's chest. But if you're driving a car pool, say, by all means use the lap belt—and position the shoulder strap behind the child's back. It's far better to use the front belt as a lap belt than to use no belt.

What makes for an ideal car?

An ideal car? Here's what our auto engineers would look for:

- A body that's light, aerodynamic, and small, yet roomy enough for five people.
- An engine that's smooth and peppy, yet economical.
- A ride that's reasonably comfortable.
- Safe, responsive handling.
- Effective braking.
- Mechanical reliability.

What to look for in a car's performance

Here's what our auto engineers look for when testing begins on a new car. Some of the criteria we use in judging a car's performance may help you when you shop for a new car.

Engine and transmission. A car's engine should have excellent "drivability." It should start quickly, without stalling. And it shouldn't stumble or hesitate, even when it's cold.

A manual transmission should shift easily and precisely, and the clutch should engage smoothly rather than abruptly. An automatic transmission should shift without lurching.

A car's acceleration should be good enough to let the car merge safely with expressway traffic and pass slow vehicles easily.

Labeled fuel mileage may be somewhat optimistic, but it's a useful figure for making comparisons between cars.

Handling and braking. A car should steer where you want it to go without being twitchy and overly sensitive. Nor should the steering be too heavy. Power steering shouldn't be so light that the driver can't "feel" the road.

Brakes can sometimes be too sensitive. A tap of the brake pedal should not result in a hard stop.

Some convenience features to consider

When you're deciding which car to buy, few factors rank higher than reliability. Even so, considerations such as comfort and convenience play a part in how well a car will suit you.

Car seats. Be sure that the car seats have enough adjustments to accommodate you (and other drivers in your family).

Climate control. A car's climate control system should be quiet, powerful, draft-free, and responsive to its controls. The fresh-air ventilation outlets should send plenty of air evenly throughout the car. In winter, the heater should cope with 0°F weather without creating hot spots.

If the car has an air conditioner, it should keep you cool when the temperature is in the 90s. If the air conditioner is integrated with the heater, so much the better. On cold dank days, you can then quickly and comfortably defog the windows.

Loading luggage. The size of a car's trunk is important. But so is its shape. A boxy trunk with a flat floor has more useful luggage space than, say, a long shallow trunk with a multilevel floor.

A large opening and a low sill make loading and unloading easier. And a trunk lid that opens high enough so you can't bash your head on it is an added blessing.

In a hatchback or a station wagon, the rear seat should be easy to fold down. Here, too, the opening should be large and low, and the seat should fold flat.

Paying the freight

Ever wonder if you could bargain down the destination charge when you buy a new car? Don't bother to try.

Our auto engineers say the destination charge is given in the price of a new car. Unlike the list price, the destination charge is not an item you can haggle over.

What's meant by destination charge? Apparently, different things to different automakers.

■ The charge for domestic cars not only represents the cost of shipping cars to dealers, it also covers the cost of bringing raw materials to an assembly plant.

■ For foreign cars, the charge represents only the cost of shipping from a U.S. port of entry to dealers, not the cost of travel overseas. That's why you'll be confronted with destination charges on some American-made cars that are more than twice as much as those on some Japanese imports.

What to expect with front-wheel drive

If you're thinking of getting a car with front-wheel drive, here's what to expect in design and handling.

Design. A front-wheel-drive car has no center drive shaft or bulky rear axle. This brings advantages and disadvantages.

■ The car can be built smaller and lighter without sacrificing interior room.

■ The car permits somewhat more room inside for people and baggage.

■ Certain repairs may require more extensive disassembly because so many components are crowded into the front end of the car.

■ Some items that require regular service may be harder to reach.

Handling. You can expect some handling quirks with a front-wheel-drive car.

■ A characteristic of front-wheel drive is that the front tires wear more quickly than the rear tires. That's because front-wheel-drive cars tend to be more nose-heavy, and the front tires must drive the car as well as handle the steering.

■ Front-wheel drive tends to give more forward traction on slippery pavement because the weight of the engine is over the driving wheels. That means you're less likely to get stuck in snow.

■ Front-wheel-drive cars tend to wander less in a crosswind.

■ During hard cornering, the behavior of a front-wheel-drive car may depend as much on what you do with the accelerator as on how you steer. Accelerate hard in mid-corner and the car will tend to run wider. Lift your foot off the accelerator and the car will tend to turn more tightly. In extreme cases, the rear end may start to slide out.

■ When you accelerate while cornering at low speed—making an ordinary left or right turn, for example—the steering may try to return to the straight-ahead position, giving you the feeling that the steering wheel is fighting you.

Switching from heating to ventilation

In many cars, the climate control system can cause problems. Switching from heating to ventilation in these cars is accomplished with engine vacuum. When the car is accelerating hard or climbing hills, the vacuum sometimes drops too low to power the system. It becomes reluctant to change functions under those conditions.

Here's what to do when you want to switch. Shift into neutral for a moment to unload the engine. Race the engine to increase the vacuum. Release the accelerator momentarily and resume where you left off.

How safe is a small car?

Despite improvements in crashworthiness, a small light car is not as safe as a large heavy car.

Although automakers seem to be concentrating their safety research and development on small cars, they can't repeal the laws of physics. A small light car will come out second-best in a collision with a larger heavier vehicle.

Compared with large cars, small cars have less structure and weight to absorb crash forces. As the number of large cars on the road decreases and as small cars proliferate, however, the statistics should begin to change.

Drivers of small cars can enormously improve their chances of surviving a severe collision simply by buckling up.

Crash protection for tall drivers

Drivers (or front-seat passengers) who are tall should check the height of front-seat head restraints if they want to increase their chances of escaping unhurt in a crash.

Studies have shown that most people don't bother to adjust the height: They just leave the restraints in the lowest position. In that position, the head restraints in many cars won't protect occupants of above-average height from whiplash injury.

What to carry in the car

Here's a list of emergency equipment that can help you cope with the most common problems you're likely to encounter on the road. These few basic tools and spare parts could spell the difference between a slight inconvenience and a long costly delay. Some emergency equipment could even save your life.

Even if you're not an expert mechanic, you could get help from a knowledgeable Good Samaritan or a professional mechanic if you have the right parts and tools in your car to make a quick repair at the roadside.

Road emergency signals. Your first concern should be to keep other motorists from running into your car while you make repairs or wait for help.

■ Day or night, triangle reflectors are generally a more visible and reliable highway warning device than flares.

■ In dense fog, however, only flares are effective, so you'll need to carry flares too.

Car jack. Make sure that the jack in your car trunk works. Practice using it. Don't wait until you have a flat some stormy night.

Lug wrench. The lug wrench that comes with most cars may not provide enough leverage to loosen tight lug nuts. You may have to buy a large cross-shaped lug wrench. Wind a strip of tape near the proper-sized socket for quick identification even in the dark.

First chance you get—before you have a flat—unscrew, grease, and replace the wheel lug nuts one at a time to keep corrosion from "freezing" them. A tiny dab of grease on the threads is sufficient.

Wheel chocks. Using a couple of short wooden wedges about 3 inches high will lessen the chances of the car slipping off the jack when the car is raised. Chock the front and rear of the wheel diagonally across from the one you're jacking up.

Plywood jack support. Scrap wood such as ¾-inch plywood (about a foot square) will keep the jack from sinking into soft muddy ground.

Spare wheel and tire. When you check the pressure in your tires, don't neglect the spare. It's important to keep your spare tire properly inflated.

Tire pump. If a tire has a slow leak, it's easier to pump it up and then drive to a service station than to remove the wheel and mount the spare.

Flashlight. A trouble light with a long cord that plugs into the cigarette lighter will work well unless your car has a battery problem. If you carry a conventional flashlight, be sure to switch it on once a month to check the batteries.

Fire extinguisher. Keep an extinguisher in the front passenger compartment, within easy reach. Mount it securely on the floor just in front of the driver's seat (if it doesn't interfere with seat adjustment) or under the dashboard on the passenger's side. Check the pressure indicator periodically to be sure the fire extinguisher keeps its charge.

Assorted hand tools. You'll need a set of open-end wrenches, small- and medium-sized conventional and Phillips-head screwdrivers, conventional pliers and locking jaw pliers, 10 feet of 14-gauge insulated wire, plastic electrical tape, a penknife, a small hammer, and a small can of penetrating oil.

Duct tape can be used to make a temporary fix on a ruptured radiator hose. (Loosen—but don't remove—the radiator cap to reduce pressure until the hose is replaced.)

Wire coat hanger. Use it to support the exhaust pipe if a pipe hanger breaks, or to make other temporary repairs.

Metal container for fuel. Don't carry a container of fuel in the car; that's a fire hazard. But do carry an empty metal container for fuel. Many service stations won't lend you one if you run out of fuel.

Siphon. If you have a fuel container and a siphon, you might be able to buy a gallon or two of fuel from a passing motorist. Get a siphon with a squeeze bulb.

Never try to suck out fuel with a conventional hose. Accidentally swallowing or inhaling the fuel can cause injury or death.

An old blanket will protect your clothes if you have to kneel or get under the car to make a repair.

Fuses. Carry two spares of each capacity that your car requires. It's easy to blow one while trying to diagnose an electrical problem. Replacing a fuse with aluminum foil or a higher-capacity fuse could cause an electrical fire.

Booster cables can get your car started when the battery goes dead, if you can enlist the aid of another motorist.

First-aid kit. Assembling your own can save money. Include gauze bandage, adhesive strips, a menstrual pad (ideal for stopping severe bleeding), and an antiseptic—isopropyl (70 percent) alcohol. Store the kit in the glove compartment for easy access.

Medicine. If you or a frequent rider needs regular medication, you might want to keep a small supply in the glove compartment.

Coins. Tape some coins under the dashboard so you can call for help in an emergency.

Additional equipment for special needs

All drivers should carry in their car the emergency road equipment listed above. Some drivers, however, need additional equipment.

If you drive an unusual car—an import, an old car, or a model that's no longer made—we recommend that you supplement the standard emergency equipment with the items listed below.

Service manual. Even if you don't know the first thing about making repairs, you'd be wise to have a factory repair manual for your particular car model—and keep it in your car.

The manual includes specifications, wiring diagrams, and other data for your car that even an expert mechanic might not know. Some garages that don't ordinarily work on imports might be willing to do so if you have the proper service manual.

Special tools. If your car has metric fittings, be sure that the wrenches and other equipment in your toolbox are metric as well.

Spare parts. Carry a spare fan belt, radiator hose, and fuel filter. Also carry a spare set of points and a condenser (if your car has these components), a distributor rotor, and a distributor cap.

Driving for fuel economy

Driving for fuel economy is not hard, but it does require some attention.

■ Combine several short trips into one, so you drive as little as possible with a cold engine. When the engine is cold, it delivers as little as 2 or 3 mpg.

■ Don't warm up the engine for a few minutes before you drive. That does the engine no good and gets 0 mpg. As soon as the engine is running smoothly, drive off at a moderate speed. That way, *all* parts of the car (including the heater in winter) warm up—and warm up faster.

■ As you drive, keep a constant speed and try to anticipate traffic conditions. Plan ahead for changes in traffic signals, and avoid getting caught behind exiting traffic or cars making a left turn.

■ A delicate foot makes for high mileage. Some economy-run drivers try to imagine they have an egg taped to the bottom of their right shoe. The goal is to step on the accelerator and brake pedals without breaking the egg.

■ In a car with a manual transmission, don't downshift before braking. Using the engine to help stop the car wastes fuel. Downshift only when you must do so to accelerate adequately, then build speed gradually and shift up early.

■ Don't be afraid to lug the engine. You can always shift down if it won't pull the car smoothly in high gear. That advice is especially useful for diesel cars, whose engines are much more efficient at slow speeds than at high speeds.

■ If you have a five-speed overdrive transmission, don't think that fifth gear is only for expressways. If the engine will pull smoothly in fifth at lower speeds, use that gear. It will save you fuel.

■ If you drive a car with an automatic transmission, you can't do as much to save fuel. But you can learn to sense when the transmission upshifts and then encourage it to shift a little sooner by letting up slightly on the accelerator.

■ Obeying the 55 mph speed limit is probably the best known and least heeded way to save fuel. Going *slower* than 55 mph in high gear is even more fuel efficient.

■ It pays to turn the engine off if you must let the car idle for much longer than half a minute.

■ To get the most out of fuel-saving driving habits, you need to keep the engine correctly tuned and the tires inflated to the right pressure. Radial tires that are designed to operate at pressures as high as 35 pounds per square inch will save some fuel because of lower rolling resistance.

■ Don't use the car as a mobile closet. Take the snow tires, baby carriage, and similar objects out of the car, and keep luggage racks and ski racks off the roof and in the garage unless you're using them.

■ Don't think that higher-octane gasoline will necessarily improve mileage. It won't, unless your engine has been tuned to take advantage of the higher octane. And don't fall for the promises of gas-saving gadgets. We have tested many of them and have yet to see one that works.

Loudspeakers for the highway

As listening rooms, cars rank slightly above toll booths and gas stations. Getting a sound system in your car that's at least adequate will depend largely on the quality of the speakers.

If you're buying a new car, the first question is whether to buy your speakers from the dealer or from a store that sells aftermarket equipment. In past tests, we've found that speakers offered as optional equipment are generally inferior to aftermarket speakers.

Rear or door. If you want to shop for a system for your new car or install stereo speakers in your present car, you'll have to decide whether to buy rear-deck speakers or speakers designed for doors. They create very different stereo effects. Rear speakers sound more like speakers at home, except the sound comes from behind you. Door speakers, which are less expensive, give an impression more like stereo headphones.

Our tests have shown that rear speakers outperform door speakers, especially in the bass and treble. Because rear speakers are larger and placed in a better location for baffling, they reproduce bass sounds better.

However, you may like the pronounced stereo effect that door speakers provide—or not have room for rear speakers.

If your radio or tape player will accept two pairs of speakers, you can have the best of both worlds by installing door speakers and rear speakers.

Installation. Some cars have appropriate rear or door cutouts, but many don't. Installation may require cutting through the door panel or the door upholstery and some metal.

Before you buy a set of speakers, be sure to measure the installation area to see whether the speakers will fit. It's important to position door speakers so they won't get in the way of the window crank mechanism or door handle.

You can have speakers installed professionally for about $50 to $75. If you're fairly handy, you can install them yourself. Be sure you have the option of returning them to the store. No matter how carefully you measure, you may find that there just isn't room for the speakers you've chosen.

Choosing a luggage carrier

People who regularly take long trips would be best off with a clamshell type of luggage carrier.

Clamshells, which get their name from their distinctive shape, cost much more than other types of carriers. They are much easier to pack, however. Nothing has to be tied down, and they provide protection from the weather.

Most clamshell carriers have two sets of hinges. In some models, the cover opens either toward the front or toward the rear, and we found these carriers easiest to load and unload. With the cover open, we had access from either side.

It's no big task, however, to remove any clamshell's cover entirely. With the cover off, loading and unloading proved equally easy with all the clamshells we tested.

Basket carriers probably make more sense than a clamshell for occasional use because they're much cheaper. But they expose their contents to the elements.

Bar carriers are the simplest type. The load rests across both bars and is strapped to them.

- Bars about 60 inches long are best suited for large cars.
- Bars that are 42 to 45 inches long are best for small cars.
- Bars that measure 52 to 54 inches can fit all car sizes, but they would extend beyond the edges of the roof of a subcompact.

Using a luggage carrier

Here are two bits of advice about using a luggage carrier.

- Don't overload the carrier. Never exceed the weight recommendation of the car manufacturer or the carrier manufacturer. Even if the car's roof could support a very heavy load, the top-heavy weight distribution could seriously affect the car's handling.
- Remove the carrier when you're not using it. Driving with a loaded luggage carrier strapped to the roof of a car costs fuel. But there's little sense to paying a fuel penalty by routinely driving about with an unused carrier on your car. In our tests, we found that unloaded basket and bar carriers increased fuel consumption by about 5 percent. One large clamshell increased consumption by about 29 percent, another by about 12 percent.

Normal oil consumption

What is normal oil consumption? Our auto engineers report that the new cars they test seldom achieve less than 2,000 miles per quart of oil.

The way a car is broken in may affect its oil consumption. But a car should get at least about 1,000 miles per quart for the first 50,000 miles. If it doesn't—or if oil consumption increases drastically—something is wrong.

Changing the oil: How often?

As a general rule, it's best to follow the automaker's recommendations for changing the oil.

■ Going beyond the interval spelled out in the owner's manual may violate the car's warranty. If you have the car serviced and the oil changed twice a year, you should have no trouble with either the warranty or the car's performance.

■ Changing the oil more often than the manual dictates won't do any harm. In the case of diesels, more frequent oil changes may be required. The oil in a diesel engine deteriorates faster than that in a gasoline engine.

■ If you do your own maintenance work, it will probably pay you to change the filter each time you change the oil (rather than every other time, as most automakers recommend). The practice makes sense—and the cost will be minimal.

Doing your own maintenance

Why work on your own car? The answer is often not only the price you pay for professional service but also the convenience—and pleasure—of doing it yourself.

You certainly save the cost of a mechanic's labor. You might also save something on engine oil, filters, and other replacement parts that are marked up by professional mechanics. And you can fix the car at your own convenience.

But there are cautions to observe. Don't take on a job unless you know what you're doing. At best, you may have to pay extra to undo any damage. At worst, a mistake could affect the safety and reliability of your car.

If you want to handle under-the-car repairs yourself, you'll need some specialized equipment to raise the car off the ground. A pair of drive-on car ramps may suffice in many cases. But you can't use them if the job involves removing the wheels.

For those repairs, you should have a sturdy stable jack that can lift the car high enough to provide plenty of working clearance.

You'll then need a pair of jack stands to support the car once it's raised. For safety's sake, you should never—repeat, never—work under a car that is supported only by a jack.

Hydraulic service jacks

If you do your own maintenance work, you'll need a jack for your garage in addition to the one you keep in your car for emergency road repairs.

The jacks that are standard issue in car trunks are barely adequate for fixing a flat along the roadside. They are often difficult to use, tip easily, and can raise a car only high enough for a wheel to clear the ground. They certainly won't do for more complicated repairs.

Instead, we recommend you use for your maintenance chores and car repairs a hydraulic service jack—a scaled-down version of the jack professional mechanics use. (You can buy one at auto-supply and department stores and by mail.) You'll also need jack stands (see below).

When shopping for a hydraulic service jack, keep the following points in mind.

■ The higher a jack can lift a car, the easier it is to place jack stands under the car at full height. Working under a car can be much easier with a few extra inches of clearance.

■ A large jack with a long handle is usually easier to position and operate under a car (especially a large car) than is a small jack with a short handle. The important measurement is the jack's "reach"—the distance from the center of the saddle to the end of the handle.

■ A jack that can be steered, raised, and lowered without having to shift the handle to different sockets is an important convenience, in our judgment.

Shopping for jack stands

Anyone who works under a car raised by a jack—even a hefty hydraulic floor jack—should use a pair of jack stands to support the car.

Here are some points to consider when shopping for jack stands.

Height at maximum setting is important for ease of use.

■ In our tests, the shortest stand was 16 inches high at its maximum setting. That's adequate for reasonably comfortable work under the car.

■ A model with a greater maximum height would, of course, be better—especially for exhaust system repairs and other jobs that require mobility and great effort. The tallest stands we tested could be raised to 23 inches, which is probably higher than necessary for most work.

Ratchet or pin. The ratchet-type stands we tested offered the greatest number of height adjustments and were quicker and easier to adjust than the pin-type stands. But they cost a good deal more than the pin-type models.

■ If you work on your car only now and then, it might be hard to justify the price you'd have to pay for a ratchet-type adjustment.

■ The stands with a pin-type height adjustment are just as useful and probably would be a more logical choice. The pin-type models we tested offered a choice of at least three heights and were easy enough to adjust for height.

Using jack stands safely

Jack stands can be deadly if they are misused. Even the sturdiest and most stable should be used with the utmost caution. Here are the most important safety rules.

■ Before each use, check the condition of your jack stands. Don't use them if you find broken, cracked, or badly rusted welds, components, or fasteners.

■ Don't exceed the rated load of jack stands. (The manufacturer specifies each stand's capacity.)

■ Use jack stands only on firm, flat, level ground. On asphalt or dirt, use a board under each stand so the legs won't gouge the asphalt or sink into the dirt.

■ Position the stands as far apart as possible when using them in pairs.

■ Position the stands so that their cradles support the axle or other chassis member securely. Lower the car onto the stands slowly and gently. If the stands shift, raise the car and reposition the stands.

■ If you are supporting only one end of the car with stands, block the wheels at the unsupported end so they can't roll.

■ Before working on the car, check the stability of the stands by rocking the car back and forth. If the car doesn't feel completely steady, jack it up and reposition the stands.

■ For added safety, don't remove the wheels and tires unless it's necessary.

Which options to choose?

Which options are worth considering? Here are some guidelines to help you weigh the strengths and shortcomings of options.

■ Some options add to a car's weight. That hurts fuel economy.

■ Some options draw their power from the engine or the battery. That also hurts fuel economy.

■ Mechanically complex options can add to maintenance costs.

■ If you're shopping for a new car, plan your purchase well in advance. Know which options you want. Cars in stock probably won't have exactly the equipment you specify. Ordering a car will involve a wait, but that may be the only way to get the precise equipment you want.

■ On some cars, desirable options are available only on top-of-the-line models.

■ Some automakers sell options in packages—several extras sold only as a unit. To obtain a certain option, you could have to buy extras you might not otherwise select.

Packs. Some dealers pack their prices with options such as undercoating that are applied to all the cars in a dealer's stock. Avoid packs if you can. You're paying for more things than you want or need.

■ Aftermarket rustproofing is not recommended. Most new cars carry at least a three-year warranty on rust perforation. Dealer-applied rustproofing is at best a risky matter. The quality of protection you get with aftermarket rustproofing would depend on the competence of the applier.

■ Paint and upholstery preservatives are another dealer pack you should resist. This option can be very expensive, and is no better than treatments you could apply yourself. In any case, the preservatives improve the luster of paint or upholstery for only a short time.

Automatic vs manual transmission

If you're deciding between automatic and manual transmissions, here are some guidelines from our auto engineers.

■ If you want a large car, you have little choice. Automatic transmission is standard on large cars and on many medium-sized models as well.

■ If you're buying a domestic car, we recommend you stick with an automatic transmission.

■ If you're buying a small import, a manual is likely to be a better bet.

■ The main advantage of a manual transmission is that it improves fuel economy. Overdrive (usually a fifth gear) helps increase fuel economy even more and reduces engine noise.

■ Manual transmission is not recommended on cars with a pedal-operated parking brake. Cars with that combination can be hard to drive away on a hill—you won't have a foot free for the brake.

Air conditioning

If you're thinking of air conditioning for your new car, in most cases you should insist on a factory-installed unit. It's usually preferable to one installed by the dealer. Some imports, however, offer only dealer-installed air conditioners. In that case, insist on the unit made for that car by the car's manufacturer.

There's little doubt that air conditioning reduces noise (you can drive with windows closed). It delays the onset of driver fatigue, increases comfort, and improves window defogging and fresh air ventilation. If your car has tinted glass, that will reduce the sun's glare and the load on the air conditioner.

Adding air conditioning will not require a larger engine. Yet you do pay a price for all that comfort. Our auto engineers say that air conditioning cuts fuel economy by up to 4 mpg. And it also will increase service costs.

A diesel engine: Is it for you?

A diesel engine is not for everyone. Although it improves fuel economy 20 to 35 percent over a gasoline engine of the same size and provides reliable drivability, it has definite disadvantages.

■ If you live in a cold climate, you should not buy a diesel. Cold weather thickens diesel fuel to the point where it can clog the fuel lines and filter and stall the engine. A remedy is to pour the proper amount of kerosene into the fuel tank—before a cold snap—to keep the fuel from thickening. Below 0°F, a diesel usually won't start unless the engine is warmed.

■ A diesel requires more frequent servicing, and the oil needs changing more often than with a gasoline engine.

■ It is not as powerful as a gasoline engine.

■ A diesel puts a greater load on the battery during starting. If you generally drive short distances, you may have to give the battery an occasional overnight trickle charge to assure reliable starting.

■ A diesel is noisy and smelly, and sometimes smoky.

■ Diesel fuel is not as widely available as gasoline.

■ A diesel engine usually costs considerably more than a gasoline engine.

Radio/tape player

Unlike a radio, a tape player offers consistent sound quality, given the limitations of a car's noisy environment.

If you want a sound system in your car, we recommend buying it from an audio shop. That way you'll get choice and potentially higher quality at a lower price.

It may not be best to buy a sound system from the new car dealer. When bought as an option, a sound system is usually overly expensive. What's more, your choice is limited to very few components.

Trailer-towing package

A trailer-towing package is a must for routine trailer-towing. It will do a better job for you than just a trailer hitch.

When you buy the package, you also get the engine cooling, suspension, and electrical system upgraded to tailor the car for towing.

The package is usually offered only on larger cars. It should be bought with automatic transmission, power brakes, and a larger engine.

Do cars benefit from polishing?

Do new or nearly new cars really benefit from polishing? We doubt it. Given the excellence of modern auto finishes, polishing your car might not be worth the time and effort.

There are other points of view, however. Certainly, no car will suffer from a careful polishing now and then. And a regular polishing schedule for an older car may eventually pay off by enhancing its resale value. But don't overdo it. Polishing too often can remove a car's finish down to the primer.

Liquid polish or paste: Which is easier?

Liquid auto polishes enjoy a reputation for going on easier than pastes. But when we tested auto polishes, we found no appreciable difference between the two types. Nor did we find any difference between soft pastes and hard pastes. All spread easily.

Steps to proper tire inflation

Here are four steps to follow for proper tire inflation.

1. All recommendations for tire pressure are for cold tires. So always try to measure pressure before the tires run far enough for friction to heat up the air inside. Say you take a reading on the car as it stands in your driveway. The tire gauge shows 21 pounds per square inch, and the recommended pressure is 25 psi. When you put air in your tires at the service station pump, add the 4 psi difference even if the trip to the station raised the pressure to 23 psi. Adding 4 psi to 23 psi gives you 27 psi, which, in this example, equals 25 psi measured with cold tires.

2. Use your own gauge to measure the air in your tires. Bleed the tire or add air according to your gauge's readings. Never rely on the accuracy of the gauge on the service station air pump. Our experience has shown that service station operators rarely check the calibration of these gauges.

3. To minimize heat build-up in prolonged high-speed driving, most carmakers recommend pressures higher than those for everyday driving. To find out the proper pressure, consult the owner's manual or check the information plate affixed to the body of the car or to the door of the glove compartment.

4. If the manual calls for differences in pressure between the front and rear tires, be sure to maintain the difference. Because tire pressure tends to rise with the thermometer, you may have to add air in winter and bleed air in summer to maintain proper pressures as the seasons change.

Why proper tire pressure is important

Safety and comfort are two excellent reasons to keep automobile tires inflated to the proper pressure. Tires kept at the proper pressure can also prevent needless outlays for fuel and new tires.

Underinflated tires can impair normal braking and traction. They are also likely to overheat and increase the possibility of a blowout, especially when a car is heavily loaded or traveling at high speed.

A car with underinflated tires uses more fuel than it should. At low pressure, tires suffer from rapid wear on the outer edges of the tread. Underinflated tires can make a car handle awkwardly or even dangerously.

Overinflated tires lack the "give" that may help avoid damage from road hazards. And overinflated tires wear faster at the tread's center. Overinflation also makes for an unnecessarily rough ride.

Choosing and using a tire pump

Equipping your car with a reliable tire pump makes sense.

■ You can use a tire pump to top off a slow leak or a tire that has lost pressure over time. You can also pump up a flat, of course.

■ If you're not very active or accustomed to exertion, consider a foot pump rather than a hand pump. When we tested tire pumps, users found a foot pump less strenuous than a hand pump.

■ An electric pump is the easiest to use but it's slow. Pumping up a flat tire took our testers from 3½ to 7½ minutes, but it required no exertion at all. All you have to do is plug the pump into the cigarette lighter.

■ Of course, an electric model is the one to choose if you must avoid physical exertion.

Used cars: How to reduce the risk

You're taking a chance with a used car. But you'll have plenty of company. Used cars outsell new cars three to one.

Once you've found a likely candidate, however, you can reduce the risk.

■ Inspect the car thoroughly. Look it over very carefully, in daylight, and drive it around for half an hour or so. Do the checks described below.

■ If the car meets your requirements, ask an independent mechanic to inspect it thoroughly. Mention any problems you've noticed when you checked the car. If the mechanic approves of the car but finds a few things wrong, ask for a written repair estimate. You may find the estimate useful in your negotiations with the seller.

When you inspect a used car

Here are some of the things you should check when you inspect a used car. But remember that if the car passes your inspection, you should have an independent mechanic look it over next.

Exterior. Look for rust, especially in the wheel wells, and examine the paint. If it isn't exactly the same color all over the body, the car may have been in an accident. Ask the seller what happened.

Interior. Check the pedals and seat springs for signs of wear. Roll the windows up and down.

Tires. Is there excessive or uneven wear on the tires, including the spare? That could be evidence of an accident. If the odometer says 10,000 and the tire treads are thin, the odometer may have been rolled back or disconnected, or the car may have been driven very hard.

Suspension. Push down hard on each corner of the car and try to make it bounce. If it keeps bouncing after you let go, the car may need new shock absorbers. Grab the top of each front tire and rock it in and out. If the wheel seems loose or makes a clunking sound, the bearings or joints may need work.

Brakes. Before you take a test drive, start the engine, step on the brake pedal, and hold it down for a minute. If the pedal continues to sink, there may be a leak in the hydraulic system. On the road, take the car up to 45 mph and brake fairly hard. The car shouldn't veer, and the brakes shouldn't grab or vibrate.

Alignment. If there's a puddle, drive through it in a straight line and then check the tracks. The front and rear wheel tracks should be right on top of each other. (Or have a friend drive the car away from you slowly so you can see whether the wheels are lined up.)

Steering. Turn the wheel back and forth before you start your drive, and do it again with the car in motion. The steering should be smooth and precise, without vibration or free play.

Gauges and controls. Check to make sure everything works.

Transmission. Try the transmission in forward and reverse gears. It should work smoothly and easily.

Acceleration. Acceleration with stumbling or hesitation, knocking, or rapping could mean the engine needs a tune-up. It could also be a sign of a more serious problem.

Oil consumption. If you're checking a gasoline engine, drive at highway speed after the car has warmed up. Take your foot off the accelerator for a few seconds. Then step on it again, hard. If you see blue exhaust smoke, the engine may need an overhaul.

Maintenance and repair costs for used cars

If you're shopping for a used car, you may want to figure into your costs the likely expenses for maintenance and repairs.

We have estimated the average maintenance and repair costs for cars in the model years 1976 through 1980, to give you a rough indication of what to expect.

In practice, these costs increase with a car's age, and also with the number of miles driven each year. High-mileage cars usually have costs up to double those of low-mileage cars.

Model year	Average cost
1976	$330
1977	300
1978	250
1979	200
1980	110

Energy conservation

Exterior caulking

Caulking, like weather stripping, helps save energy by reducing the amount of cold air that leaks into the house. Just as important, caulking helps preserve the house structure by keeping water out of cracks and joints.

■ The obvious places to caulk are around door and window frames, and at the corners of the house (there may be gaps where the siding joins). But there are other important places that may need to be sealed.

■ Check first for gaps between the house framing and the foundation. To spot cracks there, stand inside the basement and look along the top of the basement wall. If you can see light, you need caulk.

■ Another place to check is the space between the siding and the sheathing. Caulk behind the siding helps block the flow of cool air, so the house can retain its heat longer.

Oil vs gas: Should you switch?

We think it makes sense to consider a conversion from oil to natural gas only if your existing oil furnace needs replacement or substantial upgrading.

■ You're likely to benefit most if you concentrate on reducing your overall energy consumption with such measures as insulation, caulking, weather stripping, furnace derating, and space heating. Investments in energy conservation will continue to pay off regardless of the price difference between oil and gas. Indeed, as you reduce your energy requirements, the price differential becomes less important.

■ If you find that your oil furnace is too decrepit to be upgraded at a reasonable cost, then it might make sense to convert to gas—but be prepared to spend a good deal on equipment. The simplest and cheapest conversion is to replace the burner in the furnace. A new high-efficiency oil-to-gas conversion burner could then be an improvement worth considering.

■ A more expensive alternative is to replace the entire furnace.

Vent a dryer indoors?

A reader from Calgary, Alberta, told Consumer Reports that the family's electric clothes dryer was being vented indoors, thus adding "much-needed moisture" to the house during cold dry winters.

Our engineers replied that venting a dryer indoors is not always a good idea. In some cases—a Canadian winter being one—the heat and moisture from a dryer's exhaust would be welcome. But a dryer might expel too much heat or too much moisture for the typical laundry room. If that's the case, you'd need a fan to circulate warm moist air to the rest of the house. And, unless the vent has a very effective filter on it, the dryer will put unwelcome lint into the air.

You may want to install a diverter to direct dryer exhaust indoors in winter, if your electric dryer is in a space you normally heat. (Gas dryers should not be vented indoors under any circumstances because their exhaust contains toxic gases.) But we think you should first be sure you won't find indoor venting objectionable: As a check, redirect your present ducting indoors to experience the heat—and moisture—you would gain.

If you then decide to buy a diverter to make a more permanent arrangement, try to place the duct so the moisture it emits isn't blown directly onto floors or walls. And be sure to clean or replace the diverter's filter.

We tested two types of filter-equipped exhaust diverters.

■ One type of diverter was essentially a T-shaped, 4-inch duct with one or two internal baffles that moved when you adjusted an external handle. A socklike filter fit over the leg of the diverter's T and had to be cleaned regularly.

■ Another type of diverter was a much larger and more substantial device, a wall-mounted metal box that used a replaceable 14×20×1-inch furnace filter. The filter had to be replaced when it became clogged, but it should go longer without attention than the socklike filters, which required cleaning.

Steps to a more efficient fire

There are several ways to make an open fire more efficient. Most of these are cheap and easy.

■ Take out the grate, if you have one in your fireplace. Removing the grate will make for a slower-burning fire and reduce the amount of air drawn out of the room. If you insist on using a grate, leave plenty of ashes under it to help cut air flow and keep the embers warm longer.

■ When laying a fire, pile the logs at the back of the fireplace, with the largest at the back. The fire will then warm the back wall, and the biggest log will act as a reflector. The net effect is that extra energy will be radiated toward you.

■ Open the fireplace damper only enough to keep the fire from smoking. Leaping flames are a sign of too much air.

■ Build small fires. The flames shouldn't extend up behind the lintel of the fireplace.

■ Once the fire dies down, close fireplace doors (see below) to trim the loss of heated air. If you don't have fireplace doors, get them.

■ To reduce the amount of air the fireplace steals from the rest of the house, close any doors that open onto the fireplace area and open a window near the fireplace a crack. (A window on the same wall as the fireplace is best; one opposite will create a draft that sweeps the room.)

■ If you're using your fireplace to supplement central heating, turn down your thermostat as far as possible while the fire is burning.

Glass doors for the fireplace

If you think you can save energy by building a fire in your fireplace, think again. An open fire can draw more heat from the rest of the house than it supplies to the room it's in. Even in that room, about 90 percent of the heat from wood burned in an open fireplace escapes up the chimney. For every $150 cord of wood you buy, $135 worth will be wasted.

If you persist in looking to your fireplace for auxiliary heat, your first move should be to get a set of tight-fitting glass doors across the front of the fireplace. (Doors of almost any material can be used, but glass doors let you see the fire.)

Tight-fitting doors stem losses up the chimney while a fire is burning. More important, they cut the loss of centrally heated air after a fire starts to die but before it goes out completely. You can't close a fireplace damper at that point, lest your house fill with smoke and noxious fumes. But if you close glass doors, we found, you'll substantially reduce the loss of already heated air up the chimney.

Will a flue damper save energy?

The chances are pretty good that you can reduce your fuel bills by having an automatic flue damper installed—if you heat your house with oil.

But what if you heat your home with natural gas? Our tests showed that a flue damper saves energy on a gas furnace only under certain very specific circumstances.

A damper—typically, a motor-driven disk installed in the furnace flue—stays open while the furnace is on and closes when the furnace shuts off. The damper on an oil furnace saves energy and money by holding in heat that would otherwise escape up the flue and be wasted. It can reduce fuel bills by 5 to 20 percent a year, judging from tests conducted by our engineers and by others. However, there is no consensus on the amount of energy you can save with a flue damper on a gas furnace. Tests have shown that savings range from slight to none at all.

Unless your gas-fired heating system meets certain criteria, you're probably better off investing in other energy-saving materials such as storm windows, an automatic-setback thermostat, or insulation.

■ If the gas furnace is located in or near an area you normally heat, then a damper can be beneficial. For example, a flue damper could pay for itself if a gas-fired furnace is just off a heated basement recreation room and would otherwise draw already heated air into the burners and the draft hood. But suppose the furnace is in an unheated basement, or in the attic. A flue damper would save next to nothing then because the heat that would otherwise go up the chimney would be diverted to areas you don't normally heat, so the reclaimed heat wouldn't do you much good.

■ A flue damper might also be useful if you have a hot-water or steam system, rather than a forced-air system. With a hot-water system, for example, closing the flue would cause the boiler to cool down at a slower rate, so less heat would be needed to reheat the water.

■ A damper could be cost-effective if you have a flue that's larger than the typical 5-inch diameter. An oversized flue represents a heat escape route that's larger than necessary. All other things being equal, an 8-inch-diameter flue produces more than three times the heat loss of a 5-inch-diameter flue. In Michigan, where building codes required 8-inch flues, tests have shown that flue dampers can reduce gas bills by 20 to 30 percent a year.

Investing in a new water heater

If you are thinking of replacing a standard electric water heater, you may want to weigh the costs and benefits of investing in new equipment.

■ An energy-saver water heater, which is better insulated than a standard water heater, can save you something like $45 a year.

■ A heat-pump water heater is also worth considering. It costs about half as much to run as an energy-saver electric water heater, although it's considerably more expensive to buy.

■ A solar hot-water system costs even more to buy and install than a heat pump. (Local and federal tax credits for solar can help narrow the difference.) But a solar water heater could save more energy: The yearly saving would be about $200 from using a solar water heater instead of an energy-saver electric water heater.

Low- or no-cost ways to save

Before you make an expensive investment in new hot-water heating equipment, consider whether you've exhausted all available low- or no-cost measures with your present heater.

■ Save $100 a year or more by reducing the amount of hot water you use. Shower instead of taking baths—and take shorter showers. Install low-flow shower heads or put flow restricters in existing shower heads. Do the laundry with warm or cold water. Operate the washing machine and dishwasher only when they are full. All this can make a healthy dent in the amount of hot water you use.

■ Turn the thermostat on your water heater down to 120°F and save about $45 a year on operating your washing machine and dishwasher, which use fixed amounts of water. (Lowering the temperature could reduce the performance of your dishwasher, however.)

■ For about $20, you can buy an insulating blanket for an electric water heater. That will save you about $25 a year with a standard water heater and about $15 a year with an energy-saver.

Insulation kits for water heaters

You can cut your hot-water bills by wrapping an extra layer of insulation around the tank. A fiberglass insulation kit is designed to let you do just that.

A water heater loses a considerable amount of heat while it's storing hot water. Even a well-insulated energy saver can accumulate about $45 worth of storage losses (for an electric water heater) or $25 (for a gas one) over a year's time.

Older water heaters or standard models (which are less well insulated) could lose twice as much. By adding insulation to the tank, you could reduce the amount of heat lost through the walls of the water heater, thus reducing the amount of energy required to keep the water in the tank hot.

We tested fiberglass insulation kits for both gas and electric water heaters. The kits reduced storage losses for the gas energy-saver water heater by about one-sixth. On the electric water heater, the kit we installed reduced storage losses by about one-third.

We could usually install a kit in less than an hour. Kits with a top plate often took a little more time. The job was generally easy, and the only tool we needed was a pair of scissors.

When installing one of these kits, be sure to keep insulation away from the heater's controls and wiring. Some instructions omit that advice. And in choosing an insulation kit, be sure it's the right size to fit your water heater.

Heat pumps: Efficient but slow

If you had a choice between a conventional electric water heater priced at about $250 and a heat-pump model at about $1,100, which one would you consider the bargain?

In the long run, the $1,100 model might well be the better buy. And if your household doesn't use too much hot water, it could pay you to consider a heat pump.

Heat-pump models cost about half as much to run as energy-saver electrics, but they do not heat water as fast. A heat-pump water heater should pay for itself in less than ten years, at the national average rate for electricity (6.75 cents per kilowatt-hour) and at the average rate of hot-water use (450 gallons a week).

Because a heat pump is slow to heat water, it might not be the right choice for people who do enough bathing and laundering to drain the tank faster than the heat pump can supply fresh hot water.

Switching from electric to solar

The graphs below were developed by our engineers to show what a hypothetical family would spend each year to operate an energy-saver electric water heater and a solar water heater, under various conditions. As the graphs make clear, it might pay you to switch from an electric to a solar water-heating system, if you have very high electricity rates.

■ The first set of graphs (the "average" case) shows what the family spends now. The graphs for the average case are based on these assumptions: The family pays 5.6 cents per kilowatt-hour for electricity, uses 450 gallons of hot water per week, heats the water 85 degrees (from 55° to 140°F), lives in a low-sun area such as New York, and has a solar water-heating system that heats 55 percent of the water. Switching from an energy-saver electric water heater to a solar water heater would save about $180 a year.

■ The next set of graphs illustrates annual operating costs at an electricity rate of 11 cents per kwh—a more typical rate for the northeastern U.S. In this case, switching to solar would save the family about $345 a year.

■ The third set of graphs shows how conservation efforts would affect our hypothetical family. Simply cutting back the amount of hot water used to 300 gallons a week would save $95 a year. If the family then switched to a solar water heater, there would be an additional $155 saving. (Because our family is putting a smaller demand on the solar water-heating system, more of the water can be heated with the sun, and less by the solar system's electric backup heater.)

■ As the fourth pair of graphs shows, lowering the water temperature has an effect similar to cutting back on hot water. With an electric water heater, the family would save $45 a year. Switching to solar would save an additional $175.

■ The last set of graphs shows a further variable: the amount of sun in your area. Up to now, our examples have been based on a system installed in a low-sun area. But most of the country gets considerably more sun, permitting a solar water heater to heat a greater fraction of a family's water. Switching from an energy-saver electric water heater to a solar water-heating system would save our family about $225, if the sun heated 70 percent of the water over the course of a year—$45 more than in low-sun New York.

Costs of electric vs solar

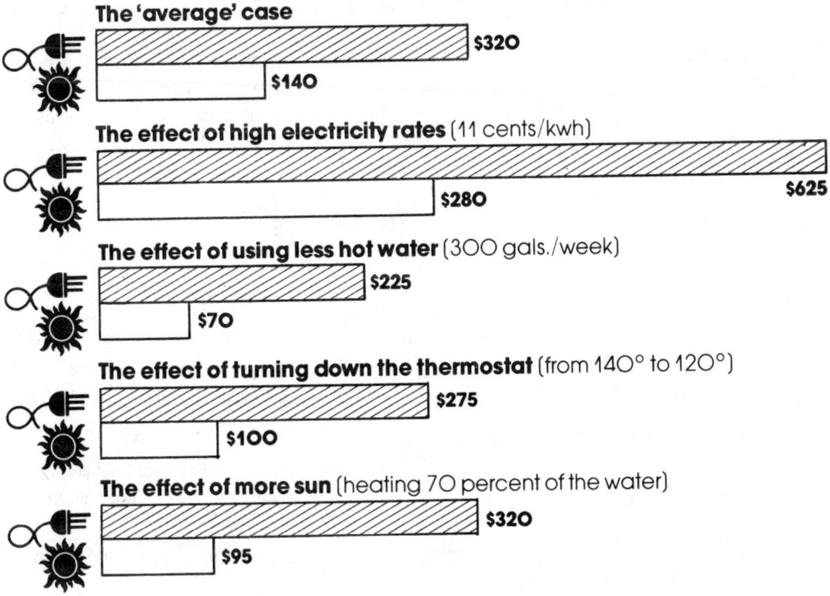

Switching from gas to solar

If you have a gas-fired water heater and are thinking about converting to a solar hot-water system, more often than not it would be a poor bargain. Our engineers suggest you apply the following rule of thumb before committing yourself.

Trade a gas water heater for a solar heater only if you are paying more than 75 cents per 100 cubic feet of gas (one therm) and paying less than 5 cents per kilowatt-hour for electricity. (A low electricity rate is important because a solar water heater uses electricity for pumps, controller, and backup heating.)

Will a solar water heater save?

There's little doubt that a solar water heater saves energy. Whether it saves money is less certain.

Switching to a solar system from a standard electric water heater could cut the cost of heating the water you now use by one-half to two-thirds.

To obtain that saving, however, you'd have to spend some $2,000 (perhaps more than $3,500), plus an additional $1,000 or so for installation. The payback period for a system so costly would be very near the hoped-for life of the equipment.

Federal and state tax credits could bring the cost within manageable range. Without such tax credits, there would be little financial reason for installing a solar water heater.

■ In 1982 the federal tax credit was 40 percent of the cost of an active solar installation, up to $10,000. On a $3,000 solar water heater, that would work out to a saving of $1,200.

■ About half the states add a tax credit or other incentive onto the federal subsidy.

■ Many states (about half—but not necessarily the same ones that provide tax credits) also exempt a solar installation from raising the valuation of your house for property tax assessment.

■ For specific information about tax credits and other benefits in your state, call the Conservation and Renewable Energy Inquiry and Referral Service, a federally funded clearinghouse for information on conservation and alternative energy sources. Its toll-free number is 800-523-2929, except in Pennsylvania (800-462-4983) and Alaska and Hawaii (800-523-4700).

Will solar work for you?

Should you invest in a solar water heater? Even if the equipment and installation costs are heavily subsidized by tax credits, it still might not make sense for you to make the change.

The decision to switch—or not to switch—to solar water heating is a complex one that requires thorough research. Investigate alternative, less costly ways to save on heating water. Even if other options are ruled out, there still are additional points to consider.

■ Before going any further, be sure your house has a suitable site for solar collectors. They must be installed on a south-facing site, usually a roof. In good weather, the site should receive unobstructed sunlight for at least six hours a day, both in winter, when the sun is low, and in summer, when deciduous trees are in leaf.

■ Finding a competent installer is crucial to the success of an installation. The skill and reputation of the installer you find could be a more important consideration than the brand of solar water heater you choose. In fact, a particular brand of solar water heater often comes with a particular installer. Before you sign a contract, get at least two estimates and thoroughly check an installer's qualifications. Ask for references from past customers and call the references.

■ You can enhance your saving if you're willing to change your habits to suit the sun. You can postpone doing the laundry until a sunny day. Or, for the greatest saving, you can switch off the backup heater much of the time and live with whatever hot water the sun provides. (You can't eliminate your energy costs entirely that way because the circulating pumps and the temperature-sensing electronic controller would still draw some electricity.)

■ You should also take into account the annoyance of doing any major home remodeling. What's more, a solar water-heating system requires inspection and maintenance. In the end, your decision may well reflect personal priorities more than financial priorities.

Tankless coil: A costly way to heat water

On a year-round basis, a tankless coil is not a very economical way to heat water. (The tankless coil is located in the steam or hot-water chamber of the boiler and heats hot water at the same time it provides heat to the house.) To meet the demand for water, the heating boiler must be operated year-round, and it must have enough reserve capacity to supply both heat and hot water on the coldest days. So, for most of the year, the boiler will burn much more oil than it would if supplying heat alone.

Assuming that oil cost $1.23 per gallon and that 64.3 gallons of hot water would be needed daily (the amount the average family uses), the tankless-coil burner we installed in our laboratory would have used an estimated $320 to $370 worth of oil per year. That's $40 to $85 higher than the annual operating costs we calculated for electric water heaters, based on an electricity rate of 6.75 cents per kilowatt-hour.

Saving with a portable heater

A portable heater can help you save energy when all you need to heat is one room or part of a room. Because a central heating system is the single biggest energy consumer in the house, anything that helps you set the central system's thermostat a little lower is likely to save energy in the long run.

You might use a portable heater to warm the kitchen during breakfast while leaving the central system's thermostat at a low nighttime temperature for an extra hour or so. Or you might use a heater to take the chill off an early spring day, turning off the central heating as soon as possible after winter.

For some uses, you may prefer a radiant heater, for others a radiant/convection heater, and for still others a convection-only model.

■ You may want concentrated heat—and want it fast—when dressing in a chilly bedroom on a cold morning. A radiant heater, such as a quartz heater, is good for quick spot heating. An upright radiant/convection heater combines good whole-room heating distribution with the ability to concentrate warmth near a desk or favorite armchair. An upright model is also easy to move from room to room and easy to store.

■ In the comparatively mild weather of an early spring or late fall, a convection-only model could well be a room's main heat source. It will give you heat evenly distributed, with relatively small temperature swings.

Using a thermostat

Turning down your thermostat is the simplest way to lower your heating bills.

■ Begin by lowering your normal daytime thermostat setting to the coolest comfortable temperature.

■ If you set back the temperature further at night or when the house is empty, you will add to your saving.

How much will you save? Both the kind of heating system you have and the weather conditions in your locality will affect the actual amount of money you save.

■ In general, the greater the setback—the difference between high and low settings—and the longer the setback period, the greater your saving will be.

■ The warmer your locality is, the higher the *percentage* of saving, though probably not the *total* saving. Homeowners who face cold winters run up very high fuel bills, and thus their overall dollar saving will probably be higher than for people living in warmer climates. In other words, it's more helpful for people in Chicago to save 20 percent of their fuel bill than for people in Los Angeles to save 80 percent of theirs.

Automatic-setback thermostats. You can achieve a saving with a standard thermostat, of course. But you may find that turning a thermostat down at night is a chore easily forgotten. And you may not like getting out of a warm bed in a cold house to turn the thermostat back up in the morning.

You can do away with the nuisance with an automatic-setback thermostat. By installing and using a thermostat that controls to two temperatures, you'd achieve a substantial saving on fuel. The heat would be automatically turned down at night and up again before you get out of bed the next morning.

Automatic-setback thermostats come in two basic types. With a clock-type unit—which can be electromechanical or electronic ("computerized")—you set the temperature changes you want and they're repeated until you reset the thermostat. With a timer-type unit, you set the number of hours the heat is to be turned down each time you wish to reduce the house temperature—and the heat will come back up after the number of hours you designate. The latter type would be preferable if your household routine unpredictably varies too much from day to day to allow use of the preset cycles of a clock-type thermostat. Of course, with the timer-type thermostat, you have to remember to make your settings every time you need a setback.

■ Whether it's worthwhile for you to buy an automatic-setback thermostat would depend on several factors: where you live, how long it takes for your home to get warm, whether you're likely to forget to lower the thermostat at night, and personal preference.

■ You might find that, when you no longer get up to a cold house, you'll set your night temperature even lower.

Saving with a thermostat

Consumer Reports engineers say that it saves you money when you lower the thermostat setting at night or when the house is empty. One reader questioned this strategy:

"The electric company tells me just the opposite, saying it takes more energy to bring the house back up to the desired temperature. Who's right?"

The answer: We are. You should lower the thermostat (unless you have a house heated by a heat pump). The amount of heat you save by lowering the thermostat more than offsets the heat needed to raise the house temperature when you want warmth.

But don't lower the temperature so much that you run the risk of freezing water pipes located in outside walls. Our engineers judge that lowering the thermostat to 50-55°F will give you a margin of safety as well as a sizable saving on your heating bill.

Improving windows

Improving your windows can be an easy and often inexpensive way to save energy. Loose windows cost you money. Your furnace must run longer than it would otherwise need to in order to replace the heat that escapes through the windows

■ We've found that simply locking the windows during the winter can help keep out some drafts.

■ If you want to achieve more than that, you should inspect your prime windows and make improvements where necessary. If you do nothing else to your windows this year, at least be sure the caulking and weather stripping are adequate. There should be no gaps or cracks in the caulking, and the weather stripping should be in good repair.

■ If you already have storm windows on your house, it will pay to keep the weather stripping on those windows in good repair. We found that replacing the weather stripping when it was in poor condition reduced overall air leakage by an average of 30 percent.

Shopping for storm windows

If you're in the market for storm windows, it will pay to shop carefully. Don't just take what a dealer has in stock or buy on the basis of a come-on price. Rather than depend on showroom displays or a sales pitch, inspect the windows closely.

The construction characteristics may not affect the initial performance of a new storm window by much. But we judge that the better made the storm window, the more satisfactory the service will be over a longer period.

Here are the important details to look for.

Rigid frame. The pieces of the frame should be put together securely, so that the sides don't bow away from the sash and the frame doesn't twist. With a rigid frame, a storm window will be better able to resist wind pressure. Corner joints should be neat and solid, with no cracks where the pieces come together.

Tie bar. This stiffener connects the sides of the frame at the middle, where the sash meet. It helps prevent the sides of the window from bowing apart.

Weather stripping. Typically, only the sides of each sash will have weather stripping. Sometimes, the stripping is installed in the tracks, rather than on the sash itself. It would be better, we think, to have weather stripping all around the sash, to block air leakage at the top of the window and at the sill.

"Marine" glazing. Look for a bead of plastic or rubber sealant all around the edge of the glass on both sides of the pane. We think this "marine" glazing makes for a stronger tighter sash. With "drop-in" glazing (the other commonly used method of sash construction), sealant is applied only to one side of the glass.

Tight-fitting sash. The glass and the screen should fit into their tracks snugly. On a well-constructed window, you shouldn't be able to jiggle a sash up and down when it's locked in position.

Sash interlock. Where the two sash come together, they should physically lock together. That is, a flange along the top of the lower sash should interlock with a similar flange along the bottom of the upper sash. To test how well this interlock works, close the window and try to force the two sash apart. If you can separate them, it's a sign that one sash doesn't sit quite right in its track and thus can't interlock with the other sash.

Some windows have weather stripping, rather than an interlock, where the two sash meet. That could be as effective as an interlock, provided the rest of the window is rigid.

"Anti-bow" pins. These are small wedges that help keep the sash pressed tightly into their tracks, as a further protection against wind gusts. If the storm windows you want don't have them, you can improvise by wedging small blocks of wood into each track.

Weep holes. The storm window frame should have two small holes (roughly ¼ inch in diameter) along the sill. They are intended primarily to allow water to drain away from the inside of the storm window frame during the summer, when the screen may let rain into that area.

Contractor-installed storm windows

Installing triple-track storm windows is not a do-it-yourself project for most people. Unless you're reasonably handy with tools—and not daunted by the prospect of spending several hours up on a ladder—you'll probably decide to hire a professional to install storm windows, or buy them with installation included.

To minimize problems that might arise between you and the installer, you should take the precautions we describe below. (Some of these suggestions would apply to any arrangement you make with a home improvement contractor.)

■ Avoid door-to-door salespersons offering suspiciously low prices.

■ Deal with an established reputable company. Friends and neighbors may be able to recommend a competent contractor.

■ You should have a written contract describing the windows in detail: size, color, brand and model designation if it exists.

■ If the windows don't have a brand name, the contract should specify the type of glazing, the type of weather stripping, and other details.

■ The contract should also include details about the installation itself. It should say, at a minimum, that the job will be done "in a workmanlike manner." The contract might also spell out the color of caulking to be used.

■ The contract should include a warranty on the installation, as well as the manufacturer's warranty on the windows themselves. The longer the warranty period on the work, the better.

■ The terms of payment should also be specified in the contract. We think it's best if the contract allows for partial payments as the work progresses, rather than payment in full before any work is done. Equally important is a "hold-back" clause, which allows you to make the final payment thirty days or so after the work is finished.

■ Inspect the windows when they are delivered, to be sure you've got what you ordered.

■ Inspect the installation before the workers leave. Be sure the work crew completes the installation according to your specifications. If you find a window that's not up to par, the crew will still be there to fix it. Check the caulking to see that it seals the storm windows tightly to the frame of the prime windows. (The caulking shouldn't block the weep holes in the frame, however.) Be sure the storm windows are level and that the sash move easily in their tracks.

Weather stripping

Don't expect too much of weather stripping. It can't compensate for large gaps where a window sash fits into the frame. Such a window needs to be fixed or replaced. And weather stripping won't eliminate the need for storm windows. But weather stripping will reduce the loss of heat due to air leakage from windows and doors.

In buying weather stripping, decide on the type that's best for your use, regardless of brand, and then price-shop. Our tests showed little quality variation among brands of a single type.

Tension strips are the longest-lasting type of weather stripping, but they tend to be expensive.

- They can be used for just about every kind of door and window joint, including that difficult spot where the two sash of a double-hung window meet.

- The self-adhesive plastic tension V-strips are easier to install than the metal ones, but both types of weather stripping should last a long time.

- The self-adhesive prefolded tension strips are particularly convenient to install around doors.

Self-adhesive foams seem to be a quick and easy way to weather strip, especially if you want the strips out of sight once they're in place. But they don't always stick and they aren't very durable if subject to friction or abrasion.

EPDM and closed-cell vinyl foams are likely to hold up the longest, but EPDM is the most expensive.

Open-cell polyurethane is the least durable, but it's cheap and a good choice for quick or temporary fixes.

Reinforced felt, foam strips, and tubular gaskets require about as much work as nailing in tension strips.

Nonreinforced felt can be installed fairly easily with a staple gun or a tack hammer. (If the stripping is to be exposed to moisture, however, use nonrusting staples or tacks; ordinary fasteners rust quickly.) Because nonreinforced felt is cheap, it may be the right choice where appearance is secondary.

Tape isn't pretty, but the low price makes it an option for attic or garage windows. Tape can be perfectly adequate, particularly if it's installed on the inside. But when tape is removed, it could pull up paint or leave a residue of adhesive that's hard to remove.

Which type of window insulation?

If you have bare windows and decide to cut down on energy losses, should you use storm windows or another type of insulator?

■ Although insulated shutters and shades provide the greatest saving, they require a good deal of your attention. You gain considerable heat by day if you let the winter sun shine in. To pick up that free heat and keep it indoors, shutters or shades on windows facing east, south, and west would have to be opened or closed according to the time of day and the level of sunlight. Such careful management takes some effort.

■ Shades and draperies are useful for windows that are too large to be covered with conventional storm windows, or for skylights and other glassed-in areas that may be easier to insulate from inside.

■ Storm windows (either a conventional storm window or an interior plastic window) require much less attention than the other types of insulators. That's one reason storm windows may well be the product of choice for most homeowners with bare windows.

■ Remember that the first layer of insulation you add will yield the greatest saving. Piling on even more insulation will not yield a proportionately higher saving. If you already have storm windows in place, it may be wise to look for other ways to save energy.

Installing a wood stove safely

Fire authorities generally agree that poor installation is a frequent culprit in home fires related to wood-burning.

A stove placed too close to an unprotected wall or directly on the floor creates a fire hazard. A chimney that is old and cracked or full of creosote is also dangerous. A stovepipe attached to an existing chimney without the proper heat-resistant adapters only adds to the danger of a fire.

In our judgment, installing a wood-burning stove is not a do-it-yourself job. Leave it to a qualified professional. But be sure to take the cost of installation into account before deciding whether to buy a wood stove. Installation of the stove and the chimney you need could more than double the cost of the stove.

Before arranging to have a stove installed, check with the local building or fire department to find out the requirements in your area. Also check with your insurance company to find out if the installation will affect your insurance rates.

Once the installation is complete, ask your insurance company and local authorities to inspect it to be sure it passes muster.

Getting less smoke with a wood stove

Here are ways you can minimize the nuisance and potential hazard of smoke from a wood stove.

■ Buy the smallest stove you need for the area you want to heat. If the stove is too big, you'll tend to turn the fire down to a smolder to avoid overheating the room. The slower the fire, the more smoke it will produce.

■ Use only well-seasoned hardwood if possible. Green or wet wood burns less completely and gives off more noxious emissions. Hardwoods (ash, birch, maple, and oak, for instance) will provide considerably more heat per cord than softwoods such as cedar, hemlock, and pine.

■ When starting a fire, let the wood burn briskly for fifteen minutes or so before adjusting air inlets and dampers to reduce the size of the fire. Don't reduce the air supply to the fire to make the stove burn as long as it can. Keep air inlets open at least a crack. If the chimney is still belching clouds of smoke a half-hour after you've rekindled a fire, you should open the stove's air inlet a bit more.

■ Don't overstuff a stove. Big loads of wood create oxygen-starved areas, which tend to burn poorly.

Buying wood

Firewood can be expensive. If you're buying wood to save on your fuel bills, you should take some precautions to make sure you spend your money wisely.

■ The standard measurement for firewood is the cord—a tightly packed stack of logs measuring 4 × 4 × 8 feet and weighing about two tons. Watch out for the "face cord"—a 4 × 8-foot stack that looks like a full cord from the front but is only a foot or two deep. A face cord should be one-fourth to one-half the price of a full cord.

■ Watch out, as well, for wood sold by the "truckload." Until it's stacked, you have little idea how much you're getting. (After all, a half-ton pickup truck can't carry a two-ton cord of wood.)

■ Be sure to buy only well-seasoned hardwood, if you can get it. The logs should have dark ends, with cracks radiating from the center. Unseasoned wood will give you a lot less heat. So will a cord with softwood mixed in.

Finance

End your escrow account?

Many lenders insist on setting up an escrow account to accumulate money for taxes and insurance as a prerequisite for giving you a mortgage. As a result, banks and savings-and-loan associations can use such accounts for their own purposes without paying interest to the mortgagees. If you think you could handle payment of your tax and insurance bills yourself, consider contacting your lender to see whether your escrow account can be ended.

Ending an escrow account. The need for an escrow account is often a matter of negotiation between you and the lender. Some lenders require such an account in all cases. Other lenders will let you pay tax and insurance bills if you can convince them that you'll pay the bills on time.

Making an inquiry of the lender could pay off. One member of our staff succeeded in having his escrow payments eliminated simply by sending a written request to his bank.

When escrow accounts are required. Some homeowners must use an escrow account. Virtually all borrowers in certain categories are required to pay their property taxes and insurance through an escrow account:

- When the mortgage is insured by the Federal Housing Administration or by the Veterans Administration.
- When the loan is for 90 percent or more of the value of the house.

When escrow accounts are acceptable. There are two instances in which escrow accounts may be less objectionable.

- Some homeowners welcome an escrow account despite the loss of interest. They prefer the "forced savings" that this method of payment requires. With an escrow account, they pay one-twelfth every month instead of having to come up with the entire amount when the taxes and insurance become due.
- About a dozen states require lenders to pay interest on escrow accounts. But the required interest rates in states with such laws range only from 2 to 5.2 percent—less than the rate even on a passbook savings account.

Buying vs renting

The table below has assumed certain mortgage rates, present and future interest rates, and housing-cost rate increases. The same form may be used to make comparisons using other assumptions. Because interest rates and inflation rates fluctuate constantly, you should adjust the assumptions for the conditions that apply when you are making your calculations.

Our example assumes a house that can either be purchased for $100,000 or rented for $8,400 the first year. If you buy the house, you will put $20,000 down and take out an $80,000 mortgage loan for thirty years at 15 percent. If you rent the house, you will put the $20,000 into a money-market fund paying 15 percent a year and reinvest the proceeds in the fund each year. We've assumed that the housing expenses (including rent but not mortgage interest) will increase 12 percent a year, that the house will also appreciate 12 percent a year, and that your marginal tax rate is 40 percent. The table shows the results of the two options at the end of the first and fifth years.

First-year summary	**Buying**	**Renting**
Gross gain		
Appreciation of house	$12,000	
Interest from money-market fund		$ 3,000
Expense		
Mortgage interest (less tax saving)[1]	7,194	
Property tax (less tax saving)[2]	1,200	
Fuel, utilities	1,800	1,800
Insurance	300	150
Repairs, upkeep	1,000	
Rent		8,400
Income tax on money-market interest[3]		1,040
Closing costs	2,000	
Total expense	$13,494	$11,390
Net gain or loss	−1,494	−8,390
Five-year summary		
Gross gain	76,234	20,228
Expense	−65,118	−73,043
Net gain or loss	$11,116	$−52,815

[1] *Mortgage interest less income tax saving (40% of first-year's interest of $11,990).*

[2] *Property tax of $2,000 less income tax saving of $800.*

[3] *First $400 of interest income not taxable; tax is 40% of balance.*

How to shop for an IRA

What should you look for when you've decided to open an Individual Retirement Account? Banks, mutual funds, insurance companies, credit unions, and brokerage houses will all be competing for your business. Take time to shop around. Your choice of IRA plans could well make a difference to you of thousands of dollars over the years.

Here are some things to keep in mind when shopping for an IRA. (These same suggestions apply if you're opening a Keogh account.)

■ Ask any potential IRA trustee about both the *current* rate and the *guaranteed* rate, if any. Current high interest rates may not hold up year in and year out for thirty years.

■ Your real return will be diminished by taxes when you withdraw the money. But if you're retired at that time, you may be in a lower tax bracket than when you opened the IRA.

■ Your real return may also be diminished by management fees. Be sure to ask in detail about the fees—both one-time and annual—exacted by any IRA trustee you're considering. The "disclosure statement" required by the Internal Revenue Service details these fees. It will be furnished to you in due course—but you should request it *before,* not after, you commit yourself to setting up your IRA in a particular institution.

■ With inflation likely to continue, the buying power of your IRA will need to be supplemented. Although IRAs are useful, other forms of retirement income will certainly be necessary.

Choosing a lawyer

Need a lawyer? When you shop for one, by all means ask about fees. But you also need to check on the quality of the service you can expect from a lawyer.

Here's some advice we published with the Virginia Citizens Consumer Council in a directory of lawyers practicing in Arlington County, Virginia:

"There is no simple way to determine whether Attorney X's $500 divorce will be more or less appropriate for a particular individual than Attorney Y's $200 divorce. . . . Consumers should ask questions about fees to learn *why* one attorney's fees are higher than another's."

Term insurance: Affordable death protection

If you are parents with young children, it's likely that you can afford the life insurance you need only if you buy term insurance. The annual premium is modest when you're young because your chances of dying are relatively small.

If you die, your beneficiary gets a specified amount of money, called the *face amount* of the policy. The annual premium for a $100,000 term policy on a 30-year-old man would typically be about $250 a year.

As you get older, the premium rises every year or every few years. As you reach retirement age, term insurance becomes quite expensive. But by then you can probably drop the insurance. Few people in their sixties are likely to need much, or any, life insurance.

Whole life insurance: Who needs it?

Who should buy whole life insurance? Relatively few people, we believe. Only if you meet one of the criteria listed below should you consider whole life:

- If you're in a high tax bracket and may benefit from its tax-shelter aspect.
- If you genuinely need a "forced savings" plan and have no better one available.
- If you know you will need life insurance after retirement age.

Cash value. Whole life's fixed premium is larger than necessary to cover the risk of death in the early years, and smaller than necessary to cover the risk of death in the late years. A $100,000 policy might cost a 30-year-old male $1,200 per year. Some of that represents savings. If you surrender your policy before it matures, you get back a cash value, which is set by a predetermined schedule written into the policy.

Most whole life policies have a cash value that builds up slowly in the early years, then somewhat more rapidly until—around age 100—the cash value equals the face amount of the policy.

The fixed predetermined rise in cash values of whole life policies amounts to an unattractive investment vehicle. The implicit rate of return on a good whole life policy, calculated under assumptions we consider reasonable, has been in the neighborhood of 6 percent (tax-deferred and partly tax-exempt)—and it's that high only if the policy is held a couple of decades or so.

Moreover, the buyers of whole life usually have no way to tell the rate of return. They pay a fixed annual premium and are never told what portion goes to pay for protection, what portion goes into savings, and what is taken out for commissions and other fees.

Mortgage term insurance

If you take out a mortgage, should you buy mortgage life insurance? That's a life insurance policy designed to pay off the balance due on a mortgage in the event of the mortgage holder's death. It sounds like a good idea, assuring that the surviving family will have a house free and clear.

But is mortgage insurance really such a good idea? We think the answer is no.

Most policies called "mortgage insurance" are really a form of term insurance known as "decreasing term." With decreasing term policies, the annual premium remains constant, but the face value, or death benefit, gradually declines.

Decreasing term insurance may have its place in special situations, but it should not be used as basic life insurance for the breadwinner of a family. Many breadwinners are underinsured to begin with, and inflation tends to make an insurance program less adequate every year. Decreasing term insurance is especially vulnerable to inflation because the coverage goes down, while each dollar of coverage is capable of buying less.

Under a few very special circumstances, a mortgage term insurance does make sense for some people.

■ Some people might already have enough insurance for their total needs at the time of buying a house. They might want the mortgage on the house to be paid off at death but might not want to rearrange an entire insurance program to accomplish that.

■ Another type of person for whom we think decreasing term insurance might make sense is a nonworking homemaker with young children. The death of a nonworking parent is likely to bring about expenses that need to be covered. Aside from final expenses (medical bills, funeral costs, and the like), there may be additional and continuing expenses for baby-sitters, day care, restaurant meals, and housecleaning, to name a few. If the breadwinner is already adequately insured and the family can afford it, insuring a homemaker with a decreasing term policy can make economic sense. The gradual decline in coverage is likely to parallel a decline in the need for coverage.

Comparing cash value with renewable and decreasing term

The table below outlines the salient characteristics of three types of life insurance.

Type of policy	Premium	Coverage	Usual coverage period	Cash values?	Sample annual premium[1]
Cash value (including whole life)	Stays level	Stays level	Lifetime	Yes	$800
Renewable term	Rises every year or every few years	Stays level	Up to age 65 or 70	Rarely	$210[2]
Decreasing term (including mortgage term)	Stays level	Declines gradually to zero	10 to 30 years from purchase	Rarely	$210

[1] *For $50,000 nonparticipating policy covering a 35-year-old buyer. Premiums for individual policies range widely above and below the examples shown.*

[2] *Rises each year or every few years.*

Should you buy a universal life policy?

A relatively new life insurance product, universal life is not a universal panacea. With a universal life policy, a specific amount of the premium is set aside for the cost of insurance protection. The remainder is considered to be "savings," which earns interest from the company on a regular basis.

Advantages. Universal life does represent an advance from the traditional whole life insurance policy in several respects, however.

■ The disclosure of fees and issuance of an annual statement to each policyholder (detailing fees, interest credited, and other information) add greatly to a consumer's understanding of policy costs and benefits. (It would be better still if the true net interest rate—not the gross rate—were disclosed.)

■ Another advantage is somewhat greater convenience in adjusting the face amount of the policy and in paying the annual premiums.

Drawbacks. But there are also drawbacks that should be understood by anyone considering universal life.

■ The substantial fees associated with universal life (even if they're lower than the fees hidden within whole life) diminish its attractiveness compared with alternative investments. Hartford Life Insurance Co. (the largest company offering universal life in 1981) was imposing a one-time fee of $575 on a $100,000 policy at the time of purchase and taking 5 percent out of each contribution a policyholder paid. Other companies were taking as much as 10 percent.

■ Simply analyzed, universal life is term insurance packaged with an investment fund. As with any package, the question is whether you can get better value by buying the components separately. If you shop for the best term insurance policy you can find and shop for the best investment you can find, we think it's likely you'll do better than if you let an insurance company do it all for you.

Comparing universal life with term and whole life

Check the table below for a quick overview of how three types of life insurance compare in four important respects.

	Term insurance	Whole life	Universal life
Premium	Increases on preset schedule	Constant	Flexible
Company-fee portion of premium	Undisclosed	Undisclosed	Disclosed
Protection	Fixed	Fixed	Flexible
Cash value (savings)	None, usually	Increases on preset schedule	Variable

Renewing certificates of deposit

Be sure to let your bank know what you want to do with a certificate of deposit before it matures.

Most banks and savings-and-loan associations will notify depositors well in advance when certificates are about to mature. Usually, the institution includes a form listing various options for reinvesting the money. It's important to respond in timely fashion and make your wishes known to the bank.

But don't count on notification by a financial institution. Mark on your calendar the maturity date of a certificate and follow up by specifying to the bank what you want done with the money. Without specific instructions, your bank may well roll over a certificate before you have a chance to select the most advantageous new investment.

Money-market funds: Are they for you?

For many consumers, money-market mutual funds are an attractive alternative to traditional bank accounts. What can they do for you—and what are their limitations?

Money funds pool the contributions of many individuals to buy short-term debt obligations (in effect, interest-bearing IOUs) issued by government agencies, banks, and corporations. The minimum initial investment at many funds is $1,000, but you may later be allowed to withdraw part of your initial investment.

What's the risk? Money funds are low-risk investments, but are somewhat less safe than bank deposits, in part because they are not federally insured, as most bank deposits are.

What do they pay? Money funds pay much higher interest than a passbook savings account. Indeed, in recent years they've paid higher interest than was generally available on certificates of deposit—one reason they've been so popular.

The fund pays you the actual yield on its portfolio, less a management fee that is typically less than 1 percent per year of the fund's assets.

Interest rates can be volatile, however. You'll want to check yields carefully before putting your money into either a money fund or a certificate of deposit. Keep in mind that while a certificate's rate stays fixed for the term of the certificate, the money-fund rate can fluctuate daily.

How do you use a fund? Like a passbook savings account, but unlike a certificate of deposit, a money fund lets you withdraw money at will, without penalty. Withdrawals can be made by written request, or with many funds, by telephone request.

Many funds also allow you to write checks against your fund account, but often the check must be for a minimum of $500. Some people have experienced delays in making withdrawals, but on the whole the funds provide almost as easy access to your money as a passbook savings account would.

How do you check pension benefits?

If the company where you work offers a pension plan to its employees, you should keep yourself informed concerning your current pension benefits. How can you find out what you're entitled to under your company's plan?

The Employee Retirement Security Act of 1974 (ERISA) prescribes the rules by which pension plans must operate, including provisions for disclosure of benefits to employees.

■ Your company must give employees a "Summary Plan Description," which highlights certain information about the company's pension plan.

■ You are entitled to receive a statement of your benefits when you leave the company.

■ If you request it, you must be given a statement of your benefits once a year. (ERISA doesn't require companies to provide it routinely, and many of them do not.) In general, ERISA requires a benefit statement to indicate both your accrued benefits and your vested benefits (the portion of your accrued benefits to which you have already become entitled under your company's plan).

Estimating retirement income needs

Does a person or family require far less income after retirement than before? We think not. Less may be needed—but not a lot less. To estimate your retirement income needs, figure on about the same income as before retirement —but deduct taxes, work expenses, and savings.

What percentage of a retired family's or individual's *gross* preretirement income would be needed to maintain the same living standard after retirement? In calculating retirement income needs, keep in mind that a retired family or individual will spend less, save less, and be taxed less.

One way to estimate retirement income is shown in the next table. It shows, for example, that a retired couple will need an income that's between 55 and 78 percent of its gross retirement income. A single person earning about $30,000, according to the table, would need 58 percent of that amount after retirement.

Equivalent retirement income

The table below was developed by the President's Commission on Pension Policy, established by the Carter Administration. The figures were calculated in 1980 for people at various income levels. The last column shows the income required after retirement to maintain preretirement living standards.

Gross preretirement income	Taxes[1]	Work-related expenses[2]	Savings and investments[3]	Net pre-retirement income[4]	Post-retirement income taxes[5]	Equivalent retirement income[6]
Single people						
$10,000	$ 2,008	$ 480	$ 240 (3%)	$ 7,272	–	$ 7,272 (73%)
15,000	3,703	678	678 (6%)	9,941	–	9,941 (66%)
20,000	5,738	853	1,280 (9%)	12,084	$ 198	12,282 (61%)
30,000	10,355	1,179	2,357 (12%)	16,109	1,282	17,391 (58%)
50,000	22,249	1,665	4,163 (15%)	21,293	3,752	25,675 (51%)
Married couples						
$10,000	$ 1,444	$ 513	$ 257 (3%)	$ 7,786	–	$ 7,786 (78%)
15,000	2,860	728	728 (6%)	10,684	–	10,684 (71%)
20,000	4,488	931	1,396 (9%)	13,185	–	13,185 (66%)
30,000	8,047	1,317	2,634 (12%)	17,999	$ 63	18,062 (60%)
50,000	17,824	1,931	4,826 (15%)	25,419	1,965	27,384 (55%)

[1] *Includes federal income tax, Social Security taxes, state and local income taxes (calculated at 19% of federal income taxes). Does not include property taxes.*

[2] *Estimated at 6% of income after taxes.*

[3] *Estimated at a percentage (shown) of income after taxes.*

[4] *Gross preretirement income less taxes, work-related expenses, and savings and investments.*

[5] *Post-retirement taxes are on income in excess of Social Security benefits, which are not taxable. Retirees without Social Security benefits would need higher retirement income.*

[6] *Equivalent retirement income as a percentage of preretirement gross income shown in parentheses.*

Basic monthly charge for telephones

When you pay the "basic monthly service" for your telephone, do you know what the billing includes? Not likely, because in most states the charges are not broken down. Even in states where they are, the breakdown is not easy to understand.

In New York State, the phone company details the charges once a year. Yet 62 percent of families surveyed by the New York City Department of Consumer Affairs indicated they had no idea what they were paying in telephone rental fees.

Here's what the charge for your basic monthly service could include:

■ Rent for the phone.

■ An "access charge" (a payment for the right to be hooked into the phone network).

■ Charge for a certain number of message units or for unlimited calls within a specified local area.

■ Charge for renting the phone wiring in your home.

■ Charge for a special phone line if you use a push-button tone phone.

Buying a phone: Does it pay?

If you do a little arithmetic, you might find it costs you dearly to rent your phone instead of buying one.

Even in states where the rental charges are relatively low, the payback period if you buy a phone might be no longer than two or three years. The saving can mount up over time. A standard tabletop phone can last for fifteen or twenty years and needs a repair only every seven years, on average.

Use the worksheet on the facing page to help you decide whether you can save. Here are the steps to follow.

■ List each phone by location. Also list its type and its outlet—modular, four-prong, or hard-wired.

■ Establish the exact charges you are now paying to rent each phone in your home. Enter them under "Monthly rental." Call the business office of your local phone company and ask a service representative to detail the charges for you. You may not get complete and correct information without prompting. To double-check the information you're given, call a second service representative for confirmation. You might even call your state's public utility commission (the phone company can give you the number) to check the allowable rates for the phone or phones you have.

■ Next, ask the service representative what other saving or charge you'll incur in making the conversion. For instance, the Bell System companies won't charge to come to your house to pick up a detached rented phone. But in some areas they'll pay you (often $5) to bring your rented phone to one of their Phone Center retail stores. The payment will be applied as a credit to your phone bill. The footnote on the worksheet indicates how to take this credit into account.

■ Our calculation is based on the assumption that you will replace each rented phone by buying an exact duplicate. Do some shopping to find the best price for the look-alike phones you'd be buying. Insert a price for each phone in the appropriate spot.

■ You'll have to add to the purchase price any costs you'll incur in converting your phone outlets to accept the standard modular jack that would come on any new phone you buy. Write in the costs involved in converting an outlet.

■ Now you're ready to make your calculation. The total cost of the new look-alike phones plus the cost of converting any outlets, divided by your present monthly rental, will tell you how long it will be before you've paid off your investment. Every month thereafter, you'll be saving the total monthly rental.

Owning vs renting: How much can you save?

Phone location	Phone type	Outlet type	Monthly rental	Purchase price	Conversion cost
________	________	________	________	________	________
________	________	________	________	________	________
________	________	________	________	________	________
________	________	________	________	________	________
________	________	________	________	________	________
		Total costs	________ A	________ B	________ C*

Calculation: ________ (B) + ________ (C*) ÷ ________ (A) = ________ (Months to break even (D)).

Saving: After ________ (D) months, you will be saving ________ (A)

Deduct from this figure the payment, if any, from the phone company for return of phones.

Choosing a phone to buy

In deciding which type of phone to buy and where to buy one, there's more involved than just price.

Warranty. If the phone you own breaks down, your phone company won't repair it. You're responsible for your own repairs. In selecting a phone, therefore, the warranty policy of a store might prove more important than price.

■ Does the store offer a warranty that goes beyond the manufacturer's warranty?

■ Does it do its own repairs, or are you responsible for shipping the phone back to the manufacturer?

■ How long will it take to get the phone repaired?

■ Can you get a phone on loan in the meantime? (A loaner is particularly important if you have only one phone. You obviously won't want to be without phone service.)

■ Once the warranty has expired, what's the charge for parts and labor?

Checking the phone. When you finally buy a phone, make sure that stamped on the underside is the Federal Communications Commission registration number, the ringer equivalence number, and the date of manufacture.

■ The first two should be reported to your phone company when you plug in the phone.

■ The date of manufacture shows that you're not getting a reconditioned phone posing as a new one.

Standard vs electronic. How well do the telephones for sale hold up? We put that question to several stores that both sell and service phones. Almost uniformly, they gave the same answer.

■ There are few problems with standard phones.

■ The electronic phones, at least at this stage in their development, are much more likely to break down.

Precautions with an electronic. If you're attracted by an electronic phone, observe certain precautions.

■ Have a standard phone in addition, so that you aren't totally dependent on the electronic phone.

■ Pay especially close attention to warranty provisions, and to the problems involved in having the phone repaired. Even if you buy your phone from a store that does its own repairs, it may repair only nonelectronic phones.

The cost of push-button phones

If you replace a rented push-button tone phone (called *Touch-Tone* by the Bell System) with a similar phone you've bought, you'll still have to pay a monthly rental fee for the *Touch-Tone* line. Even though many central exchanges today are capable of handling *Touch-Tone* signals without installation of special equipment, phone companies still have the right to charge extra for providing a *Touch-Tone* line.

If you decide to give up your push-button tone phone and switch to a rotary dial, you'll have an extra saving when you buy a phone.

Affordable high style in a telephone

If you buy a phone made by the large independent manufacturers, rather than rent one from Bell System companies, a high-style phone could fall within your budget.

A *Trimline*-type phone, for instance, might seem affordable if you have to pay only $20 or so more than a standard phone as a one-time purchase price, instead of paying a hefty premium month after month for renting one.

The phone you'd buy would be a twin of one rented from Bell. Unless you happened to notice the manufacturer's name, you'd be hard-pressed to tell by appearance that the look-alike was not your rented model.

Installing a phone

In some cases, all you have to do to install a phone you buy is simply to plug it in. Even with more complicated installations, if you're reasonably handy you can probably do the job yourself.

■ If your home is equipped with a standard modular phone jack, you'll have no problem connecting your new phone. Because new phones come with a modular plug, all you have to do is plug it in.

■ Nor is there much of a problem if your home has a jack that takes a four-prong plug. Just plug in an adapter that will accept a modular plug. You can buy the adapter at a phone store or an electronics-supply store.

One side of the adapter receives the phone's modular plug. The other side has four prongs to fit into your jack.

■ If your rented phone is hard-wired into a box mounted on the wall, or directly into the wall, the installation will be more difficult. Before tackling that job yourself, check with your phone company. It's worth asking under what circumstances it might make the change without charge.

■ To do the job yourself, you'll have to get a conversion kit. The kits are available for a few dollars from phone outlets and are free from many Phone Center stores. The kits come with instructions and are not particularly difficult to use.

■ Conversion kits are also made for wall-phone outlets, because new wall phones also plug in with modular plugs.

Saving on an extension

No matter whether you rent or buy a phone, you might be able to save by wiring your own telephone extensions. Whether—and how much—you can save with a do-it-yourself installation of an extension depends on the regulations in your state.

About half the states allow consumers to do their own wiring, in one way or another. Despite this, in many cases, there is no monthly saving involved. But if you're adding an extension, you can still save on the often-substantial one-time installation charge made by the phone company.

Doing your own wiring for an extension is not difficult.

■ At a telephone equipment store or an electronics-supply store, buy what's called a "duplex jack" and extension wiring.

■ The duplex jack plugs into a standard modular phone jack, converting it to a receptacle for two modular plugs.

■ Plug the extension wire into the other receptacle. Run the wire to a new location, stapling it along the baseboard.

■ Attach a back-to-back modular jack at the end of the extension wire. Your phone can now be plugged into the other side of that jack.

When to prepare a will

The time to prepare your will is when you've acquired assets that can be passed on to someone else, or when you have minor dependents.

The main purpose of a will is to make sure your property is distributed the way you want, with a minimum of delay and expense. Also, if you have minor dependents, your will can provide for their care.

There are few eligibility requirements.

■ You must be above a certain age (the minimum varies from state to state, from 14 to 21).

■ You must be fully aware of the consequences of making a will.

■ You must be acting voluntarily.

Reviewing your will. Every few years you should review your will to make sure it conforms to your current wishes about how your property is to be distributed. Generally, you should revise your will:

■ If there's a significant change in your family's composition or health.

■ If there's an important change in the tax laws.

■ If you move to a state whose laws will affect your estate in a different way.

Should you prepare your own will?

It is perfectly legal to prepare your own will. We advise you to consult a lawyer, however, if any of the following circumstances apply to you:

■ If your potential estate, including any property you're likely to inherit in the near future, is more than $100,000.

■ If you're planning to disinherit someone in your will.

■ If one of your beneficiaries might require special care. (For example, you might have to make special arrangements for a retarded child.)

■ If you have property complications. (For example, if you own a small business, you may want to arrange for one of your beneficiaries to take it over.)

■ If you decide, after trying to prepare a simple will on your own, that it takes more care and attention than you're ready to give.

After the will: Last instructions

Once your will is completed, you should give the person you name in your will as executor a list of last instructions. It may be in the form of a letter and should contain any of the following items that are relevant:

■ A note on where your will and other valuable papers can be found. (Some states temporarily seal a safe-deposit box when the holder dies. Do not put your will in a box without asking your bank what the rules are in your state.)

■ Funeral and burial instructions.

■ An explanation of any unusual action covered by your will, such as disinheriting one of your children.

■ Your father's name and your mother's maiden name, which may be needed for the death certificate.

Food

Nitrosamines: The risk and how to reduce it

The particular nitrosamines found in bacon cause cancer in animals, and the assumption must be that they can also contribute to the risk of cancer in humans. But given the complexity of human diets, other environmental factors, and the cancer-causing process itself, no study could ever prove that eating bacon causes cancer. So we can't say how many cases of cancer a year might be attributed to eating bacon, or how much eating a certain quantity of bacon would increase your odds of getting cancer.

There's no doubt that a genuine—though small—risk is associated with eating bacon. Don't eat bacon, and you avoid the risk.

If you can't bear to give up bacon completely, serve it as an occasional treat rather than an everyday part of the diet.

There are some things you can do to minimize the risk, however.

- Try nitrite-free bacon. The brand of nitrite-free bacon we tested had virtually no detectable nitrosamines in it. Unfortunately, it didn't taste very good.

- Look for bacon with high lean-to-fat ratio—that is, the most meat. Nitrosamine levels are higher in the fat.

- Avoid cooking with bacon grease. It can contain three to four times as much nitrosamines as the bacon.

- Cook bacon at a fairly low temperature. It will take longer to cook, but less nitrosamines are likely to be formed. Or cook bacon on paper towels in a microwave oven. That method of cooking has been found to produce less nitrosamines than frying.

- Cook bacon in a well-ventilated area. Some kinds of nitrosamines vaporize during cooking, and you might inhale them along with that tempting bacon aroma.

Storing bacon

Bacon should be eaten within a week of its purchase. Be sure it's tightly wrapped—it keeps best that way. Don't freeze bacon because freezing hastens deterioration of its taste.

Homemade baked beans

If you want to serve beans that taste great, you'll have to make your own. The ones that come in cans just don't make the grade. Even the best of them tasted mediocre, as we found in our tests of canned baked beans. Our homemade version was far superior. It was judged excellent by the taste experts.

The dish had a nice blend of the flavors and aromas of beans, pork, onion, and tomato. It was just slightly sweet and salty. It was also only mildly spicy. If you like more zing, you can easily adapt the recipe: Garlic, chili powder, or cloves add interesting notes.

You'll get thirteen side-dish servings, about ½ cup each. If you like a dish lower in fat and sodium—and lower in calories—see our second version of the recipe, below.

Baked beans #1

1 pound dried navy beans
¼ pound salt pork, cubed
1 teaspoon vegetable oil
1 medium onion, chopped
½ teaspoon ground mustard
¼ teaspoon freshly ground black pepper
2 teaspoons Worcestershire sauce
½ cup tomato purée
2 tablespoons molasses
3 tablespoons dark brown sugar

Rinse beans in a 3-quart saucepan. Add 6 cups of hot water, bring to boil, and let boil for 2 minutes. Cover and let stand for 1 hour. Drain and discard the water. Add the salt pork and 4 cups of fresh hot water. Bring to a boil and simmer, covered, for 45 minutes.

Preheat oven to 300°F. Scoop the salt pork out of the water and lightly brown it in the vegetable oil in a 3-quart, range-proof dutch oven or casserole. Add the chopped onion and sauté until the onion is transparent. Stir in the ground mustard, black pepper, Worcestershire sauce, and tomato puree. Simmer for about 3 minutes. Add the molasses and brown sugar and stir well. Pour the liquid from the beans into the mixture and let simmer for another 2 minutes. Add the beans, stir gently, and cover.

Bake in preheated oven for 3 hours.

Baked beans #2

Our pork and beans had a higher protein content than any of the canned beans we tested—10.5 grams per serving. But our recipe also had 211 calories per serving—higher than any of the canned beans. Because of the salt pork, it also had about three times as much fat per serving as most of the canned versions—5.6 grams. Finally, it was higher in sodium than the lowest-sodium canned products—374 milligrams per serving.

We devised a second recipe that substituted 2½ strips of bacon (cut up) for the salt pork, that used only 2 tablespoons of dark brown sugar, and that omitted the vegetable oil. Result: Per serving, the new dish had about 8 grams of protein, 159 calories, 2 grams of fat, and only 82 milligrams of sodium. The recipe was judged very good.

If you get gas

Beans are one of those foods that cause people to say "I like them, but they don't like me." Beans do produce intestinal gas in many people.

The gas is caused by complex carbohydrates called oligosaccharides. Because these carbohydrates can't be digested, they pass into the lower intestine, where they react with normal intestinal bacteria. Humans have different types and levels of bacteria in their intestines. That's why beans get along fine with some people and not with others.

If you have the problem, you might do well to cook beans from scratch (see our recipes above). To get rid of some of the oligosaccharides, the U.S. Department of Agriculture recommends soaking the dried beans in water for a least three hours. Then discard the water, and cook the beans in fresh water. This should help alleviate the problem with gas.

Homemade beef stew

Stewing is a good way to serve beef and still stay within your budget. The long, slow, moist-cooking process tenderizes the meat, so you can use tougher, less expensive cuts. Adding vegetables and seasonings to the simmering browned meat makes a basic beef stew.

Canned and frozen beef stews are convenient, but our tests showed that few of the commercial stews tasted very beefy. And the meat was usually too chewy, the vegetables too soft.

Our own homemade beef stew, however, was judged excellent for its sensory qualities. It had lots of tender beef and firm vegetables, and the gravy tasted of beef stock. An 8-ounce bowlful had 231 calories. That's more than many of the commercial stews we tested had, but our version was also among the lowest in fat and among the highest in protein, vitamin A, and iron.

Our homemade recipe had 453 milligrams of sodium per serving. If you're on a low-sodium diet, that may be too much. You can adapt our recipe by leaving out the salt and bouillon cubes, and make up for any loss in flavor by adding some herbs. Try basil, thyme, or rosemary, or use a bouquet garni while the stew is cooking. These herbs will also spice up our basic recipe, if you prefer a stew that's a bit less plain.

Beef stew

3 tablespoons vegetable oil
2 pounds stew beef, cut into 1-inch chunks
½ garlic clove, minced
1 medium onion, chopped
2 tablespoons all-purpose flour
¾ teaspoon salt
½ teaspoon Worcestershire sauce
¼ teaspoon black pepper
4 cubes beef bouillon
4 cups water
4 cups potatoes, cut into ¾-inch chunks
2 cups carrots, cut into ¾-inch chunks
1 cup celery, cut into ¾-inch chunks
1 cup frozen peas

Heat the oil in a 4-quart pot. Add the beef, about a third at a time, browning thoroughly. Remove the beef and put to one side.

In the same pot and using the oil remaining in it, sauté the garlic until it's light brown. Add the chopped onion, then cook until it's transparent. Add the flour, cooking until it's light brown. The flour should absorb all the oil and the mixture will be clumpy.

Return the meat and its juice to the pot. Add the salt, Worcestershire sauce, pepper, bouillon cubes, and ½ cup of the water. Stir well to pick up all the browned bits from the bottom of the pot and to make sure the flour is completely blended into the water. Then add the rest of the water, and stir to mix.

Keep stirring until the stew boils. Continue to stir, letting the stew boil slowly until the thin watery gravy becomes thick enough to coat the back of a spoon. The gravy should thicken quickly just after it boils.

Reduce the heat to a simmer and cook for about 1½ hours. If desired, add herbs. While the meat is simmering, peel and cut up the potatoes, carrots, and celery.

Add potatoes and carrots, cook for 10 minutes. Add the celery and peas; cook for 7 minutes, then serve. The recipe makes eleven servings.

You can freeze any leftover stew in plastic containers. If you want to prepare the entire batch for freezing, you may want to make up the stew without the vegetables, then add them later.

Choosing a bread

If you have a child who seems to survive on sandwiches, it would make sense to prepare sandwiches with bread that's nutritious. If you are concerned about a bread's nutritional quality, check the ingredients list.

The following ingredients are likely to improve the protein quality of grain: milk, eggs, whey, and whey/soy combinations. The more of them on the label, and the higher they stand on the list of ingredients, the better.

People who eat a more varied diet can safely choose a bread for its taste or its price. The store brands we tested were usually the cheapest, often costing between 40 and 80 cents per pound. Our homemade bread (see below) cost 47 cents a pound. It was one of the cheapest breads, if you don't count your labor and household energy as part of the price.

Keeping bread

Saying a bread has no preservatives is one way to sell bread these day. But the preservative typically added to bread—calcium propionate—has never caused alarm. The additive is used as a mold inhibitor.

Science can keep bread from growing moldy too quickly, but it hasn't yet discovered a way to keep bread from getting stale after a few days. One thing that will *not* prevent bread from getting stale is storing it in the refrigerator. That hastens the cyrstallization of starch, which is what happens when bread goes stale.

Using the freezer, however, works fine. Bread put into the freezer in the original unopened wrappings will keep well for up to three months.

Homemade bread

Bread made from our recipe is the kind that you can happily eat plain. It was the only bread whose taste was good enough to be judged excellent by our expert tasters when we tested bread.

Our bread retained the subtle taste of baked wheat, and it was yeasty and more buttery than most of the commercial breads. Its crust was firm and its crumb tender without being too airy. Our expert tasters noted that it had "fast breakdown," which is the technical way of saying it melts in your mouth.

Its performance in our nutritional test was judged very good. Two slices contained 180 calories, 5.4 grams of protein, and 207 milligrams of sodium.

Bread-making can be as sensuous an activity as eating freshly baked bread. But it's one of those cooking skills that takes some practice before you know exactly what to expect at various stages in the recipe.

If you are new to bread-making, rely on a cookbook to get you started. Many cookbooks devote long sections—or even the whole book—to explaining "until blisters appear," "knead lightly," and other parts of the process.

Here's our recipe. It makes two loaves and takes about three hours.

White bread

1 package dry yeast
3 tablespoons sugar
½ cup lukewarm water
½ stick (¼ cup) sweet butter
¾ cup whole milk
1½ teaspoons salt
1 large egg, beaten
4 cups unbleached all-purpose flour

Dissolve the yeast and 1 tablespoon of sugar in the water, which should be about 85°F (use a kitchen thermometer to check). Let the mixture sit for about 10 minutes (bubbles will indicate active yeast).

Heat the milk and butter in a small saucepan until the butter is melted; set aside. Measure the remaining 2 tablespoons of sugar and the salt into a large bowl. Pour in the milk-butter mixture; blend well with a wooden spoon. Add the beaten egg and ½ cup of flour. The temperature of the mixture should be about 105°. Add the yeast mixture and stir well. Add about half the flour. Beat vigorously for 3 minutes or 300 times with the wooden spoon (the beating can be done with the dough hook attachment of a mixer). Add the rest of the flour to make a soft dough.

Lift the dough from the bowl and knead on a floured board until blisters appear on the dough's surface and the dough is elastic. Shape the dough into a ball, return it to the bowl, and butter the surface. Cover with wax paper. Let rise for 1 hour in a warm place (100° to 110°) until it has doubled in size. Punch the dough down and knead lightly.

Divide the dough into two and shape to fit two well-greased and floured loaf pans. Again, grease surface of dough with butter; cover lightly with wax paper. Let rise for 1 hour. Meanwhile, preheat oven to 400°. Bake 30 to 35 minutes. Loaf should be golden-brown and sound hollow when tapped on the bottom.

Four cakes to make from scratch

Making a cake from scratch can be as easy as pie. Our food technologists developed the four cake recipes below, which are nearly as simple as the one-bowl method of packaged mixes. But with these recipes, you won't have the artificial-flavor problem that plagued the packaged cake mixes we tested.

Start off with our basic mix, consisting of cake flour, baking powder, sugar, and salt. You can double or triple the recipe—make as much as you can conveniently use. Add the appropriate ingredients and the basic mix becomes a yellow cake with a rich buttery taste or a chocolate cake flavored with cocoa and butter. Or turn the basic mix into our white cake.

The sensory consultants for whom we baked our cakes rated our yellow cake better than any of the packaged mixes they tested. The chocolate cake was rated the equal of the best packaged mixes tested, and the white cake, which was the least successful, was rated good by our sensory consultants, as were most of the commercial white mixes in the test project.

For those who want to eat their cake and have some extra nutritional goodness too, we devised our "Everything Cake," a kind of carrot/fruit cake.

Because it's a dense cake, a slice of the Everything Cake has more carbohydrates and calories than most other cakes, packaged or homemade. It also provides a fair amount of several vitamins and minerals: vitamins A and E; the B vitamins— thiamin and pantothenic acid; and the minerals—iron, magnesium, phosphorus, and zinc.

The flavor of the Everything Cake is predominantly that of apricots and raisins, with a buttery and fruity accompaniment. It isn't as sweet as most cakes you're used to eating. The Everything Cake has other special characteristics: a slight chewiness, firmness, and an uneven crumb texture (caused primarily by the weight of the extra ingredients in the batter). It can also be a bit dry, if the raisins and apricots you use are too dry.

Our sensory consultants had one objection to all four of our homemade cakes—that they were a bit too salty. You can reduce the amount of salt in the recipes, if you like.

When you try the recipes, be sure to measure ingredients and follow directions carefully. If your oven is fairly even, the cakes should come out just fine. And if they don't, consult the troubleshooting chart, which follows the recipes, to help you locate the problem.

(continued on next page)

The basic mix makes about 3 cups—the amount you need for each of the four cake recipes that follow.

Here are our recipes and instructions. Be sure to sift together the ingredients in the basic mix after you measure them.

Basic mix

2 cups cake flour
1 tablespoon baking powder
1 cup sugar
1 teaspoon salt

Chocolate cake

3 cups basic mix
½ cup cocoa powder
½ cup softened butter
1 teaspoon vanilla
1 cup whole milk
2 eggs, unbeaten

Yellow cake

3 cups basic mix
½ cup softened butter
1 teaspoon vanilla
1 cup whole milk
2 eggs plus 2 yolks, unbeaten

White cake

3 cups basic mix
½ cup softened butter
1 teaspoon vanilla
1 cup whole milk
2 egg whites, unbeaten

Preheat oven to 375°F. Grease and flour two 8-inch round cake pans. Sift dry ingredients (the basic mix or the mix plus cocoa) together into bowl. Add the softened butter, the vanilla, and about ⅔ cup milk. Beat at medium speed (high speed for portable mixers) for 2½ minutes. Add the rest of the milk and the unbeaten eggs. Beat for 3 minutes. Pour batter into pans and bake for 30 minutes. Test for doneness with toothpick. Cool in pans for 10 minutes, then remove and cool on racks. Frost when cold.

Everything cake

3 cups basic mix
½ cup each:
chopped walnuts, quick rolled oats,
wheat germ, golden raisins,
chopped dried apricots
½ cup softened butter
1 cup whole milk
1 teaspoon vanilla
3 eggs, unbeaten
1 cup grated carrots

Preheat oven to 375°F. Grease and flour two 8-inch round cake pans. Sift the basic mix ingredients together in bowl. Add the remainder of the ingredients. Beat at medium speed (high speed for portable mixers) for 3½ minutes. Pour batter into pans and bake for 40 to 45 minutes. Test for doneness with toothpick. Cool in pans for 10 minutes, then remove and cool on racks. Cake can be frosted, but it is not meant to be layered, and it doesn't cut well until it's cold. It keeps well.

Problems baking a cake?

Our food technologists developed this troubleshooting guide to help you figure out the answers to your cake-baking problems.

If the cake... / ... the problem may be...	Oven too hot	Oven too cool	Mixed too much	Mixed too little	Wrong-sized pan	Taken out of pan too soon	Wrong type of flour	Strong or rancid flavorings	Poor quality ingredients	Eggs beaten too much	Eggs beaten too little	Underbaking	Overbaking
Is too small	✓	✓		✓	✓	✓				✓	✓		
Has peaks or cracks	✓												
Is sunken		✓										✓	
Is too dark or too pale	✓	✓			✓							✓	✓
Tastes flat									✓				
Tastes bitter or unpleasant								✓	✓				
Is coarse		✓		✓						✓			
Is too dense	✓		✓							✓	✓		
Is crumbly				✓									
Has tunnels	✓			✓									
Has thick, hard crust		✓											✓
Is dry										✓			✓
Is soggy				✓								✓	
Is tough	✓		✓				✓						✓

Choosing a cake mix

Because you can usually make a satisfactory cake with nearly any mix, you probably could choose a mix by price rather than brand. Our food technologists suggest you stick to the cheapest mixes—which are often the store brands—especially if you like icing on your cake. Most flaws in flavor and texture can be covered up with a strongly flavored frosting.

Our tests of cake mixes showed that no one company's mixes consistently outdid another's. The test results also showed that the chocolate and yellow cakes, overall, had fewer flaws than the white cakes. But the majority of the mixes tasted just ordinary; many were marred by tell-tale artificial flavors and defects of texture.

Pudding-added cake mixes

"Fluffiness" used to be what people wanted from a cake mix. Nowadays, fluffiness is out and "moistness" is the new byword, with "pudding added" the key phrase on the label.

Are pudding cakes any moister than those made from ordinary cake mixes? According to our food technologists, a cake mix plus pudding is a bit of a put-on.

The pudding-added mixes will produce a moist cake. But our sensory consultants who tested cake mixes found that those with pudding didn't taste consistently better—or moister—than those without pudding added.

Instant pudding is mainly sugar and starch, both of which can be found in puddingless cake mixes. It's you, the baker, who adds the moistness when you add an extra egg and some oil or butter to the mix.

Fried chicken: Cost of convenience

For the best fried chicken at the least cost, buy a fresh bird and cook it yourself. Use our recipe below—the results were judged excellent by our sensory consultants.

But if you're in a hurry, or don't want to cook, that's not helpful advice. Instead, you can go to a fast-food place for your fried chicken. You may get decent chicken, but you may have to pay the price of convenience.

Our consultants tested chicken from both *Church's Fried Chicken* and *Kentucky Fried Chicken.* Compared with the frozen fried products we tested, the fast-food dishes were among the better-rated. The chicken was particularly meaty—though it was expensive.

With the frozen fried products, the quality is likely to vary widely, judging from our tests of a number of these products. The price too would be more expensive than for home-fried.

Homemade fried chicken

Fry your own chicken and you should be able to serve a dish that tastes better than frozen or fast-food chicken—and can be fixed at a budget price.

Our recipe for homemade fried chicken is quite simple. It shouldn't overwhelm even reluctant cooks. Here's what you'll need.

Fried chicken

1 2½-to-3-pound broiler-fryer, cut up
½ cup vegetable oil
1 egg
¼ cup water or milk
½ to ¾ cup seasoned flour or seasoned bread crumbs

A 3-pound chicken, cut up, will yield 8 to 10 pieces that will barely fit into some 10-inch frying pans. It's best to use a larger pan or one of those particularly large electric frypans.

Pour the oil into the pan and let it preheat over medium heat.

Beat the egg with the water or milk in a shallow bowl. Then put the seasoned bread crumbs or seasoned flour in a paper or plastic bag. Dip the chicken pieces one at a time into the egg mixture, and put the pieces into the bag. Shake the bag until the pieces are coated, then take them out and put them aside.

When the oil is hot, put the pieces in the pan. Fry them on one side until browned, then turn them with tongs to brown the other side.

When the pieces are browned, turn the heat to simmer. Cover the pan. Leave the cover's vent hole open (if it has one). Simmer for 25 minutes, removing the cover during the last 10 minutes if you want crisper chicken. Remove the pieces, drain them on absorbent paper, and serve.

Frozen fried wings: A good buy?

Don't buy frozen fried chicken wings for economy's sake. Fried wings are little or no cheaper than other frozen chicken parts, and you get less meat for your money.

Our tests of wings-only products showed that the meat—what there was of it—was generally tender. When you buy wings, you get much the same amount of edible material on the bones as with other fried chicken parts. But more of the wing portion is coating and less of it is meat.

On average, the fried wings we tested provided a shade less protein, and significantly more fat and calories, than the other chicken portions we analyzed.

MSG: How safe?

If you think you are sensitive to MSG (monosodium glutamate), try to avoid food containing large amounts of it.

Glutamic acid—the "G" in MSG—is found in many Chinese dishes. One of the most common natural amino acids, glutamic acid is contained in soy sauce, in hydrolized vegetable protein (often added to processed foods), and in foods such as tomatoes and mushrooms. It is also found in the human body.

MSG and other salts of glutamic acid have the ability to enhance a food's flavor. For that reason, Oriental cooks were adding it to their foods (in the form of a seaweed) long before the chemical itself was identified.

MSG is considered a safe additive, although a small percentage of the population seems to be sensitive to it. The reaction to MSG has been dubbed "Chinese Restaurant Syndrome." Symptoms include facial pressure, chest pain, and a burning sensation in the head and chest immediately after eating a meal containing the substance.

It's not clear whether MSG is really the cause—or at least the sole cause—of the syndrome. One researcher reported an experiment in which people noted those symptoms more after drinking spiced tomato juice and coffee than after drinking a solution containing MSG.

Other researchers describe different symptoms being reported as Chinese Restaurant Syndrome. Reactions to the substance may be idiosyncratic and partly psychosomatic.

Homemade chicken chow mein

As part of our test project on Chinese-style dishes, we developed our own homemade Chinese-style dinner. A homemade dish can be much more pleasing to the palate than a dinner bought in the supermarket. Ingredients can be added or altered to suit your taste, because much of the "Chinese" in Chinese-style food is the style of preparation and cooking—finely cut ingredients stir-fried.

Our homemade chow mein had more chicken in it than any of the store-bought chicken chow meins we tested. Because it was chicken, which is lower in fat than red meat, our chow mein was low in calories—about 200 per serving.

The ingredients that take longer to cook are put in first, and all ingredients are cooked for as short a time as possible. The recipe takes about a half-hour to prepare. It serves four. You can prepare the recipe in a wok or a frying pan.

Chicken chow mein

1 raw chicken breast
1 small onion
¼ pound green beans
1 small carrot
1 large stalk celery
2 scallions
2 tablespoons chicken fat or oil
2 tablespoons soy sauce
⅛ teaspoon freshly ground black pepper
½ cup canned bamboo shoots
⅓ cup canned sliced mushrooms
1 cup fresh chicken stock
(if canned stock is used,
omit 1 tablespoon soy sauce)
2 teaspoons cornstarch
½ teaspoon brown sugar
1 cup fresh bean sprouts

Slice the chicken breast into thin strips (about ⅛-inch square and 2 inches long). Cut onion, beans, carrots, celery, and scallions into pieces of similar size, but keep separate. (Beans and scallions should be cut on diagonal.)

Heat chicken fat or oil in a large skillet. Sauté onion until transparent. Add 1 tablespoon soy sauce, the black pepper, and the chicken. Stir-fry until chicken looks firm and white, about 5 minutes. Remove and set aside.

Using the same skillet and the oil remaining in it, stir-fry the green beans and the carrots with 1 tablespoon soy sauce. Add 1 tablespoon water if vegetables start to scorch. Cook until beans start to look translucent. Add the celery, the bamboo shoots (but reserve brine), the mushrooms, and the chicken stock. Stir and cook until vegetables are slightly tender. If mixture looks dry, add ¼ cup more chicken stock.

Mix cornstarch and sugar with 2 tablespoons brine from canned bamboo shoots. Pour into vegetable mixture, stirring until it thickens. Add cooked chicken/onion mixture and bean sprouts. Stir until bean sprouts look slightly transparent. Add scallions and stir. Serve with rice or Chinese noodles.

To freeze our chow mein, stop a few steps short of completing the recipe. After vegetable mixture is thickened, remove from range, add cooked chicken/onion mixture. Put into freezer containers, seal, and freeze. When reheating, add fresh bean sprouts and scallions.

Frozen fish portions: Pros and cons

Whatever can be said for frozen fish portions can be summed up in one word: convenience.

People who like fish and people who are attracted by its low-calorie, low-fat, and high-protein levels are likely to be disappointed in the frozen portions. None of the frozen fish portions tested by our sensory consultants came even close to our standard for sensory excellence. And none was as nutritious as plain broiled fish.

Convenience. There's little doubt that the frozen product is popular. In fact, after canned tuna, most of the fish sold in supermarkets is sold as frozen portions or sticks.

■ Fish fresh from the water is delicious. But in some areas, it's frozen fish or no fish at all—though you can buy perfectly acceptable frozen fillets instead of the precoated frozen portions.

■ While fresh fish can be a bit of a challenge to prepare, and even frozen fillets might take a minute or two to ready for cooking, precoated frozen portions simply go right into the oven to bake for 20 to 30 minutes.

Nutrition. The frozen portions we tested were coated in batter, breading, or sauce, making them higher in calories, fat, and sodium than fresh or frozen fillets. In many of the products we tested, the coating outweighed the fish inside. Because of the coating, the frozen fish portions were lower in protein than the fillets, which were all fish.

Taste. Our sensory consultants found that the frozen fish portions were often either too dry or too oily, or had dark-meat flavor that was heavier than the mild taste of a good fresh white-meat fish.

Fish: Fillets vs frozen portions

If you're deciding whether to buy fresh or frozen fillets or frozen fish portions, you'll get more fish and better flavor for your money if you stick to the fillets.

You can broil the fillets with a little seasoning. Or bread them, if you're of a mind: It's not a major chore. See our recipe below.

Breaded fillets: A recipe to try

Preparing your own coated fish fillets for dinner is not difficult to do—and the results are bound to be tastier than a meal based on frozen fish portions.

The best of the frozen fish portions we tested were judged to be only good. Our alternative is a little messier to prepare than the frozen fish, but we think it's well worth the extra clean-up.

You can use fresh fillets or plain, ready-to-cook, frozen fillets from the supermarket. If you use frozen fillets, thaw them overnight in the refrigerator. We tried this recipe with both fresh and frozen skinless cod fillets, and it's delicious either way.

Here's our recipe, to coat about a pound of fillets.

Breaded fish fillets

½ cup all-purpose flour
½ cup plain bread crumbs
½ teaspoon salt
½ teaspoon paprika
¼ teaspoon (scant) crushed leaf thyme
¼ teaspoon crushed parsley flakes
¼ teaspoon freshly ground black pepper
1 large egg
1 tablespoon whole milk
½ cup vegetable oil

Cut the fish fillets into serving-sized pieces if necessary, and wipe dry with a paper towel.

Put all the dry ingredients into a plastic bag. Shake well to blend, then pour into a shallow pan.

In another shallow pan, beat the egg slightly and blend in the milk.

Dredge both sides of each piece of fish in the breading mixture. Shake off the excess coating. Slip the fish pieces into the egg mixture, making sure each side is evenly coated with egg. Let the excess drip off and return the fish to the breading mixture, again coating each side evenly. Set aside on a rack.

Preheat the vegetable oil to 370°F in a frying pan, then add the pieces of fish. Cook the pieces until golden brown on one side (4 to 6 minutes), then turn them gently and brown on the other side (another 4 to 6 minutes).

Buying, storing, and serving ice cream

If you don't know which brand of ice cream to buy, it could help to check the ingredients. If you want ice cream at its best after you've bought it, be sure to store it properly.

Ingredient listing is required and you can learn a lot by reading labels.

■ Chances are you'll be buying a very good product if you find one that lists cream as its first ingredient, and sugar ahead of corn syrup.

■ If you like vanilla, look for natural flavorings. Most of the vanillas we favored when we tested ice cream contained natural flavors or a combination of natural and artificial. Most of those we rated low contained artificial flavors.

Solidly frozen packages mean a better quality product.

■ At the store, pick a package that's brick-hard, and get it home and into the freezer quickly.

■ Buy ice cream in small packages that you'll use up fairly quickly, so there won't be much time for ice crystals to grow in the freezer at home.

Proper handling at home can also keep ice cream quality high.

■ Storing ice cream in a freezer-door shelf for a few hours before serving sometimes provides the perfect consistency for scooping.

■ Return the ice cream to the freezer quickly after serving.

■ Be sure the package is closed up tight or wrapped in aluminum foil or plastic wrap to prevent moisture from escaping or off-flavors or odors from getting in.

How ice cream rates nutritionally

In the table below, we compare ice cream and ice milk with two other desserts and with whole milk and low-fat, fruit-flavored yogurt.[1] Two scoops (or a ½ cup) of vanilla ice cream is lower in calories than either a wedge of apple pie or a slice of yellow cake. That's not surprising. What's surprising is that the ice cream is also lower in calories than either the milk or the yogurt. And, of course, the ice milk is even lower in calories than the ice cream.

The ice cream and ice milk are lower in protein than the other foods, true. But they are also lower in sodium. They contain less carbohydrate than the other desserts and the yogurt. And they beat the other desserts in calcium, riboflavin, and vitamin A. The ice cream contains about as much fat as the milk—and three times as much as the ice milk or the yogurt.

Food (serving)	Calories	Protein (g.)	Calcium (mg.)	Phosphorus (mg.)	Riboflavin (mg.)	Vit. A (ugRE.)	Vit. C (mg.)	Fat (g.)	Carbohydrates (g.)	Sodium (mg.)
Vanilla ice cream (½ cup)	140	2.3	88	67	0.17	67	0.4	7.9	15.9	42
Vanilla ice milk (½ cup)	101	2.1	88	65	0.17	26	0.4	2.2	18.2	50
Homemade apple pie (5 oz.)	363	3.1	13	31	0.03	4	1.4	15.7	54.0	427
Yellow cake with chocolate icing (3.5 oz.)	365	4.2	68	112	0.08	16	trace	13.0	60.4	208
Whole milk (8 fl. oz.)	150	8.0	291	228	0.4	76	2.3	8.2	11.4	120
Low-fat, fruit-flavored yogurt (8 oz.)	225	9.0	314	247	0.4	27	1.4	2.6	42.0	121

1 Values for ice-cream and ice milk are averages for brands we tested for a report on ice cream. Values for other foods are from the U.S. Department of Agriculture.

Buying milk

Much of the milk sold today could be fresher, more wholesome, and more nutritious. Based on tests of milk samples bought in two different areas of the country, we think the failure of milk to be uniformly excellent in quality in some localities is due to lax standards of production and distribution.

Until regulations are strengthened or properly enforced, there are only a few things you can do to make sure you're buying the best quality milk available at the store where you shop.

■ Check the "sell-by" date (or last day of sale) on a milk container and buy only the freshest product.

■ Take home only as much low-fat or skim milk as you can use quickly. Our data indicate that they spoil faster than whole milk.

■ To extend storage life, buy milk in opaque containers. (Light passing through the walls of translucent plastic jugs can affect the flavor.)

■ Compare prices. Take advantage of any price difference between the store's house brand and other brands of milk.

■ If you use a lot of milk fairly quickly, buy half-gallon or gallon containers. You'll save money.

Which milk is which?

With just three basic types of milk, it shouldn't require a scorecard to tell them apart. A brief list may be all you need.

Whole milk. The federal government (for milk shipped in interstate commerce) and nearly all the states require whole milk to contain at least 3.25 percent milk fat.

You can expect about 151 calories from a glass of whole milk.

Low-fat milk may contain anywhere from 0.5 to 2.5 percent milk fat (the amount is declared on the label). Such products must be fortified with vitamin A. Vitamin D may also be added.

There are about 121 calories in a glass of low-fat milk.

Skim or nonfat milk contains less than 0.5 percent milk fat in most states. Skimming removes whole milk's vitamins A and D, but skim milk must be fortified with added amounts of vitamin A (addition of vitamin D is optional).

You can expect about 86 calories from one glass of skim milk.

Storing and using milk

If you don't keep milk refrigerated properly, you risk losing more than that cool refreshing taste. Even at an ideal storage temperature of 40°F, bacteria in milk that could affect aroma and taste may double in number every thirty-nine hours.

There are ways you can protect the quality of the milk you buy.

■ Get milk last when you shop, to minimize the time it's out of refrigeration.

■ Once home, keep milk cold and the container tightly closed.

■ Pour only the amount of milk you need and return the container immediately to the coldest part of your refrigerator.

■ Use up older milk before opening fresh cartons.

Your daily calcium

Milk has a reputation as a good source of calcium. But you'll need more than milk if all you drink is only one glass a day.

A daily 8-ounce glass of milk yields about one-third of the calcium recommended for anyone from childhood on into middle age. But if you don't drink three glasses of milk a day (or use milk in cereal, say), you should get calcium from other dairy products—or drink more milk.

Processed orange juice: Frozen is best

Frozen concentrated orange juice has a better chance of approaching excellence than any other type of processed juice. In taste tests of frozen concentrates by our sensory consultants, only a hint of the processing required to make orange juice convenient intruded on the aroma and flavor of fresh oranges.

The bottled or cartoned juice you find in the supermarket refrigerator case, called "chilled" juice, generally tasted more processed to our consultants. And canned orange juice bears little resemblance to fresh orange juice.

Frozen orange juice can be kept for months without any loss of quality, if it's kept frozen. Look for cans that are frozen hard and are free of frost.

To make juice from a frozen concentrate, don't hold the can under hot water. The hot water can soften the cardboard, making the pull tab or can opener hard to use.

Chilled orange juice

Although in our tests chilled orange juices didn't taste as good as the best of the frozen concentrates we tested, the chilled juices as a group still had as much vitamin C and other nutrients as the frozen juices.

Chilled juices that come in bottles, although they may be kept in the refrigerator case, are actually processed more like canned juice, and may not need to be refrigerated until they've been opened.

Most chilled orange juices, as a reading of the labels shows, is "reconstituted"—made from concentrated orange juice. The manufacturer has merely saved you the trouble of reconstituting the juice.

Even the best of the chilled juices we tested tasted distinctly of cooked oranges, but they still retained some fresh orange flavor and aroma. The rest of the chilled juices that were reconstituted tasted entirely of processed, or even overprocessed, oranges. Many suffered a flavor defect known as "oxidized citrus"—the deteriorated citrus flavor common in canned citrus juices.

Chilled juice is attractive to manufacturers for several reasons. It's cheaper to ship bulk concentrate from Florida to packing plants near the intended point of sale. The final product often commands a higher price. And, under federal standards, bulk concentrate can contain fewer oranges than the frozen concentrate sold directly to consumers.

Canned orange juice

Canned orange juice can cost you in more ways than one. Despite its insipid taste, it is generally priced in the same range as frozen concentrates. But there's another objection to canned orange juice besides its taste. Lead can leach from the solder used to hold the tin can together, especially when what's inside the can is acidic.

The U.S. Food and Drug Administration has warned against leaving canned fruit juices in an opened can. FDA studies have reported that lead levels can increase as much as sevenfold when open cans of orange juice are stored for five days in the refrigerator.

An occasional glass of juice with that much lead won't hurt you. But if anyone in your household drinks a lot of orange juice, it shouldn't be canned orange juice—at least not until manufacturers have completed phasing out lead-soldered cans in favor of welded cans. Meanwhile, store canned juice in another container once it's opened.

Oranges for home squeezing

The best juice oranges may be ugly. In fact, they may not even look ripe. But partly green oranges are just as ripe as completely orange oranges.

Valencia oranges—in season in spring and early summer—make an excellent juice that's deep orange. But hues closer to yellow-orange are acceptable in an excellent orange juice. Like pulpiness, color is largely a matter of personal preference.

More important than its looks in choosing an orange for juice is its feel. You want an orange that's heavy with juice and that has no soft spots. If your supermarket permits you a choice of oranges, weigh them and see which one gives you more pounds for your money.

Although oranges don't ripen after they're picked, they do continue to breathe. Keeping them in plastic bags or other closed containers smothers them and encourages mold to grow. If stored in a cool place with good air circulation, oranges can keep for several weeks.

Improving your glass of OJ

A Consumer Reports reader suggests a way to make good orange juice even better.

To get the zestiness of fresh juice—with only a minimal increase in price per serving—the reader adds the juice of one fresh orange squeezed into a container along with a can of reconstituted juice. See if you think the added taste is worth the extra trouble.

Here's another suggestion to try: Give the orange juice container a vigorous shake or two. Aerating the juice will improve the taste.

What orange juice contributes to the diet

Orange juice is the main natural source of vitamin C in the American diet. Tests conducted for us showed that, on average, a 6-ounce glass of orange juice usually provides about 100 percent of an adult's Recommended Daily Allowance of vitamin C, which is 60 milligrams. Differences in vitamin C content among the types of juice were inconsequential.

Several labels for orange juice products bear the words "unsweetened" or "no sugar added," which help distinguish pure orange juice from the many products on the market that are only part orange juice. But the lack of *added* sugar shouldn't be mistaken for a lack of sugar or calories.

A 6-ounce glass of orange juice contains the equivalent of about 1½ tablespoons of sugar and 70 calories. The 1½ tablespoons of sugar in a glass of orange juice is about the same amount as in a soft drink, although the acidity of orange juice disguises the sweetness.

Orange juice is one of the best natural sources of potassium. That mineral is in so many foods that it's not often in short supply in a person's diet. But potassium is important for people who are taking diuretics (to control high blood pressure), which deplete the body's supply of potassium.

Pizza: A nutritious snack or meal

Pizza is nutritious, whether you eat it as a snack, a lunch, or part of a dinner.

A slice of pizza supplies a reasonable percentage of a teenager's Recommended Daily Allowance of protein, calcium, and some vitamins. And a light meal of two slices of pizza with salad and milk would be nutritionally adequate for a youngster.

But pizza doesn't have everything. The fact that a pizza is smothered in tomato sauce might make you think it contains a wealth of vitamin C. It doesn't. The high temperature at which pizza is cooked destroys much of the vitamin.

Another nutrient in short supply is iron. Unfortunately, one available in abundance is sodium: Pizza can contribute a large part of a person's daily intake of sodium.

Frozen chicken pot pies

When we tested frozen meat pies, we found the commercial products were inferior to our own excellent pot pies. It takes time and work to prepare our homemade recipe, but we think the results well worth the effort.

Our recipe for superb-tasting pies yields eight one-serving pies. We estimate that an average cook can make the pies in about 2½ hours.

Note that the recipe is for *frozen* pot pies: It allows for some liquid to be lost during freezing. If you want to cook and eat one or two pies right after you make them, you'll have to spoon out a tablespoon or two of liquid from the filling.

The pies are 10-ounce pies. To make them, you'll need eight 5-by-1¼-inch aluminum pie pans. We've listed the ingredients for the three parts of the pie—stock, filling, and pastry—separately, but the instructions are given together. (Note that we made our pies with only a top crust. A bottom crust tends to get soggy anyway.)

Chicken and stock

4 cups water
2 frying chickens, halved
2 stalks celery, chopped in large pieces
1 large carrot, chopped in large pieces
1 medium onion, quartered
2 bay leaves
Bouquet garni (15 peppercorns, 1 tsp. leaf sage, ¼ tsp. rosemary, ¼ tsp. thyme, and ⅛ tsp. celery seeds tied in a small piece of muslin or cheesecloth)

Filling

1 tablespoon vegetable oil
1 small clove garlic, minced
1 medium onion, chopped
1½ teaspoons salt
¼ teaspoon freshly ground black pepper
2 tablespoons flour
4 or 5 cups chicken stock (from recipe above)
4 cups cubed chicken meat (from stock above)
1½ cups potatoes, in ½-inch cubes
1 cup carrots, in ½-inch cubes
1 cup frozen peas

Pastry

2 cups sifted all-purpose flour
½ teaspoon salt
⅔ cup vegetable shortening
6 tablespoons cold water

Start the stock. Combine chicken and stock ingredients in a large pot. Bring to a boil and cook for 30 minutes.

Start the pastry. While the chicken is simmering, sift flour and salt into a large bowl. Cut in shortening with pastry cutter or two knives until it has a grain the size of corn kernels. Sprinkle water over mixture, 1 tablespoon at a time, while stirring lightly with fork. Continue until dough is moist but not sticky. Press dough into ball. Chill.

Prepare the cooked chicken. Remove the chicken after it has cooked in the stock for 30 minutes. Remove meat from skin and bones. Put meat aside to use in filling. Return skin and bones to simmering stock pot. Let simmer about 30 minutes longer.

Make the filling. While the stock is simmering, collect and prepare the filling ingredients. (Note: For someone on a restricted sodium diet, substitute garlic and herbs for the salt. That way you can reduce the sodium content without too much loss of flavor.)

By this time the stock should have cooked long enough. Strain it into a bowl. Heat the vegetable oil in the large pot. Add garlic; brown. Add onions; cook until transparent. Add salt (or herbs), pepper, and flour; mix in well but don't let flour brown. Add 1 cup strained stock to onion mixture; mix well. Add remainder of stock and bring to boil. Add chicken, potatoes, and carrots; bring to boil. Cover and simmer for 10 minutes. Fill each pie pan with about ¾ cup of this mixture. Let cool.

Roll the pastry. Divide pastry into eight small balls. Roll out each ball between two pieces of wax paper until the crust is about ½ inch larger than the diameter of the pans.

Finish the pies. Distribute the frozen peas on top of the cooled filling in the pie pans. Cover with pie crust; crimp edges. Dust crust lightly with flour and prick with fork. Place pies in individual freezer bags, and freeze.

To cook the pies. Preheat oven to 450°F. Put frozen pies on cookie sheet and place on rack in center of oven. Bake the pies for 40 minutes, or until the crust is golden brown.

Potatoes and calories

The potato need not be a fattening food. Eaten plain, a medium-sized, 3.5-ounce baked potato yields only about 93 calories and virtually no fat.

Load that same potato with fats of one sort or another and you pay the price in calories. A tablespoon of sour cream, for instance, will add 29 calories. A pat of butter contributes 50 calories.

Much the same thing happens, of course, if you convert the potato into french fries. Frozen fries, in fact, may get a double helping of fat—once when they are fried at the factory and again, if you heat them in oil, at home.

When we heated fries in our oven for a test of the frozen product, they averaged 185 calories per 3.5-ounce portion (about a cup). Potatoes we deep-fried from scratch, using our own recipe (see below), were 224 calories per portion.

Homemade french fries

Here's our recipe for homestyle french fries. They'll be delicious (but they'll also be 224 calories per portion).

French fries

For four to five servings, start with five to six medium-large baking potatoes (Russet Burbanks are a good choice).

Pare and wash the potatoes, leaving them in cold water as you work. Slice the potatoes into ⅜-inch-square strips about 2 inches long.

Drain the strips and pat them dry with paper towels so that their moisture won't cause splatters when the strips come in contact with the cooking oil

Pour enough vegetable cooking oil into a frying pan or deep-fat fryer to cover the potatoes (in a 10-inch frying pan, about 2 cups of oil should be enough). Heat the oil to 375°F.

Add half the strips and fry them to a light golden brown, turning, or stirring as needed. They should be done in about 10 minutes. Then cook the rest of the potatoes.

If you want to have fries available in your freezer, follow the same procedure but remove the fries from the oil just as they start to brown.

Lay them out on a paper towel for at least 5 minutes to drain and cool. Then put the fries into a plastic freezer bag, seal it, and store the package in your freezer.

When you want to serve the fries, just return them to hot oil to finish the cooking.

Fast-food fries

How good are fast-food fries? To find out, we sent our taste experts to six big chains *(Arby's, Arthur Treacher's, Burger King, McDonald's, Roy Rogers,* and *Wendy's),* all in the New York City area.

Our experts judged the fries on the spot, and then again as a takeout order, fifteen minutes after receiving them. They repeated the procedure in a second restaurant of each chain.

French-frying methods at *McDonald's* seemed to pay off. Our tasters rated its shoestring potatoes very good, the highest rating any fast-food fries received. The fries were consistently hot, crisp, and golden brown, with tender insides, a distinct potato taste, and a light flavoring of oil. While they didn't match our homemade fries (see above), the *McDonald's* fries were as good as the best of the frozen products we tested.

McDonald's potatoes did however, suffer in takeout orders. As they cooled, they became soggy and less flavorful. They also tended to arrive with too much salt, but they could be ordered salt-free or with "light" salt.

French fries at the other five fast-food chains did not equal those served by *McDonald's,* though several samples were judged good by our taste experts.

There was no discount for quantity at *McDonald's,* by the way. The small and large orders cost the same per ounce of fries. And it didn't pay to buy the large size at *Wendy's* and *Burger King.* It cost more per ounce than their small package of fries.

Frozen fries: Cost of convenience

When it comes to frozen french fries, what is the cost of convenience?

Saving time. Starting with frozen french fries instead of fixing potatoes from scratch does not necessarily save you time.

An oven needs about fifteen minutes to preheat and stabilize at the 425° or 450°F suggested on most labels of the frozen products. Actual cooking typically takes about twenty minutes more. So some brands of frozen fries may need a half hour or longer before they're ready for the table.

When we made our own fries from fresh potatoes, it took only about 1½ minutes to peel and slice each potato for cooking, fifteen minutes to preheat a pan and oil for deep-frying, and another ten minutes for actual cooking.

You can cut the total time it takes to prepare frozen french fries to less than twenty minutes if you pan-fry or deep-fry them. But that produces a greasy pot to wash, adds fat to the fries, and often makes for messy splatters.

Saving money. When we bought fresh potatoes to compare our home-made french fries with the frozen products, we paid about 32 cents a pound, yielding cooked fries that cost about 15 cents for a 3.5-ounce serving. The frozen fries generally cost us less than that per serving—but only if we bought them in packages of two pounds or more. In sizes of less than two pounds, the prices generally worked out to several cents a serving more than the fresh potatoes.

You're apt to save 3 to 5 cents on each serving if you buy a supermarket brand rather than a national brand.

The question of taste. When you prepare frozen french fries, a sure sacrifice is in taste. Only six of the thirty-six brands tested by our sensory consultants merited a rating of very good; sixteen were merely good, and almost as many were just fair.

Making your own french fries from scratch means peeling, cutting, washing, drying, frying, draining, and a pan to wash—but it should also mean tastier fries.

Frozen fries: What's in them for you?

What can you expect, in terms of nutrition, from frozen french fries? Here are some of the facts we found, based on our tests.

■ While a 3.5-ounce serving of the frozen fries we tested provided, on average, 3.3 grams of protein, potato protein is low in quality. So a serving of the fries wouldn't go far toward meeting your daily dietary need.

■ On average, a serving of the frozen fries we tested would supply less than 3 milligrams of vitamin C. (An adult's Recommended Daily Allowance of the vitamin is 60 milligrams.)

■ Other nutritional benefits are more reliable. A serving of fries would yield 11 to 12 percent of a teenage or adult male's daily niacin needs (14 to 16 percent for females of those ages).

■ You'd also get nearly 400 milligrams of potassium, more than the amount contained in a cup of whole milk.

Pilchard: A low-cost substitute for tuna

Pilchard neither looks nor tastes like tuna, but it's just as nutritious and a much better buy. You'll like the price—and you just might like the taste. Mixed with mayonnaise, onion, and celery, pilchard makes a nice sandwich filling.

A member of the herring family, pilchard is a large sardine and is found in abundance off the coast of Peru. Seafood marketers sell it like tuna, packed in oil or water in a little can.

Unlike tuna, the pilchard we tested had an aroma that was strongly fishy and slightly briny and tinny. The flavor tended to be very salty, sour, and oily—more like that of large skinned sardines than tuna. The flesh was deep beige and somewhat flaky. It wasn't firm like that of tuna.

How nutritious are sandwiches?

When we checked the nutrient content in several sandwiches popular with children, we found that bologna would not be the best choice on almost any count, including price.

■ In our tests of bologna, we found that a three-slice serving of beef- or beef-and-pork bologna provided, on average, 9.6 grams of protein (3 ounces of poultry bologna averaged 10.9 grams). That's less protein than you'd get with 3 ounces of cooked hamburger (about 21 grams), cooked chicken (about 27 grams), or canned tuna (about 25 grams).

■ A beef-bologna or beef-and-pork bologna sandwich provides a respectable amount of a number of important vitamins and minerals, as the table on the facing page shows. It's a nutritious-enough lunch for a child or an adult. But the table also shows that a bologna sandwich has more fat, calories, and sodium than sandwiches made with peanut butter or hamburger. Only a tuna sandwich has slightly more calories.

■ Beef-bologna or beef-and-pork bologna, however, is an extremely expensive source of protein and other nutrients. On the basis of a cost per pound of protein, it's twice the price of tuna, and three times the price of peanut butter.

How four sandwich fillings compare

The table below shows how much of a 7- to 10-year-old's Recommended Daily Allowance for a number of nutrients is provided by four sandwich fillings. The RDAs are set by the National Academy of Sciences/National Research Council. Serving size, serving cost, and other measurements are determined by us or are based on data from the U.S. Department of Agriculture.

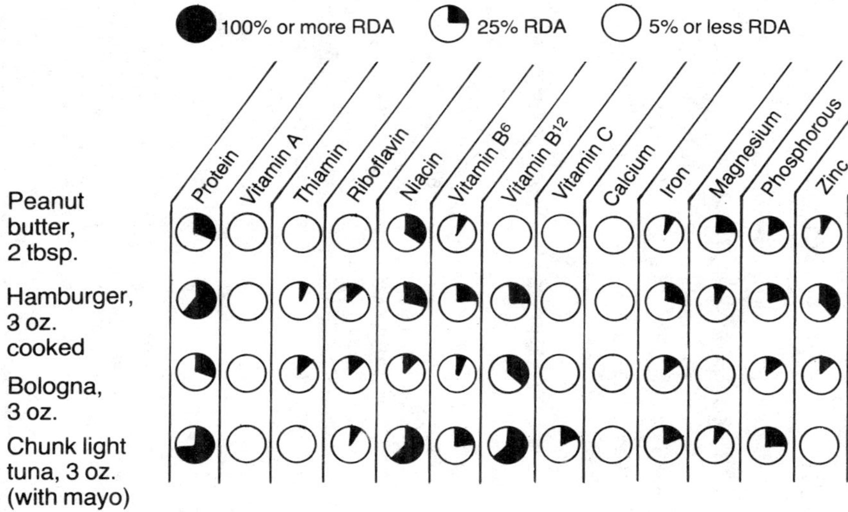

	Calories	Fat (gm.)	Carbohydrate (gm.)	Sodium (mg.)	Cost (cents)
Peanut butter, 2 tbsp.	219	18	5	149	12
Hamburger, 3 oz. cooked	243	17	0	50	40
Bologna, 3 oz.	261	24	1	1120	39
Chunk light tuna, 3 oz. (with mayo)	266	18	0	640	46

Canned soup

Canned soup is cheap and convenient and may be all-American, but it's not a nutritious meal. And few are as good as a proper homemade soup.

Even a real soup lover, however, runs short of time and patience from time to time and has to make do with canned soup.

To get a meal's worth of nutrition out of canned soup, you should eat it with two other all-American favorites: a sandwich (maybe tuna, cheese, or egg) and a glass of milk (preferably skim).

If you're making a meal of canned soup alone, stick to the chunkier soups. You'll probably get better nutrition from that variety. They generally provided more protein than the other canned soups we tested and should provide more vitamins and minerals than the thinner soups. With almost all the canned soups we tested, however, sodium content was quite high.

To increase the nutrients you get in a meal of canned soup, you can try one of these ideas from our food technologists.

■ Prepare a condensed soup with milk instead of water.

■ Stir an egg into the soup as it cooks, and accompany your meal with a slice or two of bread.

■ Simply eat the soup with a glass of milk and some crackers, and follow with a piece of fruit.

Homemade vegetable-beef soup

Our taste experts who tested soups for us didn't think much of most of the canned soups they tasted. They judged only a few to be very good. The rest were rated good, fair, poor, or variable.

Most homemade soups with good ingredients would taste better than canned soups. But we set ourselves an additional challenge: We also wanted to create a soup so full of good things that it would be a meal in itself.

Our soup was judged very good by our taste experts. It has 270 calories per 8-ounce serving—more than any of the canned soups. But our soup is also a lot more nutritious. It has all the vitamins and minerals you get when you simply cook up a pot of vegetables. And it has more protein (11.8 grams per serving) than all but one of the canned soups we tested. The recipe makes about five 8-ounce servings.

Vegetable-beef soup

5 teaspoons vegetable oil
½ pound stew meat (in ½-inch cubes)
½ cup chopped onion
1 teaspoon salt (optional)
¼ teaspoon (scant) freshly ground black pepper
5 cups water
Mixed diced vegetables:
- *1 cup potatoes*
- *¾ cup carrots*
- *½ cup peeled radishes*
- *½ cup fresh green beans*
- *½ cup celery*
- *½ cup green peas*
- *¼ cup scallions*

Heat 1 tablespoon of the vegetable oil in a 6-quart pot. Brown meat in oil. Add chopped onion and sauté lightly. Add seasoning, stir, then add water. Heat to boiling. Cover pot and simmer for about 1 hour or until meat is tender.

In a skillet, sauté potatoes, carrots, and radishes in the remaining 2 teaspoons of oil until the potatoes become slightly transparent. Stir in green beans, celery, and peas.

Add stir-fried vegetable mix to beef-water mixture in pot. Add scallions. Then heat to boil. Cover pot and simmer until vegetables become tender.

Pressure cooker soup stock

For cooks in a hurry, fixing a good soup from scratch might be impossible without a pressure cooker. Making soup stock the traditional way takes hours of simmering for the flavors to blend. Making stock in a pressure cooker takes much less time, and the fast cooking doesn't compromise quality.

Our food technologists developed the recipe for chicken stock given below. It's for a 6- or 8-quart pressure cooker (cut ingredients in half for a smaller pressure cooker) and makes 1½ quarts.

There are several advantages to the chicken stock we made.

- There's virtually no waste—just the chicken bones and skin.
- The chicken parts are a bargain, compared to commercial broths.
- You can control the amount of salt. (We added just a little.)
- You can adjust the flavor to your taste. In our stock, celery is a predominant flavor. You can omit the celery leaves from the recipe, if you prefer. Using peppercorns instead of ground pepper gives the broth a little more zip.

Chicken stock

2 pounds chicken (necks, backs, wings)
1 teaspoon salt (optional)
⅛ teaspoon black pepper (or 8 peppercorns)
1 stalk celery, with leaves, chopped
1 small onion, diced
1 carrot, diced
3 sprigs parsley, chopped
1 bay leaf
5 cups water

Cut the chicken into serving-sized pieces. Put all the ingredients into pressure cooker. Cover and lock the lid. Set control for 15 pounds per square inch (if you have a cooker with an adjustable regulator) and place cooker over high heat until the regulator indicates that pressure has been reached.

Reduce the heat to maintain pressure, cook 15 minutes, then shut off the heat and let the pressure reduce of its own accord. (That will take about 20 minutes.)

When it's safe to open the cooker, pour the contents of the pot through a sieve, and refrigerate the liquid. It will keep for about a week, refrigerated, if you leave intact the layer of fat that forms when the stock cools.

Save the chicken and vegetables, too. When they have cooled, you can remove the meat from the bones, retrieve the bay leaf, and purée the chicken and vegetables in a blender. The paste can be used to thicken soups and sauces.

Black bean soup in a pressure cooker

This black bean soup makes a hearty winter lunch. It's based on the recipe for a pressure cooker chicken stock, presented just preceding this recipe.

The quantity is for a 6- or 8-quart pressure cooker. Cut ingredients in half for a smaller pressure cooker. (The recipe for black bean soup was adapted from one provided by the Westchester County, N.Y., Cooperative Extension Service.)

Black bean soup

1½ cups dried black beans
¼ cup margarine
1 cup coarsely chopped onion
1 stalk celery, minced
1 cup chopped peeled tomatoes
6 cloves garlic, minced
1 teaspoon dry mustard
½ teaspoon black pepper
1½ quarts chicken stock (a vegetable stock or chicken boullion can be substituted)
½ cup dry sherry or Madeira
1 tablespoon chili powder
1 teaspoon grated orange peel
1 teaspoon sugar

Wash, sort, and place the beans in a saucepan. Cover them with water; allow 4 cups of water for each cup of beans. Bring to a boil and cook 2 minutes. Cover, remove from heat, and let stand for 1 hour.

Melt the margarine in the pressure cooker. Sauté the onions and celery until the onions are translucent. Add the beans, the water they soaked in, and the remaining ingredients.

Cover and lock the lid. Set control for 15 pounds per square inch (if you have a cooker with an adjustable regulator) and place cooker over high heat until the regulator indicates that pressure has been reached. Reduce the heat to maintain pressure, cook 15 minutes, then shut off the heat and let the pressure cooker cool for 5 minutes. Run cold water over the pot to further reduce pressure.

You can serve the soup as is, or purée it in a blender if you prefer a thicker consistency. We found that letting the soup rest in the refrigerator overnight produced a better blend of flavors.

Chopped parsley or crumbled hard-cooked eggs make a nice garnish.

Homemade stuffing

Stuffing is traditional with turkey. Because of the potential for contamination of stuffing from bacteria, make the stuffing and loosely pack it in the bird at the very last minute before roasting. Or better yet, we recommend that you roast the bird unstuffed and cook the stuffing separately.

We've created a nutritious fruit-nut-vegetable stuffing that cooks on top of the range. It uses the neck, heart, and gizzard that usually come packed inside whole birds. But you can substitute sausage and use the stuffing as a side dish with chicken, pork chops, or other meats. The recipe makes about fourteen ½-cup servings.

Making the side-dish stuffing is a three-step process.

Step 1

4 cups water
1 small onion, quartered
1 stalk celery, chopped
5 whole peppercorns
½ teaspoon leaf sage, uncrushed
Turkey neck, gizzard, and heart

Bring all ingredients to a boil in a 3-quart saucepan. Cover and simmer for an hour. Drain and set aside stock. Remove meat from neck and chop it, along with the gizzard and heart, into small pieces. Set those aside.

Step 2

1 cup bulgur wheat (100% natural)
2 cups stock (from Step 1)

Bring stock and bulgur to a boil in a 3-quart saucepan. Cover and simmer until bulgur is cooked to desired doneness. Fluff with a fork.

Step 3

4 tablespoons lightly salted butter
1 large onion, chopped
2 cups celery (4 stalks), chopped
1 cup canned chestnut meats, crumbled
1 large Delicious apple—cored and chopped, but not peeled
½ cup golden raisins
Cooked bulgur (from Step 2)
½ teaspoon salt
¼ teaspoon freshly ground black pepper
Chopped neck, heart and gizzard pieces (from Step 1)
1 teaspoon leaf sage, crushed
½ teaspoon leaf thyme

In a large skillet over medium heat, sauté onions in melted butter until transparent. Add salt, pepper, sage, and thyme. Add chopped meat pieces and stir-fry for 2 minutes. Add celery, raisins, chestnuts, and apple. Toss ingredients together and continue cooking for 3 minutes. Add bulgur mixture. Blend well and adjust seasonings to taste.

Substitutions. Some substitutions will work.

■ You can use boiled chestnuts instead of canned ones.

■ We used a red Delicious apple, but you can use any crispy-textured variety.

■ Some people prefer sausage stuffing. You can use two or three sausage links, about ¾ cup, instead of the chopped turkey neck, heart, and gizzard, but decrease the butter to a tablespoon.

■ Instead of bulgur, you can use brown rice or ordinary rice.

Talking turkey

Our food technologists who tested turkeys suggest these guidelines for buying turkey and preparing it for cooking.

Which type to get. For value, buy the largest turkey your family can use.

■ The larger the bird, the greater the ratio of meat to bone, so the cheaper the serving.

■ Whole turkeys are cheaper per serving than turkey breasts. But a whole turkey may be just too much meat for a small family, so for some a turkey breast may be the best choice.

■ There's nothing to recommend the turkey rolls and roasts. The ones we tested were expensive and not very tasty.

■ There's no reason to choose a basted turkey over one that's not basted. Injected basting solutions had no consistent effect on the overall sensory quality of the turkeys we tested. An injected basting solution adds weight, too. The water and the basting solution, even within government guidelines, can make up nearly 10 percent of the weight—as much as 14 ounces of a 10-pound turkey.

■ There's probably no reason to insist on a fresh-killed turkey. The one we tested didn't taste very fresh. Its dark meat was juicy, but its white meat was slightly dry.

Frozen turkey requires special handling.

■ When you buy a frozen turkey, be sure the package is in good condition and the bird is solidly frozen.

■ Put it into your home freezer as soon as you can. It will keep for about twelve months if stored at 0°F. Frozen turkey breasts, roasts, and rolls will keep for about six months at 0°.

■ A frozen whole turkey, breast, or roll should be thawed in its wrapper in the refrigerator (twenty-four hours for each 5 pounds of weight) before cooking. Roasts are usually cooked frozen.

How nutritious is turkey?

While the tests we did on turkeys left us with little to praise about their taste and texture, we found the bird to be a nutritious food.

All the turkeys we tested—whole birds, breasts, rolls, and roasts—offered a generous supply of protein. When cooked, the whole turkeys and turkey breasts averaged 26 percent protein. The rolls and roasts averaged 19 percent (their moisture content was higher).

Fats and calories. Turkey has less fat and fewer calories than many other meats. A serving of turkey has about 25 percent fewer calories than a serving of roast beef, and 46 percent fewer than a serving of pork loin. The whole turkeys, including skin, were 11 percent fat, on average. The turkey breasts, rolls, and roasts were about 7 percent fat. Calories per 3-ounce serving ranged from 100 in an all-white-meat roast to 201 in a whole turkey.

■ Most of the fat in cooked turkey is just beneath the skin and in the pan drippings. You can significantly reduce fat and calorie intake by avoiding both.

■ You can reduce your intake of fat and calories even more by eating less dark meat, which has about twice the calories of white meat.

■ Because turkey breasts are all white meat, the average calorie content of those we tested was, of course, lower than that of the whole turkeys.

■ The fat in turkey is largely polyunsaturated, unlike the fat in most meats.

Health

Nonprescription drugs for acne

Acne affects 69 percent of adolescents—some 15 million between the ages of 12 and 17. But a surprising number of adults have acne—some into their forties.

Fortunately, there are medications—several available without prescription—that can effectively control most cases of mild acne. A U.S. Food and Drug Administration advisory panel judged three ingredients in over-the-counter products to be both safe and effective in treating acne: sulfur, the combination sulfur/resorcinol, and benzoyl peroxide. Our medical consultants believe that benzoyl peroxide is the most effective of the three.

Benzoyl peroxide is the only ingredient used in nonprescription products that has been shown to prevent acne lesions. It penetrates into the follicles (where acne begins) and it apparently acts on the bacteria that contribute to acne. In addition, benzoyl peroxide appears to help prevent the plugging up of follicles.

■ All benzoyl peroxide medications can be considered relatively effective in preventing acne.

■ How benzoyl peroxide products are formulated has a lot to do with their effectiveness. A lotion or cream is less effective than a gel, which is the best formulation for penetration into the follicle. (Gels, however, are somewhat more drying and irritating than lotions or creams.) Unfortunately, virtually all nonprescription benzoyl peroxide products are lotions or creams, though you may be able to locate an over-the-counter gel using benzoyl peroxide. (We found two when we checked in 1981—*Clear By Design* and *Fostex BPO.*) By contrast, the benzoyl peroxide products available by prescription are almost all gels.

■ The FDA panel concluded that products containing from 2.5 percent to 10 percent benzoyl peroxide are safe and effective for over-the-counter use. According to our consultants, however, a product that has 10 percent is not necessarily more effective than products with lower percentages.

Sulfur and sulfur/resorcinol. These chemicals have been used in the now-outdated treatment that emphasized peeling. Removing surface skin was thought to unseat the follicle plugs and prevent them from causing full-blown acne lesions.

Doctors now recognize that sulfur products, and the peeling they induce, don't prevent pimples. But these products can speed healing of existing pimples by drying them out and peeling them away. That helps to reduce the two to four weeks it generally takes for a pimple to heal on its own. In addition, the flesh-colored tints in most sulfur medications help mask the lesions.

Salicylic acid is another traditional ingredient in acne treatments. The FDA panel decided there was not enough evidence to confirm the effectiveness of salicylic acid, but several experts on acne disagree. They cite recent studies suggesting that salicylic acid may help clear up the mild acne—mainly blackheads—that tends to be especially common among young adolescents.

Rub-on salicylic acid lotions may unplug these small lesions. Only mild acne cases are likely to benefit, however, according to our consultants. The alcohol in these products, by removing surface oil, may help cosmetically.

Self-treatment for mild acne

The majority of all acne cases (about 60 percent) are mild, which means they are limited mainly to blackheads or a few small pimples. Mild acne can be satisfactorily controlled through self-treatment with nonprescription products, though a physician might produce quicker—or better—results.

Here are some suggestions from our medical consultants to help you deal with a mild case of acne.

■ Apply medication where there are no pimples: The labeling instruction "apply to affected areas" should be taken to mean any place on your face where you *might develop* pimples. It does not mean applying the medication just to pimples. This misunderstanding results in many failures of self-treatment. The most effective medications act only to *prevent* acne. Even some professionals admit that they have neglected to advise their patients properly regarding this point.

■ Sulfur remedies are somewhat helpful in healing pimples that do appear. For cover-up, they're preferable to ordinary makeup materials, which may contain an excessive amount of oil.

■ Benzoyl peroxide is far better than sulfur as a preventive, however. It can be tricky to use because irritation—burning, peeling, and redness—is a common side effect.

■ Irritation itself bears no relation to therapy for acne. In fact, too much burning and peeling may discourage continued treatment and can aggravate acne.

■ Slight irritation, however, is a good yardstick for establishing an effective dosage of benzoyl peroxide.

■ The goal is to achieve a barely perceptible redness, a slight feeling of dryness and tightness—without peeling or discomfort. Products with a lower percentage of benzoyl peroxide may be less irritating.

■ Wait at least thirty minutes after washing before applying benzoyl peroxide. Moist skin accentuates irritation and drying. Always apply it in a thin film. If you're fair-skinned, be particularly careful when you start using a benzoyl peroxide product (apply it every other day for the first week). Don't put a benzoyl peroxide product on sensitive skin areas such as the lips, the corners of the mouth, and the skin near the eyes.

■ You'll have to build up exposure to benzoyl peroxide products gradually. At first, you may not be able to tolerate the product for more than three or four hours a day. (It can be washed off.) After a while, your skin should become "hardened" to the product's irritating effects.

■ After a week of once-a-day applications you can apply the product twice a day, and then even more often if your skin will tolerate it. If too much irritation occurs, discontinue use for a day or two and cut back on the frequency. It may take three to four weeks before you can notice improvement in your complexion.

■ Continue the medication even after your complexion is under control. The treatment is designed to control acne—there is no cure for it. If there's no improvement after three months of self-treatment, you should probably consult a physician.

Rules for taking aspirin

Aspirin is by no means a harmless drug. Used with caution, however, it can make you feel better. It reduces pain, inflammation, and fever. But used carelessly, aspirin can occasionally produce serious side effects—especially in the stomach. In fact, it leads all over-the-counter drugs as a cause of serious adverse reactions.

Here are some rules for proper use of aspirin. The risk of side effects can be reduced if these procedures are followed.

■ To minimize possible stomach irritation and to hasten the absorption of aspirin, always take aspirin with a full glass of water or other liquid.

■ The recommended adult dose is one or two standard 5-grain tablets every four hours. (A 5-grain tablet is the equivalent of 325 milligrams.) The maximum safe dosage to take without a doctor's approval is twelve tablets in twenty-four hours.

■ If you feel it necessary to take aspirin for more than ten consecutive days, consult a physician.

Aspirin: For some it's not safe

Although aspirin is safe and effective for most users, the drug should not be taken by certain people. Side effects could range from mild to life-threatening for these people.

Aspirin is not for everyone. It's long been known that aspirin is not perfectly safe for regular use by certain categories of people.

■ No one with ulcers should take aspirin, except under a doctor's care. Aspirin can make existing ulcers worse.

■ Pregnant women should avoid taking aspirin during the last three months of pregnancy. Studies have shown that ingesting aspirin may prolong pregnancy and labor and increase the risk of maternal bleeding, stillbirth, and infant mortality.

■ Arthritics should be under a doctor's care. They should not try to treat the disease themselves with aspirin. Inadequate treatment can lead to irreversible joint damage. And the large doses of aspirin required for proper treatment should be taken only under medical supervision because they increase the risk of side effects.

■ Asthmatics should be wary of taking aspirin.

■ Do not take aspirin if you are sensitive or allergic to it—if it causes skin rash or shortness of breath.

■ If you are taking any other medication regularly—for gout, diabetes, or other conditions—consult your physician before taking aspirin.

■ Children who have the flu or chicken pox should not be given aspirin. Studies have suggested that use of aspirin might be associated with a rare but often fatal childhood disorder called Reye's syndrome. The disease occurs mainly among children between 6 months and 15 years of age who are recovering from the flu or chicken pox.

Side effects. The most common side effect from aspirin is a mild upset stomach.

■ "Heartburn" or nausea apparently affects about 2 to 10 percent of people who take aspirin only occasionally.

■ Mild stomach bleeding may occur in people who take aspirin on a daily basis. But the bleeding is painless, unrelated to symptoms of stomach distress, and usually of no clinical importance.

■ People who take aspirin every day should be checked periodically for possible anemia.

■ Serious side effects from taking aspirin are relatively uncommon and occur mainly among people using aspirin regularly in high doses. Under those circumstances, aspirin can cause stomach ulcers and massive gastrointestinal bleeding.

Acetaminophen: Who needs it?

Datril, Tylenol, and other brands of acetaminophen—a nonaspirin pain reliever—cost more than plain aspirin.

For the great majority of people, the switch from aspirin to acetaminophen is unnecessary—and expensive.

Advantages. It's true that acetaminophen is less irritating to the stomach than aspirin.

■ Heavy aspirin users, such as arthritics, do face an increased risk of serious stomach bleeding.

■ From 2 to 10 percent of people who take aspirin apparently experience some stomach upset. (Irritation is an insignificant problem for most aspirin users—those who take aspirin only occasionally.)

■ For people with ulcers or others who should not take aspirin, acetaminophen can be quite useful.

Disadvantages. For all other users of acetaminophen, the price you pay for an aspirin substitute may not be necessary. What's more, acetaminophen is not without risk.

■ Acetaminophen has no advantage over aspirin as a painkiller or for fever reduction: Milligram for milligram, the two are virtually identical in effectiveness.

■ As for inflammation, there's no contest. Aspirin in large doses relieves both pain and the inflammation causing it. In arthritis, the anti-inflammatory action of aspirin can also help prevent further joint damage. Acetaminophen has virtually no effect on the inflammation of arthritis, though it does help reduce the pain caused by the inflammation.

■ Acetaminophen is by no means harmless. Overdoses can cause permanent liver damage or death.

Shopping for acetaminophen

If you're among those who should avoid aspirin, the extra price you pay for acetaminophen is worth it. But you don't need to overpay.

When we checked prices, we found that a 100-tablet bottle of generic acetaminophen sold for less than one-third the price of regular-strength *Tylenol.* Although generic acetaminophen is a bargain, compared with the brand-name acetaminophens, it still costs more than three times as much as generic aspirin.

We know of no reason why generic acetaminophen should be any less effective than a brand-name acetaminophen. But don't look for generics on the same shelf with brand-name products. Instead, ask the druggist for "acetaminophen" or "APAP"—it may be kept behind the counter.

Is Bayer better?

Commericals for *Bayer* aspirin may claim it's better than ordinary aspirin. It certainly costs more than other brands of plain aspirin.

But is *Bayer* really better? Is it worth the extra money? Tests sponsored by Consumer Reports say no on both counts.

We tested nine brands of plain aspirin—*Bayer*, two other nationally advertised brands, and six store brands from around the country. We compared their performance, using the three laboratory tests that the makers of *Bayer* called crucial for indicating therapeutic superiority. On no test did any brand—including *Bayer*—perform significantly better than any other brand.

Based on these results, we advise you to buy the cheapest aspirin: All aspirin is pretty much the same.

Buffered aspirin

Bufferin costs more than plain aspirin, but is a buffered product worth the extra price?

Only if you have to take large amounts of aspirin daily are you likely to benefit from a buffered aspirin. But there's no need to pay the premium price *Bufferin* commands. A generic buffered product will work as well as *Bufferin* and save you money.

Bufferin and generic brands of buffered aspirin contain the same amount of aspirin as a standard 325-milligram aspirin tablet, plus a small amount of two antacids. The antacids help the aspirin dissolve faster in stomach fluids.

Those who might benefit from buffered aspirin are primarily arthritics whose doctors prescribe heavy daily doses of aspirin. Such heavy users are much more likely to experience stomach distress from aspirin than would occasional users.

Our medical consultants report that buffered aspirin has eased stomach upset for some of their arthritic patients. If you buy buffered aspirin, you should try a generic version. The one we tested dissolved as quickly as *Bufferin*—and cost $2.80 less for a bottle of 225.

Anacin: What's the difference?

Anacin, the most heavily advertised of all nonprescription drug products, is probably one of the least necessary for you to buy.

Anacin contains aspirin and caffeine. Each tablet has 400 milligrams of aspirin (compared with the 325 milligrams in a plain aspirin tablet) plus 32 milligrams of caffeine (the amount in a quarter-cup of brewed coffee). The fabled "Anacin Difference" is 150 milligrams—the difference between two tablets of *Anacin* and two tablets of plain aspirin.

How fast is fast? Right on the label are the words "FAST PAIN RELIEF." Is *Anacin* faster at pain relief than plain aspirin?

To get an idea of its speed, we compared *Anacin* with plain aspirin in our dissolution tests. We also tested a generic brand with ingredients identical to *Anacin,* but costing more than 25 percent less.

Both *Anacin* and the equivalent generic product we tested dissolved at virtually the same rate as standard aspirin, suggesting that speed of pain relief would be about equal for all three.

How helpful is caffeine? Although caffeine's role in pain relief still needs more clarification, one thing *is* known about caffeine: It can make you tense. Yet for years, *Anacin* has been advertised as a tension reliever.

Nevertheless, some people may want an aspirin/caffeine combination instead of plain aspirin. If so, they should try a generic brand. The one we tested contained the same ingredients as *Anacin* and costs less.

Extra-strength: Who needs it?

Taking more than the standard dose of two plain aspirin adds little, if any, pain relief and is usually a waste of money.

Our medical consultants deplore the growing trend toward "Extra Strength" and "Maximum Strength" tablets. They warn that it's not wise to ingest extra-large amounts of a drug when standard amounts will do the job.

"Extra Strength" is a clever marketing ploy. Manufacturers simply pack more aspirin into a tablet, add an extra-large price tag, and proclaim that they've done something special.

With many drugs, there's a simple relationship between the amount you take and the subsequent effect: The larger the dose, the greater the response. Aspirin, surprisingly, does not follow this pattern.

Clinical studies have been unable to show conclusively that adding more aspirin increases the pain relief provided by two plain aspirin (650 milligrams). The so-called dose-response curve seems to level off markedly above 650 milligrams—the dosage that results in significant pain relief.

For most people with a headache, that means two tablets of an extra-strength product—a total of 800 to 1,000 milligrams—offer little, if any, more pain relief than two tablets (650 milligrams) of plain aspirin.

While a 650-milligram dose of aspirin should handle most everyday aches and pains, larger doses of aspirin may sometimes be helpful. But there's no need to buy an extra-strength product. Simply take three plain aspirin tablets instead of two. That delivers 975 milligrams of pain relief—more than in a standard two-tablet dose of many brands of extra-strength products. But take no more than twelve plain aspirin tablets in twenty-four hours—the maximum safe adult dosage without a doctor's approval.

Three expensive variations

Plain aspirin also comes in three expensive variations. What do you get for the extra price you pay? Of the three variations, only enteric-coated aspirin may benefit one group of aspirin-takers.

Enteric-coated aspirin makes sense for people who cannot tolerate the stomach irritation that aspirin sometimes causes. The specially formulated outer coating "protects" the tablets from dissolving in the stomach. Instead, the aspirin dissolves in the small intestine.

Enteric-coated aspirin, such as *Ecotrin* or less expensive generic versions, may be especially helpful to arthritics and others who need to take aspirin in large amounts. But pain relief is somewhat delayed, compared with ordinary tablets.

Timed-release aspirin tablets typically contain twice the normal dose of aspirin, released over a period of six to eight hours. They're not suitable for relief of pain or fever, because rapid relief of these symptoms depends on rapid absorption.

This product is aimed mainly at arthritics who must maintain a steady aspirin level in the blood by taking aspirin frequently throughout the day.

Timed-release aspirin offers high-priced convenience: It allows the patient to take fewer tablets less often each day.

Aspirin capsules. The main difference between tablets and capsules is price and packaging. The shiny capsules resemble many prescription drugs, and people apparently believe they're more effective than tablets. But capsules have no therapeutic advantage over tablets.

Those who dislike the taste of aspirin or have trouble swallowing tablets may prefer the capsules.

Is caffeine harmful?

There is no persuasive evidence that moderate caffeine intake is harmful to the average healthy adult. But excessive intake may lead to chronic caffeine intoxication, or "caffeinism," a medical term for the well-known "coffee nerves." Common symptoms include restlessness and disturbed sleep, heart palpitations, irritation of the stomach, and diarrhea.

Caffeine is also mildly addicting. People who ordinarily consume substantial amounts of caffeine-containing beverages or drugs may experience such symptoms as headache or depression for several days when they stop using the products.

Caffeine and pregnant women. One group of healthy adults—pregnant women—has been cautioned by the U.S. Food and Drug Administration to avoid caffeine or use it sparingly. Animal tests have suggested a possible link to certain birth defects. Because questions about caffeine's possible role in birth defects remain unresolved, our medical consultants believe the FDA's advice to pregnant women is sound: If you're pregnant, you'd probably be wise to avoid caffeine.

Caffeine and children. The possible overconsumption of caffeine by youngsters has also been a cause for concern. Children seldom drink much coffee, but they can be exposed to significant amounts of caffeine in soft drinks and iced tea, especially in terms of their body weight. There is some evidence that children who habitually consume several caffeinated soft drinks daily experience jumpiness, insomnia, and other effects seen in adult coffee-drinkers.

How much is too much caffeine? What constitutes an excessive intake of caffeine is hard to define. It varies widely among individuals. Some people are able to drink several cups of coffee or tea daily without apparent side effects. Those who are unusually sensitive to caffeine, however, may experience nervousness, nausea, and other symptoms of caffeinism from a single cup of coffee.

■ The amount of caffeine required to cause stimulant effects in a typical adult is estimated to be about 150 to 250 milligrams, the amount of caffeine in one or two cups of brewed coffee.

■ An "excessive" amount—one capable of producing some symptoms of caffeinism in adults—is estimated to range from as low as 200 milligrams per day to 750 milligrams per day.

Cutting back on caffeine in coffee

If you want to cut back on your intake of caffeine in coffee, there are several things you can do without actually giving up coffee altogether.

You can reduce caffeine content a little by changing your brewing method, and a lot by switching from brewed coffee to instant coffee. You can also switch to decaffeinated coffee.

■ The drip method of brewing produces higher caffeine content than the percolator method.

■ Brewed coffee generally contains twice the caffeine content of instant coffee.

■ Decaffeinated brands, of course, usually have only a few milligrams of caffeine per cup. You may well find that you can't detect a flavor difference between decaffeinated coffee and regular coffee marketed in the same brand line.

Dandruff

Dandruff appears to be seasonal—generally milder in the summer and most severe from October through December. Milder cases can be managed without medical measures.

Mild flaking. When it's mild, dandruff is a cosmetic problem that doesn't really require medical treatment. To control dandruff that is merely mild scaling, use an ordinary shampoo several times a week. (Even daily shampooing will not harm the hair or scalp.)

Moderate or severe flaking. Heavier flaking accompanied by scalp inflammation may indicate seborrheic dermatitis of the scalp. Excess production of sebum, the oil secreted by sebaceous glands, may be involved in causing the inflammation. To treat seborrheic dermatitis, medicated shampoos (available without a prescription) are often all that is necessary.

Safe and effective treatment. In its review of medicated shampoos, an advisory panel appointed by the U.S. Food and Drug Administration identified some ingredients that work—and some that don't.

Here is a list of active ingredients for treatment of dandruff. The concentration percentages shown in parentheses are those deemed safe and effective by the FDA advisory panel. Before buying a medicated shampoo, check the label for one of these active ingredients at the percentage listed:

- Coal tar (0.5–5%)
- Coal-tar distillate (4%)
- Coal-tar extract (2–8.75%)
- Coal-tar solution (2.5–5%)
- Salicylic acid (1.8–3%)
- Selenium sulfide (1%)
- Sulfur (2–5%)
- Sulfur (2–5%) and salicylic acid (1.8–3%)
- Zinc pyrithione (1–2%).

Home blood-sugar testing: Pros and cons

For many diabetics, it makes sense to invest in a device for self-testing of blood-sugar levels. For certain diabetics, it would be a waste of money.

Those who benefit. Blood-sugar testing is generally advised for the following groups of patients.

■ Pregnant diabetics need to maintain normal levels of blood sugar. Several studies have shown that maintenance of blood-sugar levels within the normal range can all but eliminate the increased rate of fetal abnormalities and stillbirths among infants of diabetic mothers.

■ Insulin-dependent diabetics, with regular tests, can gain insight into the effects of insulin, diet, and exercise on their blood sugar. With the help of a physician, they can learn to make adjustments accordingly. Such testing is especially recommended for those with unstable or "brittle" diabetes, who experience wide swings in their blood-sugar levels, and for those with existing complications, such as eye or kidney problems. The tests can also be used to check symptoms that might otherwise be misconstrued by patients as signs of impending insulin shock.

■ Maturity-onset diabetics requiring drugs—those whose diabetes is not controlled by diet alone—may also benefit from blood-sugar testing. It can provide important information for the patient and physician in adjusting the dosage of oral drugs or insulin. Here again, it's particularly indicated for those with poorly controlled diabetes or complications.

Those less likely to benefit. Patients with mild diabetes well controlled by diet probably won't gain much from blood-sugar monitoring. For them, it's likely to be just an unnecessary expense.

For such patients, urine tests and periodic blood-sugar testing by a physician are generally adequate for monitoring purposes.

Appetite suppressants: How much long-term effect?

Think twice if you're considering using appetite suppressants as part of a long-term weight-loss program. You might be subject to a rebound effect.

According to findings in controlled trials, patients treated with appetite suppressants regained weight faster after treatment than dieters practicing only behavior modification (a program for changing the eating habits and lifestyle that promote obesity).

One six-month trial compared results with an appetite suppressant, behavior modification, and a combined treatment program. Drug-therapy patients lost an average of 32 pounds and the combination-therapy group 34 pounds—both significantly more than the 24-pound average lost by those on behavior modification alone.

When the patients were followed up a year later, however, there was a striking reversal of the treatment results.

- Those receiving behavior therapy alone had gained back only 4 of the 24 pounds lost.
- Those who had received the drug, either alone or in combination with behavior therapy, had regained much of their lost weight: 20 of the 32 pounds lost by the drug-therapy group and 24 of the 34 pounds lost by those on the combination regimen.
- Thus, the initial benefit of an appetite suppressant could be short-lived. And combining it with behavior therapy might serve only to undermine the long-term effectiveness of the behavioral approach.

Diet pills raise safety questions

Appetite suppressants that you can buy over the counter might compromise your health.

Our medical consultants think these OTC diet aids, particularly those with high doses of PPA (phenylpropanolamine), could increase blood pressure to above-normal levels in some people, and could lead to other adverse effects as well.

They also suggest that PPA's interaction with oral contraceptives should be studied, as well as reported side effects such as transient psychotic behavior.

"Puffery" for three-speed bikes

A reader of Consumer Reports chided the editors of the magazine for writing that three-speed bikes were inferior to ten-speeds and best used for errands or trips to the train station.

"Of course a ten-speed is more efficient," the reader conceded, "but it's also expensive and temperamental. I don't care that I have to puff harder pedaling my three-speed. I bought it for the exercise."

An exercise bike: Is it for you?

If you think jogging is boring and if swimming leaves you cold, perhaps you should try an exercise bicycle. If you're uneasy about public displays of exertion, you'll have less problems with an exercise bike: You can shape up in seclusion.

The exercise bike isn't really a bicycle—it has only one wheel and doesn't move. But you ride it like a bicycle, and it can provide you with a fairly rigorous exercise program.

Because an exercise bike can cost you anywhere from $100 to $400, you have to be serious about wanting to exercise. If you're not sure whether you would really use an exercise bike, rent one for a while, if you can, from a retailer of exercise equipment.

If you decide you would like to have one around for an occasional workout, it would make sense to buy an inexpensive model. But if you plan to follow a regular exercise program, it's important to have a more expensive machine—one that's comfortable and works smoothly.

How can exercise help your heart?

Although it has yet to be proved that exercise will reduce the possibility of a heart attack, there's plenty of evidence that exercise can make your heart work more efficiently.

But it's important to choose the right kind of exercise. You won't get much cardiovascular conditioning from stop-and-go activities such as golf or softball. The best way to strengthen your heart is to engage in *sustained* activity, such as jogging, swimming, bicycling, or skipping rope.

Before undertaking strenuous exercise, however, you should check with a doctor if you're older than 35. Hard pedaling or other vigorous physical activity could be dangerous, even fatal, to someone with unsuspected coronary disease. A cardiovascular problem doesn't rule out exercise, however. In fact, cardiac rehabilitation programs often include exercise under supervision.

For best results, your exercise program should meet the following conditions.

Duration. Each exercise session should last at least ten minutes at the start, fifteen to thirty minutes after your muscles are in better shape. It's all right to rest a couple of minutes after every three or four minutes of sustained activity. It's wise to warm up gradually before exercising strenuously, and to cool down gradually after a heavy workout. But don't include rest periods, warm-up, and cool-down time when you measure the duration of the exercise.

Frequency. You should exercise at least three times a week, preferably on alternate days. Eventually, you may want to exercise even more often.

Intensity. The exercise must be strenuous enough to give your heart and lungs a workout. The best way to measure intensity is to check your pulse rate immediately after stopping the exercise.

Press the index and middle fingers of one hand against the upturned wrist of the other hand and count the number of beats in exactly ten seconds. Multiplying by six gives your heart rate in beats per minute.

The chart on the facing page shows the heart-rate threshold you should reach and the range you should stay within—*assuming you are in good health.*

AGE	HEART-RATE THRESHOLD RANGE
25-29	135 to 164
30-34	132 to 161
35-39	129 to 157
40-44	126 to 153
45-49	124 to 150
50-54	122 to 148
55-59	119 to 144
60-64	117 to 142
65-69	114 to 138

Selecting an exercise bike

An exercise bicycle can give you enough of a workout to enhance your cardiovascular system. If you plan to follow a regular exercise program, it's important to have a machine that's comfortable and that works smoothly. It will probably pay to pick a good bike—and you will probably have to pay more than $200.

Here are some guidelines to follow in selecting an exercise bike.

Single-action. Within the price range of the models we tested, only single-action models were judged likely to give a good workout. In these bikes, handlebars and seat remain stationary during pedaling.

Seat-to-pedal distance. As with any bike, the distance from the seat to the lowest pedal position should equal your crotch-to-floor measurement plus 2 inches. That will let you extend your foot for efficient pedaling.

Covered spokes. Choose a model with a solid wheel or a shield over the spokes. Uncovered spokes can be dangerous.

Smooth pedaling. A bike should work smoothly enough to allow you to develop a rhythm, especially when it's set for high resistance and you have to pedal hard. Pedals should not stop at the top of each pedal rotation, especially when the resistance setting is high.

Adjustment control. You may want to adjust the resistance while you're sitting on the bike so the controls should be easy to reach—on or near the handlebars. Controls should not be overly sensitive. If the controls change the resistance a lot when you move them only slightly, it's difficult to get a setting that's just right.

Rigidity. The more rigid the bike's frame is, the more smoothly the bike should work. The less rigid machines will flex a lot, especially when a heavy rider pedals hard.

Pedals. Models with ordinary bike pedals may be uncomfortable for bare or stocking feet. If you expect to pedal without shoes, you would probably prefer pedals with a large flat surface.

Pedal straps can help keep your feet from slipping off. They also let you pull up and push forward, as well as step down, on the pedals. If you choose a model without straps, you can always buy them at a bicycle shop—they're inexpensive and easy to install.

User-to-user adjustment. When more than one person will be using an exercise bike, the seat height, handlebar position, and pedaling resistance may have to be adjusted at the beginning of each exercise period. So you may prefer a model whose seat and handlebars can be adjusted without tools.

Fighting foot odor

Foot odor occurs because the foot's warmth and sweat provide choice growing conditions for bacteria, which decompose chafed dead skin cells.

Here's what you can do to combat foot odor.

■ Good foot hygiene can help reduce odor by eliminating the dead skin. That means washing the feet thoroughly (including in between the toes) with soap and water as part of a daily bath or shower.

■ To reduce perspiration, wear lightweight shoes that fit comfortably. Heavy or tight shoes often promote sweating. When weather permits, wear perforated shoes or sandals. Leather is probably the best shoe material because it breathes, allowing perspiration to evaporate. Even so, about 20 percent of the perspiration absorbed from the previous day's wear stays in leather shoes, which is why alternating pairs of shoes each day is a good idea. Shoes made of synthetics retard evaporation even more.

■ Hose should not be too tight and should be changed every day. Preferably, socks should be made of a natural fiber, such as cotton or wool, which absorbs moisture better than synthetics. Wool is about twice as absorbent as cotton, but heavy wool socks may actually increase perspiration.

■ Absorbent powders can also help keep the feet dry. Ordinary talcum powder is fine for this purpose and is much cheaper than specialized foot powders. Dust the feet after bathing or swimming, and shake powder into your socks and shoes.

Athlete's foot

Athlete's foot usually affects men, especially those between the ages of 15 and 40. You don't have to be an athlete to get athlete's foot, but it helps. Locker room floors act as ready sources of infection, and profuse sweating from exercise encourages fungal growth.

Keeping the feet dry is the key to preventing and treating athlete's foot.

■ Wash your feet daily and dry the spaces between the toes thoroughly but gently, so as not to tear the skin.

■ After drying, apply a foot powder, particularly if you've found you're prone to develop athlete's foot. By absorbing sweat, powder prevents the occurrence of the soft flaking skin that fungi thrive on.

■ Avoid sweat-producing shoes and thick wool or nylon socks, especially in hot weather. Sandals and cotton socks are preferable. Go barefoot when you can. (People with diabetes or poor circulation in the feet, however, should avoid going barefoot, even inside the house.)

Medication. Athlete's foot can occur despite attention to foot hygiene. When it does, there are some over-the-counter preparations that can produce good results.

■ Antifungal remedies containing either undecylenic acid or tolnaftate are both safe and effective, according to a report by a U.S. Food and Drug Administration advisory panel. Controlled studies show that products with these ingredients are equally effective, but those with tolnaftate cost about 2½ times as much as those with undecylenic acid.

■ If the medication clears up the athlete's foot and is not irritating in any way, you should continue using the product for a while to prevent the infection from recurring.

■ But if the infection hasn't cleared up after four weeks of self-treatment, the FDA panel recommends that you see a physician or podiatrist.

■ Professional treatment is also called for if athlete's foot swells, reddens, or becomes painful. That may mean that bacteria are present in addition to fungi. Antifungal products are ineffective against bacterial infections.

Athlete's foot lookalikes. People who think they have athlete's foot sometimes treat it on their own for months or years with little improvement. All too often, what they think is athlete's foot is something else entirely. A doctor can easily tell if you really have athlete's foot by taking a scraping of the skin involved and examining it under a microscope. If no fungi are visible under the microscope, the lesion is probably not athlete's foot.

■ One possibility is "shoe contact dermatitis"—an inflamed, itching rash usually caused by an allergy to one or more chemicals used in making shoes. The distinguishing feature of this rash is its symmetry: It usually appears on the tops of *both* feet and on the large toe. If an allergy to a chemical is causing the rash, a dermatologist can give you a patch test that may be able to identify the chemical.

■ Another possibility is foot eczema. This is an itching noncontagious disease of unknown cause. The appearance varies, depending on the type of eczema present. Treatment by a dermatologist may be required to clear up the foot eczema.

Corns and calluses

Ill-fitting shoes plus the repeated trauma induced by walking cause most calluses and corns (small calluses with a compact central core). Loose shoes create friction; walking and tight shoes both exert pressure.

■ Because they're composed of dead skin, calluses themselves can't "hurt." Problems develop when a callus grows so large that its bulk presses against the underlying tissue.

■ Corns generally develop over bony projections on toes, usually in response to friction or to pressure from tight shoes. Pain from corns is usually sharper and more localized than pain from calluses.

Correcting the underlying problem. The best way to get rid of calluses and corns and prevent their return is to eliminate the original pressure or friction that caused them.

■ Many cases can be solved by getting better-fitting shoes.

■ Correcting faulty weight distribution in the foot can sometimes solve the problem. In people who have high arches, for example, the heel and ball of the foot bear nearly all the body's weight, and thick calluses can form there and cause pain. An arch support or orthotic device can shift some weight to the arch. Once the stress is removed, the calluses should gradually disappear.

Trimming. When the underlying problem is corrected, trimming will help corns and calluses disappear.

■ Do-it-yourself trimming can be done on calluses, not on corns.

■ Trimming is best done when the skin is softened after a bath or shower, or after soaking the feet in soapy water for ten to fifteen minutes. After drying the foot, rub the callus gently with a moistened pumice stone or buffing pad (available from a drugstore). Afterward, apply a moisturizing lotion to help soften the skin.

■ This regimen of soaking, trimming, and moisturizing can be repeated several times a week. Attempt to remove only a thin layer of skin each time, and stop rubbing immediately if the callus starts to hurt or becomes inflamed. Diabetics and people with poor circulation in the feet should not trim their own calluses becauses serious infections may result from accidential injury.

■ Corns should be trimmed by a professional. And no one should attempt "bathroom surgery" with razor blades on either corns or calluses. Surgical trimming should be left to trained professsionals such as podiatrists.

Remedies. Most over-the-counter products to treat corns and calluses contain an acid that softens and destroys the outer layer of skin. Unfortunately, the acid can't distinguish between dead corn or callus skin and the healthy tissue around it. If applied carelessly, the products can cause serious burns.

Though podiatrists strongly discourage use of the products, a U.S. Food and Drug Administration advisory panel concluded that they could safely be used. The FDA panel suggested taking a number of precautions when using corn-and-callus products.

■ Limit application to five treatments. (Complete removal of corns and calluses is not always essential and could be harmful because they do fulfill a protective function.) If there's no improvement after two weeks of treatment, seek professional help.

■ Apply the product only to the corn or callus, not to the surrounding normal skin.

■ Diabetics and people with poor circulation should use the products only under the supervision of a doctor.

Padding can also relieve the discomfort of corns and calluses.

■ For lesions on the underside of the foot, innersoles that line the bottom of the shoe may help.

■ Our consultants preferred neoprene rubber innersoles, available in sporting-goods stores, to the softer latex-foam variety.

■ Lamb's wool or cotton placed between the toes can alleviate pain from soft corns.

■ Other unmedicated padded products—corn pads, heel cushions, metatarsal pads (for the ball of the foot)—can also help. Most are sold in drugstores, shoe stores, or shoe-repair shops.

Problems of the elderly. Podiatrists can be especially helpful to the elderly, who often have difficulty treating corns and calluses because of poor eyesight or arthritis. With aging, the loss of natural padding in the foot can make even minor problems debilitating. Simple measures such as cushioning or innersoles in the shoes can often provide dramatic relief.

Ingrown toenails

Ingrown toenails are a major source of foot pain and discomfort.

Causes. Improper cutting of the nail is usually what causes an ingrown toenail. Improper footwear—tight or pointed shoes, tight socks or stockings—can occasionally cause an ingrown toenail by forcing a free corner of the nail directly into the adjacent skin flap. Foot perspiration aggravates the situation by softening the skin and making it more vulnerable.

Prevention. Proper cutting of nails should normally prevent ingrown toenail. (Some toenails are congenitally curved and may require professional care.)

■ Cut the nail straight across, level with the tip of the toe.

■ Do not cut away or taper the corners in any way. Cutting the corners makes the nail vulnerable—it could grow back the wrong way and become ingrown. A straight cut, however, will leave the nail long enough to prevent the problem.

■ It will help, too, if hosiery is loose and shoes have a "toe box" large enough so that the toes—especially the big toe—do not press against the sides or front of the shoe.

Self-treatment. If an ingrown toenail is caught early, self-treatment can produce good results.

■ Soak the foot in warm water once or twice a day and dry it carefully.

■ Apply dusting powder to absorb perspiration.

■ Using a nail file or strong toothpick, wedge a wisp of cotton under the corner of the nail where the pain is. That will help keep the nail from penetrating the skin at the side of the nail.

■ Replace the cotton once a day until the nail clears the corner.

■ If there are signs of infection, consult a doctor. Treatment may involve removing all or part of the nail.

■ Over-the-counter products to relieve the discomfort of ingrown toenails have not yet been shown to be effective.

Bunions

Bunions can be the most painful of the maladies that commonly afflict the foot—and among the most difficult to treat successfully. They are four times more common with women than with men.

Causes. A bunion results from inflammation of the joint at the base of the big toe: It's actually a bursitis of that joint. The inflammation may be brought about by years of wearing tight short shoes.

The underlying cause of most bunions is an improper alignment of the bones of the foot, a tendency that seems to be inherited. Pressure from the shoe causes the big toe to bend unnaturally, so that it can actually overlie the next toe. The irritation by the shoe may cause the growth of an irritating spur at the end of the big toe's metatarsal, one of the long bones of the foot.

Treatment. Unlike other foot problems, bunions are not amenable to self-treatment. The bunion shields sold in drugstores offer scant relief, according to our consultants.

A bunionectomy may be performed to cut off the bone spur. That may suffice to relieve mild bunions.

But if bone realignment is needed, the patient requires a more extensive operation in which the large toe or metatarsal, or both, are cut and properly repositioned. Many people spend hundreds of dollars having a bunion corrected only to have it recur because a faulty bone alignment remains.

If the bunion is not too painful, ask yourself if your foot's cosmetic appearance is important enough to justify an operation. You may be able to relieve the pain of bunions by using bunion-last shoes.

Diabetes and foot problems

Among the complications that afflict diabetics, foot problems can be especially devastating. Because of a loss of sensation in the feet during middle age—a disorder called diabetic neuropathy—diabetics can be unaware of calluses, blisters, and minor foot injuries. Untreated, these may become diabetic ulcers—open sores that readily get infected. The infection can lead to gangrene and, possibly, to amputations.

Prevention. About 85 percent of diabetic ulcers can be avoided, say experts.

■ In part, prevention involves taking simple precautions, such as washing and examining the feet daily, using comfortable shoes and cushioned innersoles, and inspecting shoes daily for gravel or protruding nails.

■ Professional help is also essential, not only for specific advice on foot care, but for treating minor problems *before* they become severe. If you are diabetic and experience corns, calluses, or other foot irritations, consider visiting a podiatrist regularly—every four to six weeks.

■ Tell the podiatrist that you are diabetic and mention any redness, swelling, callus, or other symptom. Ask about preventive measures for diabetics, including a padding made of polyethylene foam such as *Plastizote,* which some of our consultants believe may be particularly useful as an innersole.

HMOs and hospitals

Your statistical chances of being hospitalized are less with a health maintenance organization. Studies have shown that substantially fewer HMO members are admitted to the hospital than patients of regular fee-for-service doctors. The difference is dramatic.

An HMO provides its members with almost all the medical care they'll need (except dental work), for which it charges a monthly fee. According to 1980 government figures, the hospitalization rate for HMO members was 418 hospital days a year per 1,000 members. For those covered by Blue Cross/Blue Shield, the rate jumped to 725 days. The national average rate was even higher—1,631 hospital days a year per 1,000 people.

Why are HMO members hospitalized less? It's not because HMO members are any healthier. A 1980 study by an American Medical Association group found no significant difference in overall health between HMO members and those covered by traditional health insurance programs.

So why do fewer HMO members end up in the hospital? The answer seems to be in the way HMOs operate. With traditional medical insurance plans, much more of your bill is normally covered if you're in the hospital than if you receive your care in the doctor's office. So fee-for-service doctors tend to hospitalize patients for certain tests and minor surgical procedures.

The system is far different at an HMO. Members pay a fixed fee each month no matter how many medical services they use. Doctors who work exclusively for HMOs are on fixed compensation.

Because it's the HMO that pays when members are hospitalized (not the members), the HMO has an incentive to cut costs and reduce hospitalizations wherever possible.

Thus, an HMO doctor would be less inclined to hospitalize someone with chronic medical problems, such as a sore back or a urinary infection, if treatment could be administered on an outpatient basis. And minor surgery would be done in a doctor's office or in an outpatient facility, if the procedure were suited to it.

Is an HMO for you?

Despite the substantial saving in medical bills that you can usually expect if you join a health maintenance organization, HMOs are not for everybody.

You're likely to be comfortable with an HMO, especially a large one, only if you have most, if not all, of the following characteristics:

■ Willingness to sever existing relationships with physicians in private practice or to pay them out of your own pocket.

■ Acceptance of the fact that you may not see your regular doctor if you're sick and want an immediate appointment. Instead you may have to go to a special "drop-in" center to be treated, usually by someone you have never seen before.

■ Tolerance of long waiting times to get a nonurgent appointment. You may have to wait as long as six weeks to two months, say, for a routine eye examination.

■ Patience with impersonal service. For instance, when you call for an appointment, you may find yourself listening to a tape-recorded message for several minutes.

Judging an HMO

If you're thinking of joining a health maintenance organization, here are some guidelines to use in evaluating one HMO against another.

Financial soundness. HMOs can fail, just as any business can. That could leave you without medical coverage—and, in some cases, with responsibility for medical bills.

■ Ask if the HMO carries insolvency insurance, and whether the contract contains a clause keeping individuals free from liability for medical bills if the HMO fails.

■ Check for membership in the Group Health Association of America. That gives some indication of financial soundness. The GHAA has told Consumer Reports that none of its HMO members has ever left an individual without medical coverage or responsible for medical bills because of an insolvency.

Facilities. Is there a full range of facilities and specialists?

■ What hospital does the HMO use?

■ Where are the laboratory and diagnostic facilities?

■ How convenient to your home is the HMO and its facilities?

■ What arrangements are there for twenty-four-hour-a-day emergency care?

■ What specialists are on the staff?

Medical staff. The qualifications of the medical staff are important. Ask for background information about the staff.

■ Are the physicians board-certified in their specialties (meaning they've passed certain tests in that specialty)?

■ Are they at least board-eligible (completed the required residency training in their specialty)?

Supplemental benefits. There is a difference in extra-cost benefits offered by HMOs. One or more of these benefits might be important to you. Ask about coverage for dental care, extended mental health care, physical therapy, extended home nursing, and a fixed or unlimited amount of prescription drugs.

Grievance procedure. A formal grievance procedure is nearly standard among HMOs. But there may also be an informal procedure—to get problems resolved quickly and effectively without going through formalities.

■ Does the HMO have a special person to handle member complaints?

■ Is there any member participation in this informal grievance process?

■ How well does the process work? Check with representatives of employee groups belonging to the HMO. (Ask the HMO's membership department for a list of its major employee groups, with the name and phone number of the union or company official who supervises the program.)

Drugs for menstrual pain

For 30 to 50 percent of women of childbearing age, menstrual pain (dysmenorrhea) can be disabling. Cramps and other symptoms can be very severe for some women for one or two days each month.

Prostaglandin inhibitors are effective in treating dysmenorrhea by preventing the problem rather than merely alleviating it. They work for about eight out of ten women, providing significant relief from symptoms.

Prostaglandins, hormonelike organic acids produced by many tissues of the body (including the lining of the uterus), play a major role in severe menstrual pain. Prostaglandins can cause blood vessels to change in size and can also cause smooth muscle (such as that in the uterus) to contract. Women with severe menstrual pain generally have increased blood levels of prostaglandins.

The prostaglandin inhibitors (a prescription medication) are not inexpensive, but the per-month cost is relatively modest because they are taken only a few days during each menstrual period.

No drug is problem-free, and the prostaglandin inhibitors are no exception. They may be inappropriate for women with a history of asthma or ulcers, because the drugs might aggravate those conditions.

Among women who can take the drugs, though, side effects have so far been minimal, mainly because the drugs are taken for so short a period (usually forty-eight hours). The most common problems are gastrointestinal upsets, such as abdominal discomfort, bloating, nausea, and even vomiting. Because these may be the same as the symptoms of dysmenorrhea, it's difficult at times to tell whether the treatment or the illness is to blame.

None of the prostaglandin inhibitors has to be taken until a menstrual period actually starts, so it's unlikely that women would take them during the early stages of pregnancy, when use of any medication must be considered carefully. That's an important point in the drugs' favor, because there is some concern over possible effects of prostaglandin inhibitors on very young embryos.

Psoriasis: What triggers it?

Some 2 million Americans suffer from psoriasis, a chronic skin disease. Researchers do not yet know why certain people are afflicted with it, but they have noted the triggering factors that can apparently cause psoriasis to flare up.

■ In young people, severe psoriasis has sometimes followed a strep throat.

■ Some people develop psoriasis where the skin has been injured by a cut, scratch, burn (including sunburn), friction, or prolonged pressure.

■ Emotional stress, obesity, alcoholism, and certain medications (lithium and propanolol, for example) may also cause psoriasis to appear.

Self-treatment for mild psoriasis

Fortunately, most cases of psoriasis are mild. Although there is no cure for psoriasis, there are a number of self-administered treatments that can relieve mild symptoms.

Here are some of the steps you can take to treat a mild case on your own.

Coal-tar remedies. Most of the products for psoriasis that you buy at the drugstore contain coal tar—in creams, lotions, gels, and baths. Some coal-tar products are bolstered by other ingredients that soften psoriasis scales and help remove them.

Coal-tar products are mainly useful for mild psoriasis—a few small patches on the elbows, knees, or scalp, for example. They help relieve itching and reduce redness. Most important, they help clear up affected areas by somehow slowing down the increased skin production that causes psoriasis plaque.

For as long as coal tar has been used to treat psoriasis there have been questions about the safety of its use. When an advisory panel appointed by the U.S. Food and Drug Administration reviewed psoriasis products, it recommended that coal-tar products for body use remain available without a prescription, pending future studies on the incidence of skin cancer among coal-tar users.

The panel agreed that coal-tar products are effective. Whatever their risk, it is far outweighed by their benefits, the panel concluded. One benefit is cost: The products are inexpensive, particularly when compared with prescription remedies and the cost of a visit to the doctor.

Moisturizers. These products can also help. They contain ingredients that seal in water already in the skin and keep it from evaporating.

Psoriatics may have dry skin, which can be quite itchy. Moisturizers soothe the skin, preventing the scratching that can trigger new plaques or make existing ones worse. Moisturizers also help keep the plaques from cracking and bleeding.

Moisturizers are not sold as psoriasis remedies, but they help psoriatics look and feel better and have some therapeutic value as well.

Some people can get along fine using moisturizers alone. Others use moisturizers in conjunction with other treatments. The main benefit of a moisturizer is that it helps remove scales. This enhances the action of most of the other treatments, which must penetrate to the underlying skin.

Light. Whether ordinary sunlight or ultraviolet, light is one of the best treatments for psoriasis. Apparently, the ultraviolet (UV) rays slow down the rapid proliferation of skin cells.

Physicians generally frown on sunbathing because it can cause premature aging of the skin and, in some cases, skin cancer. But psoriasis is one situation in which sunlight's proven effectiveness outweighs the risks. Extensive use of light, however, should be supervised by a physician.

Unfortunately, few psoriatics have the time or opportunity to use natural sunlight to its best advantage. And embarrassment about their skin condition may prevent many psoriatics from sunbathing in public.

Artificial sunlight in the form of UV can help overcome these problems. Standard sunlamps can treat only a small area at a time but may be adequate in mild cases. If patches are scattered, whole-body treatment with light panels or a light box may be necessary—but should be undertaken only under the supervision of a physician.

Patients can purchase light panels or light boxes for home use. Several companies now sell directly to consumers.

Professional treatment for psoriasis

Professional treatment for psoriasis is generally called for when the disease worsens, when self-treatment fails, or when psoriasis interferes with your life.

If you need professional treatment, consult a dermatologist (a physician who specializes in treating skin diseases). Most are willing to devote the time and energy often required for a successful outcome.

It pays to be patient when you start treatment. It may take several visits to find the right treatment or combination of treatments (the national average is six visits). Although the prescription drugs needed to maintain the improvement may be expensive, once the disease is under control, there's usually no need for more than one or two office visits per year.

How doctors treat psoriasis

If you decide you need more than self-care and nonprescription remedies to relieve the symptoms of psoriasis, there are several treatment programs a physician may prescribe. People who have been disappointed by professional care in the past should know that current therapies can improve most cases of psoriasis.

The major treatments now in use by physicians include the following.

Topical steroids—creams and lotions applied to the skin—are the most commonly prescribed medications for psoriasis. (They're most effective when used with some type of airtight cover—plastic wrap, plastic gloves, or even a plastic suit.) Topical steroids are more effective than coal tar (which is available over the counter), but the steroids are also much more expensive.

Injection of steroids is reserved primarily for isolated patches that resist other forms of treatment. Treating widespread psoriasis by steroid injection can lead to serious internal side effects.

Anthralin is another effective topical medication that is especially useful against thick stubborn psoriasis. Adverse effects—it stings and temporarily stains the skin, hair, and nails, and may permanently stain clothes—can be largely avoided, and some improvement still obtained, by using lower-strength anthralin formulations.

Methotrexate, a drug taken internally, has been used in psoriasis treatments for more than thirty years. But it poses a small but definite risk of severe liver disease. The risk increases the longer the treatment is continued. As a result, methotrexate is a treatment of last resort for psoriasis, even though it can produce dramatic results.

Light is an important part of both a professional and self-administered program for treating psoriasis.

■ Whole-body treatment should only be done with the advice of a dermatologist, who must first determine if UV will help (a small percentage of psoriatics actually get worse). The dermatologist can then prescribe an exposure regimen suited to the patient's skin type (a severe sunburn can make psoriasis worse, for example) and to the severity of the disease.

■ Whole-body treatment can be done either with a light panel that has an array of four 4-foot fluorescent UV tubes, or with a light box, a four-sided cabinet lined with fluorescent UV tubes. To use a light panel, the patient must turn the body to expose each side. A light box treats all sides at one time.

Coal tar and ultraviolet light are both effective psoriasis treatments. When used together, their beneficial effects are multiplied, possibly because coal tar's photosensitizing action enhances the effectiveness of UV. The combination of coal tar and UV is called the Goeckerman regimen, named after the doctor who developed it in 1925. Because of its proven record of safety and effectiveness, the Goeckerman regimen is generally the first treatment that dermatologists prescribe for severe psoriasis (cases affecting 25 percent or more of the body surface).

PUVA is one of the newest and most effective psoriasis treatments, but it's also one of the most controversial.

■ The P stands for the drug psoralen; the UVA, the high-intensity long-wave ultraviolet light (UV-A). Psoralen, which makes the skin more sensitive to UV-A, is taken orally. About two hours later, the patient stands in a light box lined with UV-A bulbs and is exposed to UV-A light for several minutes.

■ PUVA produces clear skin in about 90 percent of patients with severe psoriasis. That requires about twenty-five treatments, taken at the rate of two or three times a week. Because of its potential danger, PUVA (like methotrexate) is considered a treatment of last resort. It is generally reserved for cases in which psoriasis affects 30 percent or more of the body surface, and only for cases that have not responded to topical steroids or the Goeckerman regimen.

How often do you need a checkup?

An annual physical exam is not mandatory for every adult, according to our medical consultants. It's a waste of money for some people to get a checkup once a year. Exams are more important in middle age, when chronic diseases such as heart disease and cancer become significant causes of illness.

Here is the basic schedule we recommend for adults who believe they're healthy and have no health-related problems and no family history of inherited disorders.

Men should consider the following:

- Starting at age 30, an exam every five years up to age 45.
- From age 45 to 60, an exam every two or three years.
- After 60, an exam every year.

Women should consider the following:

- Starting at age 20, an exam every three years to age 40.
- From age 40 to 50, an exam every two years.
- After 50, an exam every year.

Tests a checkup should include

No two doctors are likely to agree on which disease-detection tests you should be given as part of a regular checkup. Out of the multitude of tests available, our medical consultants recommend seven that they believe offer the greatest benefit. Each of the seven can detect serious disease before symptoms arise. And treatment of the disease begun at that early time is likely to produce a better outcome than if treatment were delayed until after symptoms appeared.

1. Urinalysis. Perhaps the most widely used test in any complete examination, urinalysis can detect a variety of conditions. The presence of sugar in the urine may indicate diabetes. Large numbers of white blood cells (pus cells) may indicate an infection of the urethra, bladder, kidney, or (in men) the prostate. Microscopic blood in the urine requires additional testing for the presence of bladder and kidney tumors.

- Our medical consultants recommend that you have a urinalysis each time you have a physical. It's simple and inexpensive, and your physician can usually do it in the office.

2. Complete blood count. A laboratory analysis of a drop of blood taken from the finger, a blood count can detect the presence of anemia (a possible sign of internal bleeding) and of blood diseases such as leukemia.

■ Our medical consultants recommend a complete blood count each time you have a physical. As with the urinalysis, it can usually be done in the doctor's office and is relatively inexpensive.

3. Automated blood analysis. This is a more sophisticated blood study. It can detect abnormal functioning of the body's organs. Most family physicians have the test done at a commercial laboratory, where special automated machines can determine the levels of up to thirty or more blood chemistries on a single blood specimen.

Some of the chemistries are more useful than others. Our consultants consider seven to be worthwhile: blood sugar, to detect diabetes (usually done on an empty stomach); calcium, to detect hyperparathyroidism; cholesterol, to judge the risk of heart disease; creatinine, to detect kidney disease; serological test, to detect syphilis; transaminase, to detect abnormal liver function; uric acid, to detect gout.

The full battery of blood-chemistry tests usually provides the doctor with more information than is necessary or desired, and some of the information can be misleading. Sometimes, the falsely abnormal results can lead to further diagnostic procedures that can be expensive and may involve some degree of risk.

■ Our medical consultants recommend a blood-chemistry analysis, which is relatively inexpensive, each time you have a physical.

4. Tests for colo-rectal cancer. One out of every twenty-five people will develop colo-rectal cancer. It occurs equally in men and women. There are three tests that can effectively detect this cancer before symptoms appear.

The first is the digital rectal examination, done as part of a checkup by your physician, using a gloved finger. Of tests for occult (hidden) blood, the most commonly used one is the Hemoccult slide test. Stool samples are prepared at home, using paper slides and a wood applicator, and returned to the doctor for analysis. The test is very inexpensive. The third test is sigmoidoscopy, which involves inserting an illuminated tube, called a proctosigmoidoscope, into the rectum and up into the sigmoid colon.

■ Our medical consultants recommend that the digital rectal examination should be a routine part of every checkup for those over 40. After age 50, everone should have a Hemoccult test once a year and have a sigmoidoscopy every three years following two initial negative tests a year apart.

5. Tests for breast cancer. An American woman has about a one in eleven chance of developing breast cancer sometime in her life. Clinical studies suggest that early detection through use of mammography and physical examination may decrease mortality from breast cancer, particularly among women 50 and older.

(continued on next page)

Mammography—an X ray of the breasts—is the only test that can detect a breast cancer before it becomes large enough to be felt on physical examination.

If you have mammography, insist on a dose of less than one rad per breast. Because it uses ionizing radiation, mammography may itself increase the risk of breast cancer. It is always justified, however, to do further investigation of lumps that are found on physical examination.

Physical examination by the doctor involves careful palpation of the breasts for lumps. Every woman should also palpate her own breasts once a month after age 20. (The best time is one week following the onset of a menstrual period, when the breasts are less swollen and tender. After menopause, choose an easy-to-remember date for breast palpation, such as the first of the month.) Most breast cancers—at least 80 percent—are first detected by the woman herself.

■ Our medical consultants recommend that an annual mammogram be performed beginning at age 50—sooner if there is a personal or family history of breast cancer or if your doctor recommends it. Routine mammography has been shown to be of definite benefit only for women 50 or older. Women between ages 20 and 50 who have annual gynecological examinations should use that occasion to have a breast exam. Otherwise, they should have a trained breast palpation at least every two or three years up to age 40 and then once a year.

6. Pap test for cervical cancer. Evidence suggests that cervical cancer develops slowly. Invasive cancer is usually preceded by a long stage (eight years or more) of localized cervical cancer that is detectable by a Pap test and almost always curable.

■ Our medical consultants recommend that women should begin Pap tests soon after they become sexually active. Women can get good protection with a Pap test every three years, after two negative Pap tests a year apart (the American Cancer Society's recommendation). But the traditional schedule—a Pap test annually—will give women slightly better protection, especially those with multiple sex partners. Many studies have shown that women who begin having sexual intercourse at an early age or who have multiple sex partners are at higher risk of developing cervical cancer. Women who have had a hysterectomy do not need a Pap test, but they should have a pelvic examination regularly.

7. Skin test for tuberculosis. This can show if you've been infected by tuberculosis bacteria since your last test, if that one was negative. While many physicians believe the test is not worthwhile for most adults, our consultants believe it should have wider application. If the test is positive, you should have a chest X ray to look for signs of active disease.

■ Our medical consultants recommend a skin test (it's simple and inexpensive) each time you have a physical, unless a previous test was positive. (Once it is positive, it will remain so.)

Storing pills

Here are two simple rules for sensible storage of pills.

■ Don't store pills in the bathroom. That's probably the worst place in the house to keep them because heat and humidity accelerate the decomposition of drugs.

■ Even under ideal storage conditions, it won't pay you to buy more pills than you or your family can use in a year. Drugs start to break down and lose potency when stored for long periods.

Home maintenance

Choosing an electric bug killer

Investing in an electric bug killer could pay off if you like to spend your summer evenings sitting out on a patio or porch. It could lessen the annoyance of bugs and make your backyard more pleasant to use.

Not every type of bug killer is equally satisfactory, however. Our engineers who tested outdoor models suggest you consider these points before you buy.

■ Stay away from units with incandescent bulbs. They failed to attract enough insects in our tests to make much of a dent in backyard bug populations.

■ Of the units with fluorescent bulbs, avoid those with relatively low killing-grid voltage. If you make your selection from among units generating 4,000 volts or more, you'll probably spare yourself a messy chore. In our tests, the bug killers under 4,000 volts had to be cleaned every few days or so to retain their effectiveness in times of high insect activity. The clogging seemed to be due to incomplete vaporization that left insect parts clinging to the metal killing grid.

■ If it's mosquitoes you're after, be warned that opinion is divided on the effectiveness of bug killers against them. Some of our testers did find that their mosquito problems were reduced by a bug killer. But to be safe, don't buy a unit unless you can get a return privilege.

■ Listen to the "zap" of a neighbor's bug killer before you buy one. The sharp sizzling sound announces bug electrocution on the grid. But with some models, the sound intensity can seem more like a **ZAP.** A loud crackling sound might annoy you or even your neighbors, and could make the squeamish shiver.

■ Check how feasible it would be to disassemble the unit for cleaning. To clean the grid of most bug killers, it's necessary to take the unit apart—at least to the extent of taking off the sides so that the grid can be properly brushed off. This could be a nuisance if you get a model that tends to clog up fast with insect remains and that needs frequent attention.

■ Many bug killers have to be disassembled to remove the bulb. Look for a model that lets you get at the bulb through the bottom of the unit. That's a useful provision, because bulbs need cleaning and, eventually, replacement.

Using an electric bug killer

An electric bug killer will last longer and be easier to maintain if you follow some guidelines suggested by our engineers.

■ Dusk-to-dawn use is quite sufficient for an electric bug killer to be effective, even though most manufacturers recommend keeping the units turned on twenty-four hours a day. We think that's excessive. The most serious insect annoyance comes with evening. That's when you should switch on your bug killer.

■ Bulbs need cleaning to remain effective. They get coated with insect fragments and dust.

■ When your bug killer seems to be zapping less frequently, it might mean the bulb has deteriorated. It's wise to replace a bulb before light output diminishes too far. After two months of continuous use, most of the fluorescent bulbs in the units we tested had dimmed to between 50 and 60 percent of their original brightness. Manufacturers seem to agree on one thing: A bulb deteriorates long before it burns out. How soon to change bulbs, however, is another question. About half the units we tested had labels recommending replacement of fluorescent bulbs every season. Others suggested replacement every two seasons. Some only said that the bulbs will last about 7,000 hours (more than two long summers of continuous twenty-four-hour use).

■ If you've chosen a model providing reasonable access to the bulb, you should be able to handle changing or cleaning it yourself. One brand in our test group recommended that only company service personnel replace bulbs. We didn't see why. Neither special skills nor tools appeared to be needed for a bulb change.

Power cost of zaps

You can zap all night throughout the summer with an electric bug killer for the cost of one or two bottles of insect repellent.

For a fluorescent unit, power to light the bulb and charge the killing grid normally ranged from 24 to 35 watts in our tests. (During zaps, power peaked at 2 to 15 watts above the normal level.) At these rates, the cost of maintaining an electric bug killer would be minimal.

Are electric bug killers safe?

Except to insects, electric bug killers are not a serious hazard, if used properly.

In the typical bug killer, the high voltage is largely mitigated by its tiny current flow. Fingers probing to touch the killing grid would almost certainly have to be in contact with the grounded outer screen as well. Any shock you get would likely be more a painful annoyance than a hazard. Nonetheless, it's best to keep hands off a bug killer.

Our engineers have two cautions for safe use of a bug killer.

■ Don't ask for trouble by keeping a unit too close to the ground. There's no point in hanging it where it can tempt the curiosity of children.

■ Don't try to circumvent the three-wire power cord provided with each unit. Plug it into a three-wire outdoor extension cord, and plug that into a grounded outlet. Most units have a safety switch that automatically shuts off electric power when the unit is being disassembled, even if the cord is left plugged in.

Choosing an electric drill

If you plan to buy only one drill, our engineers recommend a standard ⅜-inch model. Although a ½-inch drill may provide more torque (twisting force), its lower speed means that you'll take longer to finish the types of jobs you'd ordinarily expect a drill to handle. Cordless ⅜-inch models, which can be convenient, lack the muscle and endurance needed for lengthy or heavy-duty work.

The drill you choose should be powerful enough for any job that's likely to come up, easily controlled, and convenient to use. Here's what our engineers suggest you look for.

Speed control is a particularly handy feature when you need a slow speed for starting holes or for driving screws. In our tests of electric drills, the variable-speed control on most models worked smoothly and progressively up to 80 percent of maximum speed.

A reverse switch can be useful for removing screws or for backing out the bit after you've drilled a hole. The type we liked best in our tests was a slide switch on the back of the drill, where it was easy to see. A few standard models had that type of switch. The cordless models had a slide switch, but not quite as conveniently located.

Most common was a lever switch, located above the trigger, that you flicked to one side or the other. We judged these switches good if they had labels to identify the direction of rotation, and fair if they lacked the labels.

Handle comfort, along with good balance, can reduce fatigue during long use. We especially liked molded handles.

Some drills in the group we tested, however, were judged to provide only fair handle comfort. A few were so short that you would have to grasp them high, with the middle finger instead of the index finger on the trigger. And a few had squarish corners that could dig into the palm of your hand.

Look for an extra handle in the model you're considering. Otherwise it would be tempting to grasp the drill's housing with your free hand for better control, especially when you push hard on a drill. But then you would cover the air vents, restricting the cooling air flow. A second handle offers a better place to grab.

Safe use of an electric drill

Here are some recommendations from our engineers to encourage safe use of an electric drill.

■ Don't buy a model with a metal case: Models with an all-plastic housing would be safer around wiring. Be careful not to touch the drill's chuck or any metal parts of the case when drilling into a wall or floor where you might hit live electrical wires.

■ Double insulation doesn't protect against a damaged power cord or extension cord. If you're working outdoors, you'd be wise to use a ground fault circuit interrupter.

■ Look for a model whose trigger lock is recessed or shielded. That's less convenient, perhaps, but it's safer—especially for lefties. The trigger lock keeps the drill running without constant pressure on the trigger. The feature is useful when you run the drill at a constant speed for a long time—say, when you use a polishing or sanding attachment. Most manufacturers place the lock on the drill's handle where the thumb of a right-handed user normally rests. That's convenient for a right-hander, but it also permits accidental engagement. It's even more of a hazard for a left-hander, whose palm tends to press against the lock.

■ Design of the trigger lock can also present a hazard. A quick squeeze of the trigger should automatically disengage the trigger lock. With some of the models we tested, though, the trigger lock wouldn't disengage when the speed-control knob was turned fully clockwise to the highest-speed setting. Check to make sure that the model you're considering is free of this defect. If the bit should jam in the work while the trigger is locked on, the drill could twist your wrist or wrench loose from your grip. Depending on where you were at the time—high on a ladder, to cite one possibility—the consequences could be disastrous.

Cordless drills

There are jobs for which a cordless drill—one operating on rechargeable batteries, not house current—is especially convenient. Although a cordless drill gives you a measure of freedom, its low power and slow speed do limit its usefulness. Also, it must be used frequently if its batteries are to maintain full capacity.

Whatever cordless model you select, its batteries should be deep-cycled—discharged fully and then recharged fully.

Look for these convenient features when you shop:

■ Special circuitry in the charger that reduces the chances of overcharging the batteries.

■ An indicator light that signals when the batteries are fully charged so that you can resume working without delay.

■ An indicator light that also signals when the batteries are too hot to accept a quick charge. (Batteries may heat up when they're discharged very quickly, and hot batteries are extremely slow to accept a charge.)

Caring for no-wax flooring

For new no-wax resilient flooring, you don't need to use a polish, even for cleaning. Until a no-wax floor is worn—probably years after installation—floor polish is a waste of money. You'd be better off saving that money to make up for the extra cost of the no-wax flooring.

For taking care of new or fairly new no-wax floors, we recommend using just a plain damp mop, or a little detergent and a rinse.

On a very shiny polyurethane-finished no-wax floor, a floor polish makes no real difference in appearance. On a vinyl-surfaced no-wax floor, whose shine is a bit less glaring, a floor polish does add a touch of gloss.

If you feel compelled to use a polish on a new vinyl no-wax floor, don't kid yourself that you're doing it for any reason other than boosting the shine. The amount of protection offered by a thin film of polish is insignificant compared with the protection offered by the layer of vinyl on the flooring.

But even rugged plastics such as polyurethane and vinyl can get scratched and worn over time, and an accumulation of tiny scratches will eventually dull no-wax flooring a little. In tests by our engineers, floor polishes did show some ability to fill in tiny scratches, which would tend to improve the shine on worn areas.

When the floor is so worn that it looks like it really needs a polish, we suggest you choose among the no-wax products by their price. The products we've tested all performed about the same, so let price be your guide.

Caring for wood floors

If you've coated your wood floors with a polyurethane finish, they require almost as little maintenance as no-wax resilient flooring. You can get by with just vacuuming or dusting, perhaps an occasional damp-mopping, and maybe a refinishing every few years.

If you don't have no-wax wood floors, you can expect a lot more work. Here are some guidelines from our engineers.

■ Don't use a water-based polish on wood: Water can damage and discolor wood. Stick to a product based on a petroleum solvent such as naphtha.

■ Work with good ventilation when using wood-floor waxes. The solvent fumes can be hazardous.

■ Our engineers found that the one-step wood waxes left floors noticeably duller and dirtier than the buffing waxes did. The extra effort required with the buffing waxes pays off in better results.

■ Be sure the wax you choose isn't too dark for the wood so that wax applied over a scratched floor finish won't make the scratches stand out.

■ Stripping old wax from wood floors requires the use of a solvent such as mineral spirits. Fortunately, the waxes we tested proved to be excellent at self-cleaning, so any buildup of wax would probably occur slowly.

■ A high-gloss wax can make for a slippery floor. Take care!

Using floor tiles

Tiling a floor requires several preliminary steps. Here are some of the things you should take into account.

■ If your floor occasionally gets wet, you may want to consider an alternative to tiles—sheet vinyl, perhaps. Wetness might cause tiles to lift up as the adhesive bond deteriorates.

■ In preparing to lay tiles, your most important concern should be to prepare the subfloor properly. If your floor is not smooth and flat, that may include installation of a plywood or hardboard subfloor.

■ If you use tiles that are one foot square, determining your needs should be simple. Just make sure to add 5 percent for waste, and buy all the tiles from the same lot. (Check the numbers on the cartons.) The smallest quantities usually available are boxes of forty-five tiles. (Mail-order brands may have single tiles or units of nine available.)

■ Self-stick tiles will make the job easier. Tiles are also available without self-stick backing, saving you something on the price. But you have to consider whether that saving will adequately compensate for the mess and effort of working with ordinary tile adhesive.

■ Some of the tiles bear directional markings that show, once you've started out on a pattern, which edge of the tile goes where. That, we judged, is a help in maintaining the continuity of design.

Making sense out of garbage bags

To sort out types, sizes, and names of garbage bags for a test project, our engineers divided the bags into five overall size and use categories.

Here's what we came up with.

Wastebasket. The bags we put in this category measured 22 by 24 inches, though the capacity given on the packages was variously described as "28 quarts," "32 quarts," and "8 gallons." Some of the bags were called "Large Waste" or "Medium Garbage" instead of "Wastebasket."

Tall kitchen. Except for one 2½-foot-wide bag, all in the group were 2 feet wide, and all were about 2½ feet tall. Labeled capacity varied from 11 to 15 gallons. One bag was called "Large Kitchen."

Small trash. These measured 2 feet 4 inches by 2 feet 11 inches. Some of the labels said the bags held 26 gallons. Others said they fit up to 20-gallon cans. Intended for old-style small garbage cans with a nominal size of 20 gallons, this size fit those cans very tightly. If you fill the can up to the top, you might not be able to gather the bag together and tie it.

Large trash. This category comprised two sizes—bags that fit up to 30-gallon cans and bags meant for 32- or 33-gallons cans. The most popular size of all garbage bags, the 30-gallon bags work much better in small garbage cans than the bags in the previous category. They leave plenty of extra bag to gather up, tie, and hold onto if you have to remove the bag from the can.

The 30-gallon bags we tested were about 2½ feet wide by 3 feet high. But 30-gallon bags may not fit 30-gallon cans. It depends on the shape of the can. If the can has a flared or squared top, the mouth of the bag may not be wide enough to go over it without ripping. In that case, you'll have to buy a 32- or 33-gallon garbage bag. They're usually about 3 inches wider and 4 inches taller than the 30-gallon bags, and they fit 32-gallon cans snugly.

Lawn and leaf. Most brands we tested in this category were a few inches taller than the 33-gallon bags. Though their labeled capacity ranged from 39 gallons to 6 bushels (48 gallons), the lawn and leaf bags fit nicely in 32-gallon garbage cans.

Bagging garbage: Not always simple

Choosing the right size garbage or trash bag for the need you have in mind is not as simple as it may appear. To get what you want, you'll have to read the label carefully and then interpret the manufacturer's dimensions and terminology.

During a test of garbage and trash bags, our engineers made the following discoveries.

Dimensions. A bag of a certain capacity won't necessarily fit a container of the same capacity.

■ A few labels claim a bag "holds up to" however many gallons. An open bag may be a satisfactory way of packaging leaves, but it's hardly convenient or tidy for household garbage.

■ Fortunately, most bags are described as fitting up to a certain size of container—but you do have to know the size of your container.

■ Some package labels give both the measurments of the bag and the container.

Terminology. You need to learn garbage talk. Here's a quick course.

■ According to some manufacturers, when you throw something away indoors, it's "garbage," as in "tall kitchen garbage bags."

■ Outdoors, an item discarded is "trash." A small trash bag is sometimes allowed to hold grass ("trash and grass").

■ A larger trash bag occasionally gets the whole lawn ("trash and lawn").

■ The largest bags are reserved for "lawn and leaf," sometimes condensed to "yard" or "lawn clean-up."

■ Some of the packages offer pictures to help you choose the right size. But one size of garbage container often looks like another. We thought that the pictures sometimes added to the confusion.

Buying garbage bags

How much strength do you need to pay for in a garbage bag?

How much strength? In our tests, we found only the vaguest of correlations between thickness and overall strength. Plastics technology is such that very thin plastic can also be very strong, and a bag made of it can securely hold plenty of garbage.

Our tests showed that thick plastic isn't necessary for a good quality garbage bag. Many of the higher-priced name-brand bags may actually be too good for your garbage.

What price to pay? We suggest you shop for price in several of the categories of garbage/trash bags we tested.

■ Our advice for buying wastebasket bags is to buy the cheapest. We found that all the brands we tested were strong enough for the job. Buying the largest package you can find should save you an extra penny or two per bag.

■ Most of the tall kitchen bags we tested withstood our test load well. We think you should also look for a good price here, perhaps even experimenting with a small package of a generic or store brand. The saving can be as much as 30 percent.

■ In the popular large trash size, you can save as much as 50 percent by buying generic bags. The saving in the small trash size is only about 10 percent.

■ Lawn-and-leaf bags can be expensive—about a quarter a piece. You might want to try a generic brand. It could save you as much as 30 percent.

■ In buying the "outdoor" bags, we think you should buy a brand's heavy-duty bag in preference to its regular-weight bag only if the lighter bag doesn't suffice. You may even find a generic bag strong enough to satisfy you.

A bag for yard work

We think the *Garbagger* should be a real help for anyone who bags a lot of clippings and leaves.

Staff members who tested the *Garbagger* at home decided that it was a real convenience for lawn care. They preferred it to a bag slipped inside a trash can because the *Garbagger* could be pulled up to support the bag as it's filled. And the *Garbagger* allows you to use both hands for filling the bag. According to one tester, the *Garbagger* halved the time it took to bag up clippings and leaves while mowing the lawn.

How it works. The *Garbagger* is a fairly stiff plastic sheet 2 feet wide by 5½ feet long, with a row of snaps on one end that fit into one of seven rows of holes at the opposite end. The idea is to roll the sheet into a cylinder and secure it with the snaps. The cylinder then slips inside or outside a plastic garbage bag. When the bag is packed full, the cylinder slides out easily or unsnaps.

By putting the snaps into different rows of holes, you can make the *Garbagger* fit bags ranging from 15-gallon "tall kitchen" bags to 33-gallon "lawn and trash" bags. It will even work with 45-gallon bags, although it doesn't fit them snugly.

How to buy it. You're not likely to find the *Garbagger* in stores so your best bet may be to order by mail from Garbagger Inc., 5329 Morgan Ave S., Minneapolis, Minn. 55419. The *Garbagger* cost $6 plus shipping when we checked the price in mid-1982.

Rules for storing gasoline safely

If you plan to keep gasoline on hand—for your power mower, say—do so with utmost caution.

Many communities limit the amount of gasoline and other flammable liquids you can store on your property. Some also require you to use only an approved container. Before buying any gasoline can, call your fire department and ask about your local fire code.

Here are ten rules for safe use and storage of gasoline.

1. Store gasoline only in a container specifically designed for it.

2. Do not fill a container to the top. Leave an inch or two for expansion.

3. Do not carry a filled container in your car, except to take it home from the service station. Secure the container so it doesn't slide around or tip.

4. Store gasoline in a separate garage or outbuilding. Better still, leave it outdoors under a shelter. Some air circulation is desirable to dissipate any escaping vapors.

5. Keep a gasoline container out of direct sunlight and away from heat.

6. Cap all openings, including vent holes, when you're not using the container.

7. A stopper on a pouring extension is not a secure closure. Remove and store the extension after using it.

8. Do not empty a container. If you leave a small amount of liquid inside a capped can, it will form a vapor rich enough not to explode.

9. If someone swallows gasoline, do not induce vomiting. Call for medical help immediately.

10. Keep the container out of reach of children.

Mixing your own glass cleaner

Tired of paying high prices for commerical glass cleaners? Try plain tap water instead. For glass windows that have accumulated a film of dirt, ordinary water should do routine cleaning as effectively as any commercial product.

Need to clean a lot of glass that hasn't been washed in a long while? If the glass isn't caked with soil, it can be cleaned effectively with a batch of cleaner you mix yourself.

Here's the formula we concocted—Home Brew No. 3—after searching through do-it-yourself literature on the subject.

Combine half cup of "sudsy" ammonia, a pint of ordinary isopropyl (70 percent) alcohol, a teaspoon of liquid dishwashing detergent, and enough water to make a gallon in all.

Try our Home Brew No. 3. Readers of Consumer Reports called it "sensational" and "a success." And you'll save well over a dollar a quart in the bargain.

Using a glass cleaner

No matter what glass cleaner you use—plain tap water, our Home Brew No. 3 (see above), or a commercial product—you can make the task easier if you keep the following suggestions in mind.

- We found that applying a cleaner sparingly and wiping the glass thoroughly prevented streaking and spotting.
- Use wadded-up newspapers to apply glass cleaner. But use old newspapers. Otherwise, the ink on the paper will leave streaks and smears.
- Quickly remove any drips or spray from surfaces around the glass you're cleaning. Some surfaces are more easily marred than others. When we tested glass cleaners, we found wood coated with furniture-grade lacquer more vulnerable than varnished surfaces, aluminum, and automobile paint.

Electric hedge trimmers

Electric hedge trimmers can provide welcome relief if you've been using a manual trimmer to cut back hedges and shrubs. They clip with superhuman rapidity—something on the order of several thousand clips a minute.

In selecting an electric hedge trimmer, one important distinction to observe is the cutting length of the blades. Not only does the cutting length determine the sweep of foliage that can be met with one pass (the width of a hedge, say), but, in any one manufacturer's line, it's also a fair indicator of price—the longer the cutting length, the more expensive the trimmer.

The comfort of the handles should be considered. It is perhaps more significant than weight as a fatigue factor. Only a few of the models we tested had handles that were judged easy to grip and guide in all the different trimming attitudes.

Light bulbs: Standard or long-life?

Which type of light bulb should you buy?

Fluorescent lighting aside, the answer is standard light bulbs in most cases. Among the bulbs tested by our engineers, the standard bulb provided the most light for the least money.

We found that in the long run standard bulbs are a better buy than any other bulbs of the same wattage, including long-life or extended-service bulbs. This was true across the board, no matter what the wattage of the bulb for which we did the calculations.

In areas where utility rates are high, the cost disadvantage of long-life or extended-service bulbs becomes even greater. Their total operating costs won't match those of standard bulbs unless rates are about 2 cents per kilowatt-hour. The reason for the higher total operating cost of long-life bulbs is that they have a lower light output than standard bulbs of the same wattage.

In some cases, you may not care if you're getting less light for your money. Convenience may be more important to you than economy. If you have to drag out a ladder every time a ceiling fixture bulb needs replacing, you may be willing to pay the price. A long-life or extended-service bulb is likely to save some of *your* energy.

How to save on light bulbs

There are a number of things you can do to cut lighting costs. Here are some suggestions from our engineers.

■ Light up your home only to the extent required for each area. Hallways and staircases need only enough illumination for safe passage. That level of light will also do for rooms used for conversation or TV-watching. Save brighter lighting for areas where people do reading, studying, kitchen work, shaving, and other kinds of close work.

■ Turn on lights only where you need them. Don't light up an entire room if you're using only a corner.

■ Turn off lights when you leave a room for more than a few minutes. (The number of times you turn lights off and on does, however, affect a bulb's life—though by very little.)

■ Keep bulbs and fixtures clean. Dust and dirt block light.

Premature bulb burnouts

If it seems that you're always replacing light bulbs in your house, keep track for a while. You may be able to figure out what's causing the premature burnout.

■ If the burnouts occur in one or two specific fixtures, you may be using a bulb of a higher wattage than the manufacturer of the lamp or fixture recommends. That could cause overheating of the bulb because the fixture's globe is too small. Or uneven cooling of the bulb could be the cause, because it contacts the globe in one area.

■ If you're using a bulb of the correct wattage, a faulty socket could be the problem.

■ If premature burnouts occur throughout the house, it's probably because of higher-than-designated supply voltage. Bulbs rated for use on 125 or 130 volts (usually available in electrical-supply houses) may solve the problem.

Fluorescent lighting

Consider using fluorescent lighting in kitchens and bathrooms, where strong even lighting is important. Fluorescents deliver about three times as much light as incandescent bulbs of the same wattage. And they last five to fifteen times longer.

Using dimmer controls

If you enjoy the ambience of dimmed lighting, you may want to install dimmer controls. They can help to extend bulb life, and they save energy. But don't be deceived by dimmer controls. You won't save on energy in proportion to the rate at which they diminish light output.

Is high-priced paint a good buy?

Much of the paint sold nowadays—even top-of-the-line products—may need at least two coats to cover the old paint.

But you can save some money when you shop for paint. Our paint chemists say that as you move up in price, the quality of the paint doesn't always improve accordingly.

We've noticed a general decline in paint quality in recent years. Manufacturers, faced with soaring prices for their raw materials, seem to be skimping on the ingredients that give a paint good hiding power, durability, and resistance to fading.

There's no point in buying expensive paint unless you're sure you need qualities that are available only in high-priced products. Even then, you're not likely to get one-coat coverage unless you are using a color not too different from the old one.

Paint labels can lead you astray

Be wary of label claims on latex wall paints. Some can be misleading.

One-coat coverage. Many of the latex paints tested by our chemists carried a claim for one-coat coverage over any surface. Don't believe it. Those claims usually warn that one-coat coverage will be achieved "at the recommended spreading rate," which is usually 400 to 450 square feet per gallon. When we applied paint with an ordinary roller, we always overshot the recommended rate considerably. That means you get a thinner coat of paint than you expect.

Flat or low-luster. Some names of flat wall paints suggest a small amount of luster, or gloss. But the paints are quite flat, despite the name. And some of the paints labeled flat can turn out to be low-luster. You may be stuck with returning paint that is mislabeled or misnamed.

Latex paints: When not to use them

Because latex (water-based) paints are vulnerable to standing water, they are a poor bet for windowsills, plant shelves, kitchen and bathroom trim, or any surface that's likely to get wet often. Oil-based paints are still the best products for these surfaces.

Alkyd or latex

The most important decision you'll have to make is whether to buy alkyd (oil-based) or latex paint when painting your house.

Using alkyd. Most of the alkyd paints we tested were judged good to excellent in ease of brushing. But you must start with a bone-dry surface. And you have to be patient with drying time.

■ Alkyd paint dries by oxidation, and that takes time. With most of the alkyds we tested, the first coat was dry enough to permit a second coat within twenty-four hours. (Some took as long as two days, however.)

■ The alkyds did well in our adhesion tests. After nearly a year of exposure to the elements, these paints still adhered well to primed hardboard, raw cedar, and primed cedar. Unlike the latex paints, the alkyds even adhered quite well to heavily chalked surfaces.

■ To clean up after painting with alkyds, you'll want to have a supply of solvent on hand for your brushes and your hands.

Using latex. In many ways, latex paints are easier to work with than the alkyds. You don't necessarily need to start with a thoroughly dry surface. The paint dries quickly. And, of course, water will clean up spills.

■ All the latex paints we tested were judged excellent for ease of brushing. But they didn't flow as smoothly as the oil-based paints. Brush strokes left deep ridges in the applied paint, which affects a paint's ability to hide the surface beneath.

■ Latex paints dry by evaporation, so they dry quickly. Follow the instructions on the label. Some labels on the paints we tested recommended allowing the paint to dry overnight before applying a second coat. Some said you could recoat in as little as one hour, which would permit application of two coats in one day.

■ Like the alkyds, the latex paints adhered nicely to primed hardboard, raw cedar, and primed cedar. After weathering, however, there was significantly more wood cracking with the raw cedar than there was with the primed cedar.

■ The label instructions on both oil- and water-based paints call for priming raw wood. That's especially necessary with latex paints, we think. Without priming, the wood is not adequately protected from water damage.

Peeling or flaking: What causes it?

When we surveyed Consumer Reports readers to find out why they painted their house, the reason most frequently mentioned was flaking or peeling old paint. What's more, those who responded to our survey frequently complained that the *new* paint began to peel or flake, often within eighteen months of when it was applied.

The old paint may be implicated. A number of things can cause peeling and flaking.

■ If the paint peels off right down to bare wood, the cause may be a moisture problem within the house.

■ Too many layers of paint can also lead to cracks. If thick enough, almost any paint will crack and peel.

The new paint isn't always blameless.

■ A significant number of survey respondents reported that peeling or flaking was a first-time occurrence with them, and was most often connected with latex paint applied over alkyd (oil-based) paint. Apparently, latex and alkyd paints don't shrink and expand at the same rate. As a result of this, the paint will begin to peel.

■ Because peeling or flaking is more likely to occur if latex is used over alkyd paint or vice versa, you should use the same type of paint you used last time.

Which paint to use. If you don't know what the old paint is, you can make an educated guess or try to have the paint analyzed.

■ If the previous owner was a do-it-yourselfer who painted the house within, say, the past six to eight years, chances are good that a latex paint was used.

■ Having the old paint analyzed could be expensive. Some university chemistry departments may do paint analyses for consumers. Or you could look in the Yellow Pages under "Laboratories, testing." One lab we called in suburban Connecticut said it would test paint for about $70. That's a sizable sum, but it may be less painful to part with the money than to watch the new paint peel away a year or so after you've done all that work.

Need two coats of exterior paint?

Labels on exterior paints generally recommend using two coats of paint for either appearance or durability (or both). Our paint chemists suggest you may sometimes need only one coat to do the job.

Whether you'll have to use a second coat depends primarily on the hiding ability of the paint. But it also depends on the condition of the surface you're painting.

■ If the surface is sound and if the new paint goes on uniformly, you'll need just one coat.

■ But if the surface is badly eroded, you may need two or even three coats no matter what kind of paint you're using.

Color is also an important consideration.

■ Some pigments are quite expensive, and so manufacturers seem to stint on them. For example, bright red is an expensive pigment. Thus, we weren't surprised to find that most of the bright red paints in our tests had poor hiding ability.

■ White pigments are expensive, too, but manufacturers apparently haven't cut corners with them. Our paint chemists judged even the worst of the whites to be at least fair.

■ The pigments used in the duller tones of green, gold, and red aren't very expensive. Manufacturers don't often stint on them. So you'd be better off in terms of your paint's hiding ability if you chose a duller color for your house.

Before painting your house

If you take some preliminary steps before beginning to paint your house, you'll make the task easier and the results more certain.

Do patch-ups before you start.

■ Replace dry cracked caulk around windows.

■ Fill surface flaws such as cracks and scratches. Sand them smooth.

■ Replace broken shakes or deteriorated siding.

■ Use solvent to clean knot holes or pitch streaks in the new wood. Coat the flaws with a sealer before applying primer, or they will release resins that can stain the paint.

■ Set nail heads below the wood surface. Cover old nails, the type that rust, with wood filler or putty to prevent rust stains on the new paint. If you have to replace any nails, use either aluminum or galvanized ones.

Wash down the house. All the siding must be thoroughly cleaned. You may be able to do the job with a garden hose.

■ Protected areas, such as siding under eaves, need a more thorough cleaning because these areas are subject to salt deposits from paint films or from the wood itself. Moisture brings the salt to the surface. Scrub with trisodium phosphate in water, then rinse thoroughly.

■ If your house is mildewed, clean all affected areas before painting. Look for a black or dark speckling that usually occurs in sun-sheltered areas. Test by spot-cleaning a section of siding with a half-and-half solution of liquid laundry bleach and water. Mildew will discolor and disappear within a minute. If it is mildew, clean it all.

■ Clean up old chalked surfaces, too. Pressure from a garden hose may remove light chalking well enough. For heavy chalking, use a stiff scrub brush and strong detergent, or rent a power washer. It will remove chalk, along with loose paint and dirt, easily and quickly.

Scrape and sand. Get out the scraper, the wire brush, the coarse steel wool, and the sandpaper.

■ Scrape away such imperfections as flaking and peeling sections, blisters, and cracking paint. Don't stop with the loose stuff. Get the surrounding area too. Otherwise, the paint will continue to peel.

■ Wrinkles in the old paint should be sanded smooth.

■ Sand glossy surfaces to give the new paint a better chance to stick.

■ Prime any bare wood, especially if you'll be using a latex paint.

An extra step for latex paint. If you're planning to use an alkyd paint, you're in luck. Our tests showed that alkyds adhered better to heavily chalked surfaces. If you're planning to use latex paint, however, here's a test you can run if you have any doubts that you've removed enough of the chalk from the old paint.

■ Choose a small section with a typical amount of chalking.

■ Paint the area, preferably with two coats.

■ When the second coat has dried for a couple of days, scratch a straight line through the new paint.

■ Apply a strip of cellophane tape over the scratch, leaving one end free. Then pull off the tape smartly.

■ If more than a few specks of paint have adhered to the tape, the new paint is not sticking.

■ Either go back and clean up all the chalked paint, or switch to an alkyd paint.

Ordering and checking paint

Now that you've completed the preliminaries, it's time to order the paint—and to check it once you've brought it home.

How much paint? Most labels say that a gallon will cover about 400 or 450 square feet.

■ To figure out how many gallons you'll need (assuming a house with a flat roof), estimate the distance from the top of the house's foundation to the eaves. If the roof is pitched, add 2 feet to the height. Multiply the height by the distance (in feet) around the foundation. Divide that by the coverage estimate on the paint can. That's the number of gallons you'll need for one coat.

■ For a second coat, don't double the quantity. You'll need only about half as much for another coat.

After you get the paint. Once the paint is home, there are precautions you should take.

■ Make sure all the paint cans have the same batch number to ensure evenness of color. The number is usually on the lid or the bottom of the can.

■ Open the can and, using a clean brush, apply some paint to a clean piece of glass or metal. After about twelve hours (fewer with latex), you should see any imperfections. If anything appears to be wrong, return the entire batch.

Using a paintbrush: The advantages

A brush can handle almost any household paint job satisfactorily.

■ A brush is the best tool to use on furniture, paneled doors, window shutters, exterior siding and trim, and small intricate surfaces. (But a brush can be slow going when you're painting a large flat area.)

■ Unlike pads and rollers, a brush can be dipped right into the can of paint. That's good, especially when you're working on a ladder.

Using a paintbrush: The disadvantages

A good paintbrush is not inexpensive. Nor is it as simple to use as it seems.

■ You'll need skill to get a finish that's uniformly thick.

■ It will take practice to achieve results that are free from brush and lap marks and other imperfections.

Choosing a paintbrush

It pays to buy quality paintbrushes. A good brush is much easier to use than a poor one. It doesn't leave pronounced brush marks, and it delivers paint smoothly and easily.

Price isn't always a reliable guide to a quality paintbrush. Some of the best ones we've tested cost only a little more than the junky imitators.

Here are some pointers to help you choose the best paintbrush for the job.

Natural or synthetic bristles? For oil-based paints, we recommend natural bristles. Synthetic bristles may perform adequately, but natural bristles give a smoother surface, with a minimum of brush marks.

For latex paints, we recommend synthetic bristles. Natural bristles will absorb the water in the paint and swell up. A waterlogged brush is uncomfortably heavy, and its bristles lose their resiliency.

Size and shape. A good rule of thumb is to use the largest brush—within limits—that suits the job.

A professional painter may prefer a 5-inch brush for painting a wall, but an amateur might find it too heavy to handle comfortably, especially after a few hours of brushing. A 4-inch brush (or even a smaller one) could be a better choice.

For trim, select small brushes that are available with bristles cut straight across, or in an oval shape, or on an angle.

Quantity and type of bristles. The more bristles in the brush, the more paint it can deliver with each dip. The bristles in a good 4-inch brush should be at least ⅞-inch thick near the handle. But be careful here. Flat brushes are made with filler strips—thin strips set into the handle to separate the bristles. If the filler strips are too wide, it's a sign that the manufacturer has skimped on bristles.

On the best brushes, the bristle tips are "branched" of "flagged"—very much like split ends on hair. Look closely to examine the flagging. The more flagging on the bristles, the more paint the brush can deliver. The paint will also flow smoother and easier.

Hog bristles, especially those marked "China," are best among natural-bristle brushes. Naturally flagged, the bristles tend to continue flagging as their ends wear down with use. Horsehair and other natural bristles are too stiff and have too little flagging. High-quality synthetic bristles are split or flagged during manufacture, but the flagging wears off with use.

Also check the taper of individual bristles. Untapered bristles give a coarse finish, with lots of brush marks. Hog bristles taper down from handle to tip, as do the best synthetic bristles. Horsehair bristles have little or no taper.

Length of bristles. Long bristles last longer and hold more paint than short ones. With long bristles, you won't need to dip the brush as often. Long bristles are also more resilient and leave fewer brush marks.

The bristles in a good 4-inch brush should measure at least 3½ inches from handle to tip. A good 2-inch brush should have bristles at least 2½ inches long.

Most good brushes have a mixture of long and short bristles for proper delivery of paint to the bristle tips. A brush that tapers gradually from handle to tip has a good mixture of lengths. A sharp taper indicates too few long bristles.

Judging quality. Bend the bristles back with your hand. Whether the bristles are natural or synthetic, they should feel soft and springy, with good bounce or snap. They should return firmly to shape after you slap the handle against your palm. (If you're painting a rough surface such as stucco, though, you'll want a fairly stiff brush.)

Grasp a handful of bristles and tug fairly hard. Even a top-quality brush may lose one or two bristles, but if you uproot more, pass up the brush. It's annoying to have bristles fall out and stick to the surface you're painting.

A good brush needs good care

You can get a lot of mileage out of a paintbrush if you care for it properly. A good brush can last a lifetime. Our paint chemists say that taking proper care of a paintbrush needs only a little time and patience. If you have neither, you might be better off buying a cheap brush and throwing it away after the job is finished.

Investing in a good brush can help make your painting easier and the job look better. A good brush, for example, doesn't leave pronounced brush marks, and delivers paint smoothly and easily—once you get the hang of it.

But if you want a high-quality brush to last and still offer good service, you should follow these basic do's and don'ts.

■ Don't use a high-quality brush if you're painting stucco, cinder blocks, or other rough surfaces that can wear away bristles quickly.

■ If your paint job takes more than a day, you don't need to clean the brush thoroughly every day. But be sure to suspend the brush in a can of thinner or water (depending on the paint base), or wrap the brush tightly in foil.

■ Clean the brush as soon as possible after a paint job is completed. Squeeze the bristles against the edge of a can to remove excess paint. Then brush off as much of the paint as possible on a piece of foil or an old board. We advise against using a paper or rag. The oils in paint—present even in latex paint—can burn spontaneously on easily combustible material.

■ Next, soak the brush in plenty of thinner or water (which you use depends on the paint base). Rinse the brush several times. Work your fingers into the bristles to remove all the paint. Don't be afraid to get your hands into the job. Paint comes off easily if it hasn't dried. (Or you can wear rubber gloves.)

■ You can soak the brush in thinner or water overnight or even longer before cleaning, if you like. But don't stand the brush on its bristles. You'll risk bending them permanently out of shape. Instead, make a hook from a piece of wire, and suspend the brush in a can so the bristles are fully immersed, but not touching bottom.

■ When the bristles are clean, shake out the excess thinner or water. Or, hold the brush in an empty bucket and twirl the handle in your hands.

■ Use a bristle comb (available in paint and hardware stores) to straighten the bristles.

■ When the brush is dry, store it suspended by the handle or lying flat and wrapped in paper or foil to keep the bristles straight.

Using a pad for painting

A large paint pad—or flat applicator—is the tool to use on exterior shakes or siding. It's faster than a brush and better than a roller for painting into a corner and along an edge. For painting large flat surfaces, our technicians found that a 7-inch pad was about twice as fast as a 4-inch brush, but slower than a 7-inch roller.

Advantages. A pad is a compromise between a brush and a roller.

■ Unlike a roller, a pad can work in corners; you might still need to use a brush for touch-ups, however.

■ A pad can handle the bottom edges of clapboard siding.

■ With the help of edge guides, a pad can form a straighter cleaner edge than a brush can. (But be sure the edge guides are free of paint so they won't mark adjacent surfaces.)

Disadvantages. A pad requires more skill than a roller.

■ You may have trouble applying paint evenly without leaving noticeable edge marks and fiber marks in the finish.

■ Pads are meant for flat surfaces. They don't do the job on slightly contoured surfaces, such as window moldings.

■ Pads tend to drip more than brushes and rollers do, especially when used to paint ceilings.

■ We found that paints that were easy to apply with a brush or roller were too thick for a pad. Diluting the paint with thinner or water made it much easier to use with a pad—but also made for more drips.

Choosing a pad

Paint pads are not particularly long-wearing. You'll probably have to replace a pad at least once during a major paint project. That makes ease of replacing the pad on its handle an important feature when you buy a pad. We found that some pads were quite difficult to remove.

Another problem with pads is the tray to hold the paint. Most of the trays we tested were quite unstable. Some hung precariously from a ladder on a single wire hanger. Some were constructed so that, even when they were on a flat surface, a little too much pressure on the pan could tip the tray and spill the paint.

Painting with a roller: The advantages

If you use a roller for painting, you can expect certain advantages.

■ Rollers are fast and easy to use.

■ They're particularly handy for painting walls and ceilings. For example, it took our paint technicians three times as long to paint a wall with a 4-inch brush as with a 7-inch roller.

■ Where a brush or a pad may leave marks, a roller tends to leave a uniform stippled texture that can be quite pleasing.

■ A roller is especially handy for applying latex paints, which don't flow out as well as oil-based paints.

Painting with a roller: The disadvantages

Using a roller for a paint job brings ease of application—but using one also exacts a price.

■ Paint applied with a roller is not perfectly even. It has a fine texture that looks smooth from a distance. But viewed up close, the paint has peaks and valleys that reduce the paint's hiding power. A second coat masks this effect because the valleys land in different places.

■ Watch out for the nemesis of roller painting—spatters of fine droplets that settle on woodwork or furniture you've neglected to cover. Those little droplets can drift devilishly far, and they're difficult to remove after the paint has dried. So to be safe, make generous use of drop cloths before painting with a roller.

■ You'll find that a roller doesn't work its way easily into corners and around trim. It's also ill-suited to handle the bottom edges of shingles and clapboard siding.

Choosing a roller

Rollers commonly come in 7- and 9-inch lengths, although smaller sizes are available for special jobs. A 9-inch roller will be heavier than a 7-inch one, but it will spread paint faster.

A roller set consists of three basic items:

■ A cylindrical roller cover to apply the paint.

■ A frame to hold the cover.

■ A pan to hold the paint.

Roller covers

Choosing a roller cover is more complex than finding a good frame or pan. Here are several points to consider.

Nap. A roller cover is made of a nap of either natural fibers (mohair or lamb's wool) or synthetics (nylon or polyester). We prefer the synthetics. In our experience, mohair doesn't work as well as nylon or polyester.

The length of the nap ranges from about 3⁄16 inch to 1½ inches.

- A short nap is best for smooth flat surfaces.
- A medium nap, about ⅜ inch, is recommended for light stucco and smooth concrete.
- A long nap, ¾ to 1 inch, is good for cinder blocks.
- The longest nap is for special jobs, such as painting chain-link fencing.

When we tested latex wall paints, we got our best results with a roller that had a ¼-inch nap. We could pile paint on more thickly with a longer nap, but that left thin, stippled valleys in the paint that allowed the original surface to show through.

Reliability. Select a sturdy roller cover. Avoid those with a core of untreated cardboard. They will soften and collapse in water.

To test the durability of a core, squeeze the end of the roller. If you can bend or distort it, look for a roller cover with a stiffer core.

Construction. Check the density of the fibers. Dense fibers—the roller equivalent of long thick bristles on a paintbrush—tend to carry more paint and give a smoother finish.

The cover should be perfectly cylindrical, without conspicuous seams. Fabric and core should be firmly attached at the ends. Look for a glue line at the ends. A cover whose fabric is well glued to the core is less likely to come apart.

Frame and pan

Frame. A good roller frame is made of heavy stiff wire, with flexible wires to grip the cover. (A cheap model secures the cover with two end caps.)

Pan. You should have no trouble selecting a pan. Just be sure you get one big enough for the roller and not too flimsy or too clumsy to keep steady when you're using it.

Caring for a roller cover (or pad)

Here's what to do to care for your roller cover. (The same advice applies to paint pads.) After each use, be sure to follow the steps listed below.

■ As soon as you stop working, squeeze out the excess paint.

■ Roll or wipe the cover clean.

■ Remove the cover from the frame.

■ Soak the cover in thinner or water (whichever is recommended on the paint label).

■ Squeeze the cover thoroughly.

■ Shake off the remaining thinner or water.

■ Stand the cover on end until it's dry.

Should you use a spray gun?

If you've never worked with a paint sprayer, consider the pros and cons carefully before deciding to paint with one.

Cost. The proper equipment is very expensive. Figure on spending at least $150 for a sprayer—and what you can get at that price won't be professional-quality equipment.

Technique. Compared with a brush, roller, or pad, a spray gun can produce the smoothest paint job of all—and in a fraction of the time required with the other paint tools. But unlike the other tools, you have to be an expert to take full advantage of a spray gun. In the hands of an amateur, a spray gun is a mixed blessing.

Spraying works well on intricate objects (wicker furniture, for example) or for large flat areas (house siding or interior walls). But mastering the proper technique is difficult. It takes a lot of practice to avoid depositing too much paint (which results in sags and runs) or too little paint (which results in a streaked, tiger-stripe effect).

Diluting paint. Most paint is blended for use with a brush or roller and is too thick for spraying. You'll have to dilute paint with thinner or water (depending on which type of paint you choose). We found that the diluting instructions that came with most of the guns we tested weren't very specific. Chances are you'll have to rely on trial and error and, ultimately, on your own experience.

Preparation and clean-up. You can't control the pattern of a spray gun nearly as precisely as you can the stroke of a brush, pad, or roller. So before you spray, you have to take time to mask off all areas that you don't intend to paint.

For a relatively small job, you might spend more time masking than spraying. And cleaning spray equipment can be messy.

Hazards. Special precautions have to be taken when using a spray gun.

■ We strongly recommend that you avoid airless paint sprayers. Stick to the air-atomized type, which atomize paint with compressed air. With airless models, which atomize the paint by forcing it through a small opening under very high pressure, you may risk injecting some paint into your flesh unless you use the equipment cautiously. The accident might be painless—but the resulting damage could be extremely severe.

■ If possible, spray outdoors. It's unhealthy to inhale the atomized particles of paint a sprayer produces. When concentrated in an enclosed area, they can be explosive.

■ If you must spray indoors, open the windows.

■ Don't smoke on the job.

■ If the paint contains a flammable thinner, be sure there are no electric heaters, pilot lights, or other open flames nearby.

■ Wear a face mask.

Aerosol paints: Pros and cons

It takes some practice to use aerosol paints effectively, and they are much more expensive than brush paints. But there are some jobs that only an aerosol can do really well. On balance, our advice is to limit your use of aerosols to fairly small areas that need a mirror-smooth coat or to intricate objects such as wicker chairs.

Cost. Aerosol paint is anything but cheap. If you do a thorough job, an aerosol is likely to cost you about ten times as much as ordinary brush paint to cover a given area. A major reason for this is that most of the aerosols are relatively poor in hiding ability, especially the reds and yellows. You'll need a lot of paint to cover a flat surface thoroughly so no old colors or patterns show through. At least half the paint will be wasted, too, depending on what you're spraying.

The relatively high cost of aerosols is most important if you're painting a very large area, or if you're trying to cover a color that contrasts strongly with the new paint. Cost probably won't matter much if you want an aerosol paint for minor touch-ups.

Safety. The solvents in these paints can be hazardous. And the droplets of paint in the spray can be harmful when they're inhaled. The propellant is a highly flammable gas. You'll have to take extra precautions when you use these paints (see below).

Ease of use. There's a knack to applying a coat of aerosol paint without runs or sags (see below). But once you get the hang of it, you can get a very smooth coat with an aerosol—much smoother than you would get with a brush. And there are no messy tools to clean—no brush, no roller, no pan.

How to paint with an aerosol

Painting with an aerosol isn't as easy as it seems. It can also be hazardous. Our engineers have some suggestions that can help you, based on our tests of aerosol paints.

Ventilation. Be sure you have good ventilation.

- Paint outdoors if you can.
- Otherwise, wear a face mask to cover your mouth and nose.
- Don't spray near an open flame.

Masking. Mask the areas you don't want to paint. At least half the paint you use will be wasted, either as "overspray" past the edges of the piece you're painting or as paint dust in the air. The errant paint will land somewhere, so protect nearby areas with newspapers or a drop cloth. Put masking tape or paper on any parts that you don't want to color.

Spraying distance. You'll need to practice to determine the right spraying distance. Check the label before you spray. The manufacturer can at least provide a clue about the best spraying distance. If the recommended distance doesn't seem right, you may have to improvise.

■ You'll find it helpful to make several test passes on a piece of scrap before you start your project. That's the best way to gauge the proper distance and spraying motion.

■ If the paint builds up or sags, you're spraying too close to the surface.

■ If the paint diffuses widely, you're too far away. In that case, the paint may dry before it hits the surface, which gives a dull coat.

Spraying technique. Spray in overlapping bands. Don't try to cover the surface with a single heavy spraying. That will most likely make the paint sag.

■ Spray one band—horizontally or vertically—and then spray another overlapping the first by about half its width.

■ Keep applying overlapping bands until the entire piece is covered.

■ When the first set of bands has dried slightly, apply another set.

■ Continue until you've covered all the old paint and any marks you want to get rid of.

Second coat. Check the instructions before applying a second coat. Some manufacturers are very specific about how long to wait between coats. For example, the directions for one product we tested said to recoat within two hours or after twenty-four, but not in between. That's probably pretty good advice for most paints. If you ignore it, you may find the second coat very dull and grainy.

Powdered paint removers: Be cautious

To remove common latex or oil-based paints, a powdered paint remover is worth a try. But be cautious when you remove paint.

Solvents vs pastes. We've always been wary of chemical paint removers. The organic solvents in most brands are among the most dangerous chemicals used in the home. The powdered paint removers we tested—ones meant to be mixed with water to form a paste—are as effective as solvent paint removers, but present a different set of hazards.

■ The pastes are strong alkalies, the sort of chemical used in oven or drain cleaners. They can cause serious skin burns, and splashing of the chemicals can be a hazard. Using the product requires goggles, gloves, and a face mask to keep the powder out of your nose and throat. But these alkali pastes don't create the noxious fumes typical of organic solvents, so they would be better to use indoors.

■ When we tested the alkali pastes against conventional solvent types to see how well they could remove paints that were as much as ten years old, the pastes did a better job than the solvents.

■ You'll need to use a solvent-type stripper for certain finishes. The alkaline composition of the paste products makes them ineffective with some clear finishes, baked-on enamels, and such exotic coatings as epoxies, vinyls, and phenolics. The alkali pastes we tried on a clear lacquer did not work very well either.

Getting rusty metal ready for painting

Painting iron or steel is easy. Getting the metal ready to paint—especially if it's rusty—is the hard part. If you leave any rust behind, it will lead to more rust, and you'll have to repaint sooner than you'd like.

To do a good job dealing with rusty metals, there's no escape: You must use a wire brush before you start with a paintbrush. You have to remove all the rust—down to the bright shiny metal—then apply a coat of rust-resistant primer.

Our paint chemists know of no effective shortcut: The best way to get rid of rust is to grind or scrape it off completely—and that can be a messy time-consuming task.

Pruning tools

In selecting pruning tools—whether hand pruners or lopping shears—your major choice is between an anvil model or a hook-and-blade unit. When we tested these tools, our staff members who tried using each type generally preferred the tools with anvil cutters.

■ Unless you're a horticultural pefectionist, we think you should favor a pruning tool with an anvil cutter. Such tools do confer, or seem to confer, a sense of smooth action and cutting ease superior to that of hook-and-blade pruners.

■ If you're a meticulous yardkeeper, however, you may prize above all else the special virtues of the hook-and-blade models: clean close cuts.

What to look for. Before you choose a pruning tool, give it a good once-over in the store.

■ Examine anvil models from the top. The blade should be aligned with the center of the anvil. Next, view them from the side. The edge of the blade and the surface of the anvil should mate fully, with no gaps or hairline spaces showing.

■ A well-made and properly adjusted hook-and-blade cutter should slice through paper easily. The blade should be smoothly curved. The hook should be ground flat on one side to present a sharp corner at the severing point.

Cleaning rugs

Our basic recommendation for maintaining the life and good appearance of carpeting is to vacuum it thoroughly and regularly. Even with regular vacuuming, however, you'll occasionally have to give your rugs a more thorough cleaning to remove stubborn dirt.

For most types of carpets, you can choose among several cleaning options, unless your carpets are very dirty or matted. Once rugs reach that state, it's unlikely that a household rug shampoo will do a satisfactory job in one application. If your carpet is heavily soiled, you'd better call in the professionals or rent a "steam" cleaning machine from a local store.

Professional cleaning. You could send your rugs to a commercial cleaner, but that can cost quite a bit for room-sized rugs. For about the same price, you could have a professional firm bring in a machine to do the cleaning in place. Either way, professionals will probably do better than you can do with a household rug shampoo or with equipment you can rent.

If you have an Oriental, antique, or costly varicolored wool rug, we suggest that you leave the cleaning to specialists in that type of rug. Rugs may shrink, and rug dyes are not always colorfast to cleaning chemicals. You would have no recourse if you damaged the rug when cleaning it yourself.

Do-it-yourself "steam" cleaning. For house calls, professional rug cleaning companies sometimes use a machine that sprays a hot detergent solution into the rug and simultaneously vacuums away the solution and dislodged dirt. Smaller versions of this type of equipment can be rented from some supermarkets and hardware stores. They are often called "steam" cleaning machines, even though they actually use hot water.

■ It takes a little practice to handle these machines. They are smaller than the professional variety, but still cumbersome. If you follow the instructions carefully, you should do all right. The machines usually don't require more effort than an electric rotary-brush shampooer.

■ From our tests of such equipment, we judged that a steam machine would work much better on very dirty or matted rugs than any of the household rug shampoos we tested—but probably would not do as well as a thorough professional cleaning. For lightly soiled rugs, we think you might be just as satisfied using a household rug shampoo with a rotary-brush shampooer and a good vacuum cleaner.

Household rug shampoos. It's not wise to shampoo rugs more often than necessary, but do shampoo them before they get heavily soiled. If your carpeting isn't very dirty, then a shampoo may brighten it noticeably and stave off the need for commercial cleaning.

Shampooing any large carpet is a big job. Here are some suggestions for managing the task.

■ The furniture should be removed or set up on foil or wax paper "booties" to protect both the furniture and the carpet from stains. Applying the shampoo to a large carpet can take hours, and the carpet will be out of service until it dries—anywhere from a couple of hours to overnight. If you can't close off the room until the carpet dries, you'll have to shampoo in sections. Cleaning the carpet that way could be a two-day task.

■ It's a good idea to pick some inconspicuous place to check the rug dye for colorfastness before trying a new shampoo. A simple test is to moisten a white cloth with shampoo (diluted if you're using a liquid) and rub it against the rug. If the cloth does not pick up color, go ahead and shampoo.

■ There's a knack to rug shampooing. It's easy to acquire the knack, but you might want to practice on an inconspicuous part of the rug. You have to learn through experience how big a patch you should tackle each time. Label instructions may not help you here. You have to take into account the type of pile and the equipment you're using.

■ You have to take care not to soak the carpet, because that might bring on stains or a mildew growth.

■ Rug shampoos are strong detergents that may irritate skin or eyes. They should be used with caution and kept out of the reach of children.

Stepladders

A stepladder needs to be strong, stable, and rigid. If you're shopping for a stepladder, the main choice you have to make is between a wood or aluminum model.

Wood ladders. We think wood ladders have a slight edge over aluminum.

■ Wood ladders are a lot more rigid than aluminum ones. They're stronger and more stable. They don't conduct electricity, and they're usually a bit cheaper than aluminum ladders.

■ But wood ladders are quite a bit heavier than aluminum ones, and when you're handling something as cumbersome and awkward as a stepladder, an extra 6 to 8 pounds can be quite a burden.

■ Wood ladders also require some care in storage because wood left exposed to the elements can be damaged by insects or by rot.

Aluminum ladders. The singular advantage of light weight makes aluminum ladders worthy of first consideration for some household applications.

■ Most of the aluminum ladders we tested weighed between 10 and 12½ pounds, as opposed to between 16 and 20½ pounds for wood models.

■ The main disadvantage of an aluminum ladder is that you have to be very careful when you're working around electricity, particularly outdoors. An aluminum ladder should not be used where it could come in contact with electrical power lines or circuits. Moreover, when you're using a power tool on an aluminum ladder, be sure that the tool is grounded or that it's of the double-insulated type.

Choosing a string trimmer

Odd parts of the lawn are best handled with a string trimmer, the modern-day version of the scythe. With a long extension cord, you can use a string trimmer to cope with untidy tufts of grass and weeds that spring up close to rocks and walls, at the base of trees, along paths and sidewalks, and close to other spots where your mower can't do the job.

How extensive a trim job your lawn requires can determine the type of trimmer you should get.

One-handed trimmers are meant for light-duty cutting on a smallish lawn. Most of the one-handed models we tested proved too awkward to use as edgers. And if you're tall, you'd have to do some bending with a one-handed trimmer. With most models in our test group, the trigger switch was about 27 inches off the ground as you trimmed. The trigger on three of the models, however, was about 3 inches higher. Those extra inches could help a tall gardener.

Two-handed trimmers have a second "helper" handle that can be adjusted to suit a particular gardening activity.

■ A two-handed model is best for those who do extensive trimming or who have to battle dense growths of heavy weeds.

■ All the two-handed models in our test group edged effectively, including the slowest trimmers, especially when the line of separation between sod and sidewalk was pretty clear.

String trimmers: Safety cautions

Safe use of a string trimmer requires some care in selection of a model and sensible use of the equipment.

■ Check for double insulation. (A double-insulated string trimmer will have only two prongs on the plug.) It's a big plus in a portable electrical tool meant for outdoor use because it relieves you of worry about properly grounding the tool to avoid a shock. When equipment is double insulated, no exposed metal part will be electrically live even if the insulation fails. Without double insulation, proper grounding is necessary for the safe operation of a trimmer.

■ No trimmer, double-insulated or grounded, should be exposed to water. The manufacturers of the models we tested quite properly warn against trimming wet grass or working in the rain.

■ Although many trimmers have a guard around the rear of the motor housing, it's prudent to wear goggles or safety glasses when using a trimmer.

■ The whirling string can draw blood if it hits bare skin, so keep hands and feet clear of the nylon line. Wear long pants and sturdy shoes—no sandals—when trimming.

■ Always unplug a trimmer when replacing the cutting line.

Toilet bowl cleaners

There's no way to keep a toilet from getting dirty. And an in-tank "cleaner" won't do the job for you. So it's on with the rubber gloves and out with the sponge or scrub brush.

■ We think in-tank products offer very little for the money. They won't clean an already soiled bowl, or even spare you the need for a periodic scrubbing. At best, they will merely slow or disguise the rate at which soil accumulates and slightly extend the time between cleanings. (With an in-tank product, the water in the toilet may not be safe for pets to drink, so keep the toilet lid closed.)

■ An ordinary liquid household cleaner should clean the bowl easily if it's just lightly soiled.

■ If the soil and stains are stubborn, a specialized in-bowl toilet cleaner will clean the toilet better. But be careful how you use an in-bowl cleaner. Because of the acid content, these products can be harmful when they get into the eyes or onto the skin or clothing. Labels on the products properly urge caution, and all warn you to keep them out of the reach of children.

■ In-bowl cleaners usually claim they disinfect toilet bowls. Our medical consultants say there's little if any medical importance to disinfecting the bowl, even temporarily.

Using an upholstery cleaner

Commercial cleaning of upholstered furniture is expensive: It can cost as much as $200 for a pair of large chairs and a matching sofa. A more economical alternative is to do the cleaning on your own, with a do-it-yourself cleaner. But proper precautions are required if you do the job yourself—and results are not likely to be satisfactory.

Our engineers have a few suggestions for you, if you decide to try your hand at rejuvenating upholstery that has lost its bloom.

■ Don't rush into upholstery cleaning. Try to get by with frequent dry brushing and vacuuming for as long as you can. An upholstery cleaner, even if applied with proper care to a suitable fabric, may cause unalterable changes in the feel, shape, texture, warmth of coloring, or overall look of the fabric. After cleaning, a flat-textured fabric might take on a blurry plushy look because the cleaner has raised fibers here and there. And plushy pile fabrics may become matted.

■ If you must use a cleaner, do the cleaning with all possible gentleness. And use the least amount of cleaner that will do the job: It's far better to re-apply a cleaner than to be overgenerous the first time.

■ To protect your hands, wear rubber or plastic gloves when applying the cleaner.

■ Before using the cleaner, test the fabric's color or texture. Simply apply a bit of cleaner to an inconspicuous patch of fabric, following the label instructions, and see if anything happens. Do that test no matter what the instructions say: The label may not tell you everything.

■ A plastic brush or brush-and-sponge combination works well as an applicator on vinyl, which surrenders dirt to bristles more readily than to cloth and is none the worse for rubbing. But brushes can be hard on flat-surfaced textiles, especially after the yarn has been tenderized by wetting with cleaner.

■ For flat-surfaced fabrics, an old terry cloth towel makes a gentle and effective applicator.

■ After the cleaned upholstery has dried thoroughly, brushing won't hurt and may even help. With velvets and velours, brushing is essential to restore the fabric's nap.

Setting up a home workshop

A first-time homeowner, particularly someone setting up a home workshop, may wonder which tools to buy.

Our engineers suggest that you invest in an electric drill—in addition to the obvious hand tools. It should probably be the first power tool you buy. You'll need it to drill holes for screws, bolts, anchors, rivets, and dowels.

Socket wrench sets

A set of socket wrenches is necessary if you hope to achieve mechanical self-sufficiency. The assorted wrenches in your tool drawer may be enough for assembling a tricycle or tightenting the bolts on a porch swing. But you need a socket wrench set to be proficient at such do-it-yourself chores as working on your automobile.

The value of socket wrenches lies in their speed and in their ability to deal with nuts and bolts in cramped, hard-to-reach, or hard-to-see places. The set you buy should last a lifetime.

Hammers: An essential tool

Even the most rudimentary home workshop needs a hammer.

For most users, the preferred shape is the familiar claw hammer. The preferred size is the "16 ounce," which is the weight of the head alone. The handle, which can be made of steel, fiberglass, or wood, adds another 8 ounces or so to the hammer's weight. Wood-handled hammers are usually the lightest.

Don't buy a hammer without holding it and swinging it a few times. If one model feels too heavy or if its handle feels too fat or too skinny to be comfortable, try another.

For occasional users. A hammer with an oval wood handle is the cheapest type and would probably be the best choice for someone who needs a hammer only now and then. We don't think it makes much sense to pay more than $10 or so for a hammer that will spend most of its time sitting in a closet or a toolbox.

For do-it-yourselfers. If you spend a lot of time building things or fixing up around the house, you'll probably be most satisfied with a hammer that has a fiberglass or steel handle. You can expect to pay at least $15 to $18 for such a hammer. These hammers are generally the strongest, and they were the ones our staff members most preferred when we tested hammers.

Using a hammer. No matter which hammer you choose, it deserves the careful attention you should give any good tool. And you should take proper safety precautions.

■ Use a claw hammer only on ordinary nails. If you pound hardened steel nails, masonry, or some other hard substance, you risk ruining the tool. You also risk injuring yourself if pieces of steel or concrete fly your way.

■ Don't use a hammer if the head is loose or badly chipped, or if the handle is cracked.

■ We suggest wearing safety goggles even when driving nails.

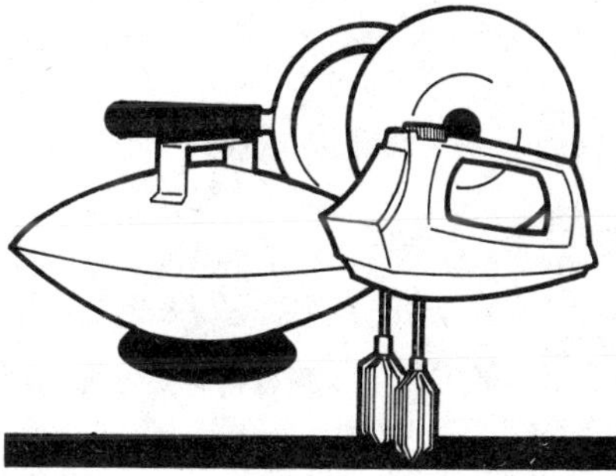

Kitchen

Grinding coffee

Here are some suggestions for people who like to grind their own coffee.

■ We think it's best to store only a small amount of beans in a grinder. Keep the rest of the beans in an airtight container in the freezer, so they stay fresh.

■ We also think it's best to grind only enough beans for immediate use.

■ The finer a coffee bean is ground, the more flavor it can yield. A very fine grind, we found, can make a pound of coffee go further. An expert taster who sampled our brews concluded that coffee quality remained good even when we reduced our recipe to 4 grams (2 level teaspoons) of ground coffee per cup.

■ If you want a good cup of coffee, keep your grinder clear of oily ground-coffee residues. Coffee oils go stale after only a few days' exposure to air and will turn rancid not long thereafter.

Thrifty dishwashing

Here are some suggestions to help you make yourself into a thrifty dishwasher.

■ Some labels on dishwasher liquids suggest that you measure out your cleaner with the bottle cap—a good starting point if you're interested in thrift.

■ Better still, try this: Measure out a teaspoon of cleaner and mix it into your dishpan. (A teaspoon holds about three-quarters of a capful.) If the suds outlast the dirty dishes, try a bit less cleaner next time. If the dishes outlast the suds, add a little more cleaner. Do that each time you wash dishes until you have a good idea of the amount you need. You may be surprised at how little that is.

■ Reform of your dishwashing habits may provide a further saving, this time in the energy to heat the water you use. Washing dishes under a constantly flowing stream of hot water can cost you more in energy than you'd pay when using an automatic dishwasher. Consider using two dishpans, one filled with comfortably hot sudsy water and the other with lukewarm rinse water. Or, if your sink has a spray hose, wash the dishes in one dishpan and put them, unrinsed, in a drying rack. When you accumulate a rackful, spray-rinse them all at once.

Why buy an electric frying pan?

A case, of sorts, can be made for the electric frying pan. It comes in handy at parties, doubling as an extra cooking element or a tabletop chafing dish. Its portability lets you cook snacks, or even meals, where there's no range—in a family room, for example, or a college dormitory.

An electric frying pan can heat quite evenly. It can also pan-fry, simmer, stew, and stir-fry. You can deep-fry small items such as french fries, but not large pieces of chicken. And you can steam, with the lid in place. You probably won't find it satisfactory for roasting or baking, no matter what certain manufacturers claim.

Choosing and using an electric frying pan

If an electric frying pan makes sense to you, you should limit your choice to the large frying pans. In our view, they offer greater flexibility than the smaller models.

Though the small frying pans performed well in our tests, we'd say they are worth considering only if you have severely limited storage space or if you travel a lot and need to include cooking gear. Even cooks in a single-person household may sometimes find the small frying pan inconvenient—when making pancakes, say, or cooking for guests.

Here are the features our engineers suggest you look for in selecting an electric frying pan:

■ "Buffet-style" handles for ease of carrying and storing.

■ Nonstick interior coating to facilitate cleaning—but use plastic, rubber, or wood utensils to cut down on scratching the surface.

■ Vent hole in the lid.

■ Square shape—it's more versatile than round. (The large square pans we tested could comfortably hold five full strips of bacon, for instance.)

Safe use. Be careful when using an electric frying pan. Our engineers suggest the following cautions.

■ Some large frying pans have flat lids with rather small knobs—a combination that makes for tight clearance for fingers. When such frying pans are hot, use a potholder to take the lid off.

■ Before moving a hot pan or pouring out the contents, remove the pan's control and attached cord.

■ Pour carefully (the large models can be clumsy in pouring).

■ If an extension cord is needed, use a heavy-duty cord.

Portable food mixers

Despite the popularity of the food processor, the old-fashioned portable food mixer still has its place in many kitchens. So does that other kitchen staple, the blender. All three kitchen appliances have their special uses, but in a small crowded kitchen, the portable food mixer has particular advantages.

■ The food processor's main talents are slicing, grinding, and making pastry dough. But it's often expensive, and it's a hefty machine that must usually be stored right on the counter top.

■ The blender is best at pureeing large amounts of food. A blender can be a lot cheaper than a food processor, but it too must usually take up counter space.

■ The portable food mixer is handiest for mixing up cake batter and instant pudding, and it's the appliance of choice for whipping cream or beating egg whites. A portable food mixer is inexpensive, light, and compact. It can be used wherever kitchen space allows, then put out of the way in a drawer or hung up when the work is done.

Using a portable mixer. With proper use, a mixer can give satisfactory results.

■ We advise running a mixer at the lowest speed that will get the job done. That should help keep splatter to a minimum.

■ We also advise mixing in a bowl large enough to contain most of the splattering, but small enough to permit submerging the beaters sufficiently for good mixing.

■ It's not advisable to use a portable mixer regularly for heavy mixing jobs. Such use will shorten the life of any portable, however sturdy. Very heavy dough, for instance, should be kneaded by hand or with a sturdier type of machine than a portable mixer.

■ It's our judgment that most portable mixers will give good service for many years if you use them under light or medium load—but not if you use them constantly for heavy work.

Choosing a food processor

Food processors provide hurry-up haute cuisine, onions without tears, even baby food. They blend, chop, crumb, emulsify, flake, grate, grind, mince, purée, shred, and slice. But what chores do you really need your food processor to perform?

■ If all you want to do with your food processor is chop vegetables, blend hollandaise sauce, or mix up a pot of chowder, we see no reason to spend a lot of money for an expensive model.

■ For processing vegetables and salad fixings, making mayonnaise, and doing other light-to-medium-duty chores, some of the inexpensive models can be an excellent value.

■ The top-rated processors we tested earned their top ranking mostly because they were superior at such heavy jobs as kneading dough, chopping meat, or grating cheese.

A nontoxic oven cleaner

Cleaning an oven is never a pleasant task. Often it can be hazardous as well. When we tested oven cleaners, we found a nontoxic aerosol, *Arm & Hammer,* that did a good job of oven-cleaning. One or two applications did the trick.

Arm & Hammer can be safely used without rubber gloves or other paraphernalia. It won't irritate your eyes or nose, and it won't damage kitchen surfaces. We top-rated it for safety.

When you clean the oven with other products, we recommend that you wear an apron, rubber gloves, safety goggles, and a face mask. Unlike the nontoxic *Arm & Hammer,* the other products contain lye—one of the most dangerous substances you can use around the house. The labels on the toxic cleaners appropriately state that the products could burn skin and eyes. Most of the labels warn about the hazards of inhaling fumes. They warn about ingestion. They outline first-aid treatment in case an accident occurs.

Not only do you have to worry about protecting yourself from a toxic oven cleaner, but you must also take care to protect nearby floors, counters, and other surfaces. Most of the cleaners' labels correctly advise spreading newspaper on the kitchen floor. Be careful not to splash the cleaner on aluminum, chrome, copper, baked enamel, or painted surfaces.

Arm & Hammer carries no such warnings—and needs none. Instead of lye, it contains nontoxic ingredients (a combination of organic salts) that, when heated, work as lye does to loosen oven grime by reacting with the fats and oils in the grime.

Choosing pots and pans

Here's what our engineers suggest about buying pots and pans.

■ For all-around durability, ease of cleaning, and high conductivity of heat, stainless steel with an aluminum bottom or core is the best choice of material.

■ Before you buy a particular pan, pick it up and see how it feels. You may find some handles more comfortable than others. And there may be some pots and pans whose balance you like better.

■ There's much to be said for taking the eclectic approach to pots and pans. Some pans are better suited for one kind of cooking than another. If your budget is tight, save your money for a good sauce pan. If you want a big kettle for boiling water to cook pasta or corn, look at an inexpensive line: Poor heat distribution in a pot used for such things matters little. And a plain cast-iron frying pan, if properly seasoned and cared for, is fine for frying bacon, eggs, and other foods.

■ Cookware coated with Silverstone makes better sense by the piece than by the set. Although tougher than Teflon, Silverstone is bound to wear out before the pan. So buying an entire set of Silverstone-lined pans is not a good investment. But a Silverstone skillet or omelet pan would be a good addition to a cook's complement for its easy cleaning and its ability to cook without butter, margarine, or shortening.

■ Resist buying pots and pans that are sold door-to-door. Such cookware may or may not be of good quality, but because of the salesperson's commission, it's likely to be far more expensive than utensils of comparable quality bought in a store.

Saving energy with pots and pans

The amount of energy used during cooking on top of the stove depends more on your cooking habits than on the kind of pot you use. A few good cooking habits will not only save some fuel but might improve the quality of your food and make your cookware easier to clean.

■ Use the lowest heat setting possible. Turn the burner up to bring water to a boil, but then turn it down as low as possible to maintain the boiling. Few foods need more than low-to-medium heat to sustain their cooking. Many manufacturers caution against high heat, even for the very best pots and pans. And for those pans with inferior heat distribution, keeping the burner at a low setting minimizes hot spots.

■ Use the smallest pan that will hold the food, and cover the pot or pan whenever possible. Water boils faster and foods cook quicker in a covered pan than in an uncovered pan.

■ On an electric range, match the pot to the element. Besides wasting heat, putting a small pan on a large element can overheat the handle and discolor the outside of the pan.

■ Don't use utensils that wobble on the element. The bottom of a pot on an electric burner should be as flat as possible when the pot is hot.

Should you buy a pressure cooker?

If you like homemade soup, stews, and pot roast, but don't like the time it takes to prepare them, it could pay you to buy a pressure cooker.

Advantages. A pressure cooker is very good at what it does best—reduce cooking time without reducing quality.

■ It will cook some foods in as little as one-fourth the time that an ordinary pot or oven would take. In fact, a pressure cooker is sometimes as fast as a microwave oven—and a lot cheaper.

■ For some stews, pot roasts, and soups, pressure cooking can be a convenient one-pot process. If a recipe calls for sautéing onions or searing meat before cooking, it can be done right in the pressure cooker.

■ If you're careful about the combinations you put together, you can also cook foods separately in a pressure cooker—at the same time and in the same pot. Most models come with a rack that keeps food away from the bottom of the pot. The rack can be used for a dinner consisting of, say, stuffed fish fillets, zucchini, and tomatoes. With each item placed first in a small oven-proof container or a pouch made of aluminum foil, the pressure cooker does the job of three pots.

■ A pressure cooker can also be used to steam foods such as casseroles or custards. They cook in their own oven-proof container, placed on the pressure cooker's rack.

Disadvantages. A pressure cooker has limited uses. You should not have unrealistic expectations of what it can do for you.

■ Unless you make stews, pot roasts, or soups often, a pressure cooker could be just another kitchen gadget that takes up more space than its infrequent use warrants.

■ It's no simple matter to get vegetables cooked to perfection in a pressure cooker. In our judgment, it's not worth the trouble to drag out a heavy pressure cooker for a task that can be done more accurately and more easily with an inexpensive vegetable steamer.

■ Cooking a stew in steps with a pressure cooker is a bit more inconvenient than cooking one in steps with an ordinary pot. You have to allow pressure to rise at the beginning and fall at the end of each step. And, if the food isn't done, you have to wait for pressure to build again before you can resume cooking. (But we didn't mind the wait between steps because that gave us time to peel and cut vegetables for the stew.)

■ The speed of a pressure cooker doesn't translate into a significant energy saving. The amount of energy expended on cooking is very slight, unless you use your oven quite often. In our tests, pressure-cooking a pot roast saved us about 4 cents worth of electricity.

Choosing a pressure cooker

Your ease in using a pressure cooker—and perhaps the frequency with which you take it out to cook with—can depend on the type of pressure cooker you select. Here are some guidelines from our engineers.

Range-top or electric. The electric models, which usually cost a bit more than the range-top cookers, offer no particular advantage in use or convenience, based on the models we tested.

Stainless steel or aluminum. Whether you choose stainless steel or aluminum is largely a matter of personal preference. Stainless steel models are heavier, but easier to clean unless food has been burned on.

■ While not entirely stainless, the steel models usually look nice and are fairly easy to care for.

■ Stainless steel doesn't conduct heat as well as aluminum does. To improve heat transmission, the stainless steel pressure cookers have a core of iron. (This explains the rust we discovered around the flanges in the stainless steel models we tested.)

■ We checked to see how well two stainless steel pots and two aluminum pots handled burned-on food. After soaking in hot sudsy water, the aluminum pots came clean with a sponge. The stainless steel models required vigorous scouring.

4- or 6-quart. For maximum versatility, we recommend you buy a 6-quart model if you have room to store it. Actually, most models we tested held half to three-quarters of the amount they claimed. But, for most cooking tasks, that's plenty.

Pressure settings. We see little if any need to choose a pressure cooker with more than one pressure setting—15 pounds per square inch. Some models we tested also had settings for 5 and 10 psi. We found that 15 psi worked well for almost everything we cooked.

Handles. For ease of carrying, choose a unit with handles on opposite sides of the pot.

■ With range-top models, look for a short handle opposite the long handle that's used in locking the lid. In our tests, the small second handle made lifting and carrying a lot easier.

■ The electric pressure cookers we tested had a short handle on each side of the pot that made them fairly easy to work with.

Cleaning. The lid of a pressure cooker is especially annoying to clean.

The flanges and the crevice around the gasket tend to trap food. It should ease cleaning of a pressure cooker if you can put the pot in the dishwasher.

■ With some models, you're warned the dishwasher could dull the shiny finish.

■ The electric pressure cookers we tested were totally immersible for cleaning.

Pressure cooker gaskets

Taking proper care of your gasket can save you money and effort in using a pressure cooker.

Replacing the rubber gasket is likely to be your only additional expense once you've paid for the pot. Eventually, a gasket loses its flexibility, but it will last longer if you store the pressure cooker lid upside down on top of the pot, as manufacturers recommend. Storing a pressure cooker with the lid in the locked position could deform the gasket.

Safe use of pressure cookers

With a few precautions, a pressure cooker is a safe kitchen appliance, according to our engineers.

Selection. When buying a pressure cooker, you're likely to find only safe models to choose among. But our engineers suggest that it would still be wise to check for the following.

■ Look for an Underwriters Laboratories listing. To obtain this imprimatur of safety, the handles on a pressurized cooker must be able to withstand a pull of 100 pounds of force and the lid must stay sealed. All the models we tested had a UL listing.

■ Look for an emergency pressure-release device. It's a plug that will blow free if the pressure rises too high. All the models we tested had the device.

■ If you can find one, look for a model with the safety plug under the handle. The concealed plug is the safest, in our view, because the plug is prevented from flying across the room.

Use. With proper care of your pressure cooker, you'll probably never need to witness the emergency release in action.

■ If you make it a point to check the vent tube beneath the pressure regulator before each use to see if it's clear, you could prevent any mishaps with your pressure cooker.

■ If the tube does become clogged, use a pipe cleaner or toothpick to clean the tube.

■ Even if for any reason the emergency release fails on a UL-listed pressure cooker, the cooker should be able to withstand five times the pressure allowed by the regulators, as a further safety measure.

Toaster oven or broiler oven?

If you're thinking of buying a counter-top cooking appliance, take time to consider which type you need. Otherwise you may be spending more money than you have to and cluttering up your kitchen counter with an appliance you won't be using regularly.

■ If you're interested only in toasting bread, buy a plain toaster. A good two- or four-slot model should certainly cost considerably less than a toaster oven. The heating elements of toaster-oven/broilers and ordinary toaster ovens are set at some distance from the bread. They tend to dry out the bread a bit before the surface reaches the proper color. But counter-top ovens are usually handier for items such as English muffins or rolls, which are often too plump to fit a standard toaster.

■ If you want to bake potatoes and meatloaf, warm rolls, heat frozen foods, and grill a cheese sandwich too, a toaster oven is probably a good choice. In our tests of counter-top ovens, we found they all matched our regular range in baking four ½-pound potatoes, which came out with crisp skins and well-cooked interiors. But for most oven tasks, you should not expect counter-top ovens to bake as well as a range. Nor will they handle large orders of food with as much finesse.

■ If you want all those things and a broiler too, a toaster-oven/broiler may offer the versatility you need.

■ If what you want is merely an auxiliary oven, the answer may be a broiler oven. The plain broiler ovens tend to be roomier than toaster ovens. And some broiler ovens offer a special feature: a motor-driven skewer that can be used for rotisserie cooking. For regular broiling, however, our tests showed that our kitchen range did better than the counter-top broilers—in some cases, a good deal better.

Safe use of toaster ovens and broiler ovens

In using a toaster oven or counter-top broiler, follow these safety precautions suggested by our engineers.

■ Don't use an extension cord unless absolutely necessary. If you do, use a short cord rated to handle at least 15 amps.

■ Beware of sharp edges on the sheet metal. A number of models we tested had razor-sharp edges on their crumb tray, drip pan, door, or the cabinet itself. Inspect the counter-top oven you buy and file smooth any sharp spots you find.

■ The glass doors of counter-top ovens can get hot enough to burn you. So can some metal parts on the outside of the toaster ovens or broiler ovens. Only those models having plastic sides with molded-in handles can be moved safely when hot.

Stir-frying in a wok

Stir-frying is something like sautéing. It involves moving food quickly across an intensely hot surface.

To stir-fry in a wok, you cut food into bite-sized chunks and whisk it through a small amount of hot oil in the bottom of the utensil. The concentrated heat sears in juices and cooks the food quickly and thoroughly.

A wok's sloped sides are designed to make it easy to lift and turn food during stir-frying, so that all sides can be cooked.

As a technique, stir-frying owes its origin to an early Chinese concern with energy conservation. Chinese stoves had openings in their top into which the woks were placed. Thus, a small fire could be concentrated on the wok's rounded bottom, and the shape conducted the heat up from the center. Traditional woks were usually made of thin tempered iron.

Leisure

No outdoor FM antenna?

FM reception is usually best with a good outdoor antenna—one specifically designed for FM. But you may find an FM antenna costs too much or your landlord won't let you mount an antenna on the roof.

There are three things you can do to improve FM reception.

- Try connecting the FM receiver to an outdoor TV antenna, if you have one.
- Invest in a standard indoor dipole antenna.
- Look into a rotatable indoor antenna.

Connect to outdoor TV antenna. Our electronics engineers think it's worth a try to connect your FM receiver to an outdoor TV antenna. The fact that the antenna is up and away from things probably ensures better performance than you'd get with an indoor antenna. Such a connection would require a signal splitter—an inexpensive accessory available at most electronics-supply shops.

Dipole. An indoor dipole antenna—the standard T-shaped "ribbon" tacked behind a bookcase or stowed under a rug—might provide tolerable reception. But it's not ideal, especially with the dipole in a fixed position.

Because a dipole is most sensitive to signals arriving broadside, it works most effectively when you can aim it to pick up each station's signal at its best. Even with a strong signal, a dipole aimed in the wrong direction can aggravate multipath interference—noise and distortion caused by broadcast-signal reflections that reach the antenna along with the original signal.

Rotatable antennas. Several indoor antennas marketed for FM reception are rotatable: They can be adjusted to function better than the dipole at reducing multipath interference and at receiving weak signals.

Depending on where you live and what stations you receive, you may be able to improve FM reception with a rotatable indoor antenna. Because these rotatable models can be moved around the room, the improvement in reception can be dramatic.

Installing an FM antenna

If you have a high-quality FM system that suffers from reception difficulties, you may find it a worthwhile investment to install an FM roof antenna. So too might a hobbyist who likes to search out distant FM stations.

The indoor antenna that comes with most stereo receivers rarely provides first-rate FM reception: Geography interferes. But you'll have to pay a price for improved reception. With all possible accessories added, an FM antenna installation may well run more than twice the price of the antenna alone.

Assembling and putting up an antenna is a fairly straightforward job, but one probably best left to a professional if the roof is steeply sloped or the footing is unsure.

Roof antennas come with all the hardware needed to mount them, after assembly, to a mast. But you'll have to buy the mast and more hardware to mount it firmly somewhere on the roof.

Here are the procedures to follow when you install an FM antenna. For safety's sake, be sure to work as far as possible from power lines—and be aware that it's easy to misjudge distance on a rooftop. If you do misjudge distance, you could be electrocuted.

■ Install the antenna away from metal objects such as pipes and fire escapes, and at least 5 feet from any TV antenna. Installation on the same mast is possible if you observe the 5-foot rule.

■ Before attaching the antenna to the mast, shift the antenna up and down several feet to test for the best signal.

■ All the antennas can be connected to "twin-lead" (ribbon) cable, which has a 300-ohm impedance. Twin-lead cable is fine if the down-lead from the roof to the receiver is direct and away from electrical wiring, gutters, and other metallic objects.

■ Otherwise, coaxial cable is preferable. (Coax can also lessen spark interference from the electrical motors of oil burners, electric razors, and the like.) But, with coax, you'll also need a balun transformer (available in electronics-supply stores) to match the antenna to the cable—and maybe another at the FM receiver, if it's not equipped for coax.

■ If the coaxial cable is longer than 100 feet, a significant loss of signal strength can occur. To beef up a badly weakened signal, you could add an amplifier at the antenna. In weak-signal areas, an antenna rotator could also be useful. It lets you change the antenna's orientation for optimum reception of distant signals coming from different points of the compass.

■ If gain is still not satisfactory, check with your dealer about "stacking" two antennas on the same mast, one atop the other. Stacking can effectively double the gain of an antenna.

■ In addition, it may make sense to protect an antenna from lightning. Electronics-supply stores offer do-it-yourself devices to guard against overload in a near miss. But only a professional lightning-arrestor installation can protect the antenna, the stereo equipment, and the house itself from a direct hit.

Need a roof TV antenna?

If you live in a strong-signal area and if your TV set is equipped with a built-in antenna, you may be able to do without a roof antenna for your TV. To find out, check the quality of the picture you get with a set attached to an indoor antenna. The picture should be clear and crisp.

If you live in a weak-signal area, one plagued by ghosts, or far from a transmitter, the result is a jittery picture flecked with "snow." Good reception may then require a roof antenna.

If you live between two cities and can receive TV pictures from both, you may find an antenna rotator useful. Without one, a TV antenna can't simultaneously receive signals from more than one general direction.

One way to judge how elaborate an antenna system you may need is by observing the kind of antennas your nearby neighbors have installed.

Choosing a bike

Before you buy a bicycle, here are some points to consider, based on our tests of bikes. Most of these points apply to both ten-speed and three-speed bikes.

Frame. If a frame lacks rigidity, some of the energy you put into pedaling will be dissipated by the flexing of the frame.

■ Closed-frame ("men's") bikes tended to rate higher in our tests than open-frame ("women's") bikes. That's because a closed frame (with its top tube) is usually more rigid.

■ Those who like a step-through frame might consider the so-called mixte, a frame pioneered by Peugeot and now used by other manufacturers. A mixte has a pair of tubes slanting down from the top of the steering column. They are attached to the seat tube and straddle it, continuing down to the rear axle. The mixte style gives less step-through clearance than an open-frame bike, but usually offers far better rigidity.

Pedaling ease. The single most important attribute of a good bicycle, in our judgment, is pedaling ease. In general, the bikes that combined light weight with high frame rigidity performed well when actually on the road.

Pedaling ease is also affected by a bike's gearing.

■ The lower the gear, the fewer feet traveled with each pedal stroke—and the less force you need to pedal because a given pedal effort doesn't have to move the bike as far.

■ The higher the gear, the farther your bike goes with each pedal stroke—but the more effort you must put in.

■ For a three-speed bicycle, with its relatively inefficient pedaling posture (using upright handlebars), gearing on the low side is preferable, in our opinion. That becomes especially true for riders who are somewhat out of condition. For example, a three-speed bicycle with 45-60-80 gearing had what we felt was a useful low gear, a medium gear (desirably) on the low side, and a usable high gear.

Handling is best judged by means of a test ride. But you can get some inkling of how a bike will ride from the shape of the handlebars. Some of the three-speed models that we judged poor in handling had excessively back-swept handlebars. They caused our test rider to assume a very erect riding posture, putting little weight on the front wheel.

Braking must also be judged on a test ride.

■ The braking response should be smooth and easily controlled, with each increment of effort producing a corresponding increase in braking action.

■ Besides being effective, brakes should be easy to control. Models in our tests that exhibited good brake control, or modulation, provided a gradual response to pressure on the levers. Their levers moved over a fairly wide range, offered a good feel, and required no more than moderate effort.

Seat comfort is especially important with a three-speed bike. With upright handlebars and a more erect riding posture than on a ten-speed, the seat bears almost the full weight of the rider.

■ The seat should be large enough for good support, but not so large as to interfere with leg movements in pedaling.

■ The padding should be fairly generous and reasonably firm.

Alignment. You can usually see if the wheels aren't aligned with one another.

■ But to make sure, hold the bike by its saddle, keeping the frame vertical, and walk the bike briskly across the floor. If it pulls to one side, it may be misaligned.

■ A properly aligned bike will track straight ahead when you ride it hands-off.

Getting the right fit is important when you buy a bicycle. Don't buy a bike that you can't try on for size. Fit is determined by the frame size, which is measured from the center of the pedal crank housing to the top of the frame's seat tube. Sizes usually range from 18 to 25 inches.

■ With a closed-frame style, you should be able to straddle the horizontal top tube with both feet flat on the ground and perhaps an inch to spare between the tube and your crotch.

■ With an open-frame or mixte style, a frame size 9 or 10 inches less than your inseam (crotch to floor, in stocking feet) is about right.

■ For all types of frame, the saddle height is right when your leg is almost fully extended at the lowest part of the pedaling stroke. At that point, your knee should be slightly flexed, with the ball of your foot on the pedal. The seat post should not have to be raised more than 2 or 3 inches. Futher extension might place the seat too high with respect to the handlebars. For the most comfortable ride, seat and handlebars should be at about the same level.

Shifting gears on a ten-speed

Because a bicycle has ten gears—or even twelve—doesn't mean you have to use all ten. But to make optimum use of the bicycle, experienced riders often do. Inexperienced riders rarely use all ten gears.

On a ten-speed bicycle, "gear" is related to the number of inches you can move with one complete revolution of the pedals. (The actual distance is the gear number times *pi.*)

■ Some derailleurs (or gear-shift mechanisms) have a wide gear range—about 33 to 100 gear—which is the best choice for individuals who aren't very athletic. Those extra-low gears provide an extra advantage when you have steep hills to climb.

■ A moderate gear range—about 38 to 100 gear—should be fine for people in reasonably good condition.

■ An athletic cyclist would probably prefer a narrower gear range—44 to 100 gear—which allows subtle choices among the more closely spaced intermediate gears. Expert riders try to keep pedaling effort and pedaling speed constant, uphill and down. They accomplish this with small adjustments in the gearing as they pedal.

■ When you do shift gears, you don't have to shift through them consecutively. You can, for example, shift from seventh gear down to third gear to climb a hill without using any of the gears between.

Learning how to shift a ten-speed takes some practice.

■ You don't select a gear by the numbers: You do it by feel. You upshift or downshift as necessary until the pedal pressure feels right at your normal cadence.

■ There's a 2-gear derailleur at the front of the bicycle, near the pedals, and a 5- or 6-gear derailleur (depending on whether it's a ten-speed or twelve-speed bike) on the rear wheel hub.

■ Moving two small levers, located near the handlebars, mechanically shifts (or derails) the bicycle chain from one sprocket to another. Shifting the rear derailleur to larger sprockets provides lower gears. Shifting the front derailleur to its smaller sprocket provides the lower ratio of a gear. Thus, in the lowest gear, the chain rides in the largest rear sprocket and the smaller front sprocket. In the highest gear, the chain is in the smallest rear sprocket and the larger front one.

Why three-speed bikes?

With ten-speed bikes so widely available, why do some people still prefer three-speed bikes? Although three-speeds are less popular and less efficient than ten-speeds, they have advantages for some riders.

■ A three-speed bicycle can be a durable and cheap form of transportation —well suited for errands or trips to the train station.

■ The shifting mechanisms of the three-speeds we've tested are generally rugged and require minimal maintenance. Those of ten-speeds tend to be more delicate, and more easily knocked out of kilter.

■ Repairs aside, some riders prefer the simplicity of three gears rather than ten.

■ And some prefer the erect riding position that upright handlebars allow. The underslung racing-style handlebars typical of most ten-speeds require some getting used to.

Shooting pictures through glass

If you want to take a photograph through glass with a flash camera, you may not always get satisfactory results. Glare or images reflected from the glass could spoil the picture. Our photo-optical specialists have a suggestion for you: Put the lens flat up against the glass.

Choosing a cassette deck

The electrical and mechanical quality of today's cassette decks—and other stereo hardware—is so high that you may well choose a deck for its features or its ease of use.

Here are some points to consider when you buy a cassette deck.

Controls. The power-assisted controls on most decks we tested worked quite effortlessly.

■ Some models had old-fashioned "piano-key" controls that needed a firm push.

■ Most of the decks we tested responded almost instantly when we touched a control. A few delayed a half-second or more. The delay would make it hard to cue a tape precisely.

■ When searching for a particular passage on a tape, it's helpful to be able to go directly from Play or Record to Rewind or Fast-Forward without having to push Stop. With one model we tested, you could go directly from Play to Record, or from Record to Play. The latter would be helpful when recording over unwanted narration. Another model could be set to play a tape automatically after rewind: You just press the Play and Rewind controls and let the deck take over.

■ Almost all decks have a separate eject button. With a few, you have to press the Stop control once to stop the tape, and a second time to eject the cassette.

Recording-level meters. The meters on most decks show where the music "peaks," or approaches a level that could cause distortion.

■ The meters are typically lighted segments, rather like an illuminated bar graph. By observing the display, you know how to adjust the deck's recording level. The lights generally give a more precise idea of peaks than the traditional "twitching needle" meter found on some models.

■ The more segments in the display, the better your feel for the rise and fall of the sound level (otherwise you're just watching blinking lights).

■ The recording-level controls on most of the decks we tested are ganged. You could set the right and left channel level either separately or together, using only one hand. Ganged controls help maintain the balance between left and right channels when adjusting recording levels. They also are useful for certain special effects, such as "fading out" the applause at the end of a musical selection.

■ A separate control for each channel might be useful for some live recording. For any other situation, however, we found it an inconvenience.

Tape protection. To guard against accidentally erasing a tape, you can always snap off the small tabs at the edge of a cassette. But a well-designed deck should also provide built-in protection against accidental erasure. Think twice about getting a model that requires you to press only Record instead of Record and Play at the same time.

Use with timer. Inquire whether you can use a household timer with the deck to record a broadcast in your absence. Most decks permit you to do this. Just connect deck and timer, press Pause and Record, set the timer to "off," and release Pause. When the timer comes on, the deck will start recording. (You can use the same technique for waking up to music.)

Audio cables and jacks. Most of the decks we tested have detachable audio cables. Plugging and unplugging the cables repeatedly could loosen their ground contacts, causing hum and interference. A deck having cables with spring-grip ground contacts should forestall the problem.

Microphone use. All the decks we tested had inputs for microphones. Some models also had a line/mike switch that let you shuttle between the mike and the deck's input for recording. If you want to record your own spoken introduction to a piece of music, the line/mike switch would be welcome. Without it, you'd have to disconnect the microphone before recording.

Cassette-compartment light. If the cassette compartment is back-lit, a glance at the deck will tell you roughly how much tape is left for recording or playing. Without a light we found the tape hard to see in a dimly lit room.

Cassette decks: Making your own tapes

Even with low-priced cassette decks, it's possible to make tapes of very high quality. Here are some suggestions from our electronics engineers. They should enable you to make recordings that will probably be better than many commercial tapes.

Types of tape. A deck's recording performance usually varies with the type of tape used. Tapes fall into four main categories.

Type I is "ferric" or "normal bias" tape. (Bias is an inaudible signal needed only to *record* on tape.) Type II, more expensive, is "chromium dioxide" or "high bias." Type III is "ferrichrome" tape. It's never been popular, and few decks provide for it. Type IV, "metal" tape, is quite expensive and may be justified only if you're devoted to recording live performances.

For most home sound systems, the tapes to buy are Types I and II. Differences between the two are slight. The better Type I tapes now perform nearly as well as Type II tapes. Their frequency response with most of the decks we tested was also better. In fact, we judged that Type I was the tape of choice for most of the decks we tested. Type II, purportedly more advanced, was a bit quieter.

Because different brands of Type I and II tapes often perform better with one bias than another, you can expect small tape-to-tape differences when recording. But the slight variations in frequency response that may occur when you record with different brands will usually be tolerable. If small differences are very important to you, however, you can buy a deck with adjustable bias, which will correct for such differences.

Testing a tape. When in doubt about a tape, try this simple test.

■ Tune an FM receiver to an interstation "blank" on the dial, switching off the muting feature to produce a hiss.

■ Record the hiss at a level of about −15 on the meter.

■ Play back the tape. Carefully compare the original hiss with the taped version, using the deck's tape-monitor switch to shuttle between the sounds. (Use the volume control to ensure that both sounds are equally loud—otherwise the comparison may be misleading.)

■ Unless the taping sounds excessively "bright"—over-emphasizing the treble—or excessively "dull"—understating the treble—there's no need to try another brand of tape.

For high-quality recording. To make the best use of a deck's dynamic range, you should record at the highest level possible without distortion, using the deck's recording-level meters as a guide.

Here's what you should do to be sure you get high-quality sound on the tape.

■ Depress the deck's Pause control, then set the deck to record.

■ Play the loudest passages to be recorded, and set the recording-level controls so that the deck's meters just reach the manufacturer's maximum recommended setting. If the music has unusually loud treble sounds, you may want to reduce the setting by a digit or two, especially with decks whose dynamic range in the treble is low. You may need to repeat this procedure several times to get the maximum recording-level setting that sounds best to you. Make a note of the setting you decide to use (so that you will have it for future recording sessions).

■ Now, start the music over as you release the Pause control.

When color prints are poor

Color film processors may claim that they provide quality control—inspection of prints by human eyes. But tests by our photo-optical specialists showed that many labs do inferior work. Based on this experience—and a survey of Consumer Reports readers who use color film—our advice to you is to refuse to pay for poor prints, or to return the prints and negatives to the processor for another try (but include a written explanation of what was unsatisfactory).

If you sometimes feel as though you're the first human being to look critically at the poor prints you've received from a lab, you could be right. To keep costs low, processors seem to leave it up to you to inspect the prints and ask for new prints when necessary.

If you get back prints that you aren't happy with, complain to the processor. Some have a money-back guarantee "if not completely satisfied." And most processors will remake a print without argument or charge.

If you used a mailing envelope. When you use a mail-order lab, you pay for the processing before you get the results. If a negative isn't printed, you usually can't get your money back in cash.

■ Of the companies we tested, only one let you return a coupon for credit or cash.

■ About half the other mail-order companies we tested gave you a credit slip good for a portion of a future processing order. You have to use that same processor again to get your money back.

■ The rest gave a coupon good for a reprint instead. If you happen to want a reprint, that form of credit is usually a better value. The cost of a reprint generally exceeds the cost of an original print.

If you used a store. If you have your film developed through a store, you shouldn't have to pay for prints that weren't made.

■ If some of your shots weren't printed, look at the negatives to make sure they were truly unprintable.

■ Many of the people who participated in our survey of color film users complained that a processor had failed to print flawless negatives. They weren't charged, but they didn't get the pictures, either.

Trying again. When you return a poor print and its strip of negatives, enclose a note to the processor.

■ Explain in writing what's wrong with the print: "foreground too dark" or "the car should be yellow, not gray-green," for example.

■ If the negative is undamaged and not badly underexposed (which shows as a low-contrast print whose dark areas are muddy rather than black), you should be able to get a decent print the second time around.

Care of film and camera. Careless handling of film and camera can cause problems with prints.

■ Film, both in and out of the camera, should be kept away from high temperatures. Leaving a camera in a closed hot car is the classic example of such abuse.

■ Film also deteriorates in high humidity.

■ Fumes from mothballs or from perfume spilled in a purse can alter film's emulsion.

■ Don't let a roll sit in the camera month after month while you wait to take the last shot or two. Even if exposed film is kept dry and cool, the undeveloped image will eventually deteriorate.

Poor camera work. Problems with pictures aren't always the processor's fault.

■ Many a photographer now and then snaps a picture without focusing or setting the proper exposure.

■ Sometimes an attempted shot is impossible. Don't try to use a flash in an arena to photograph something hundreds of feet away, for example.

Ordering color reprints

Getting extra color prints made has its problems. Here are some suggestions from our photo-optical specialists to make it easier to get good reprints.

Handling negatives. Negatives are easily damaged and shouldn't be handled unnecessarily.

■ When selecting a strip for reprints, handle it only at the edges.

■ To identify the picture you want reprinted, use the frame numbers on the film.

■ From a processor's view, a customer who wants reprints should never cut the negatives apart.

Matching colors. The color of the reprint probably won't quite match that of the original print.

All the processors we talked with make reprints on the same type of machine they use for making the initial prints. But day-to-day variations in the chemicals, photographic paper, and equipment—and broad standards for an "acceptable" print—all can make for differences in color.

If having an identical print is important to you, look for a processor that recommends sending the original print to use as a guide. (Kodak recommends sending a "guide print" only if the order is for twenty-five or more reprints.)

When your film's not returned

The risk of a color processor losing your roll of film is less than one in a hundred. It doesn't seem to affect the odds whether you send your film through the mail or use a store.

If your film has not been returned by a processor, there's still a chance it may turn up.

■ Film lost by the post office has been known to arrive months later.

■ Film without mailing information is generally processed and then sent to a company's "lost and found." If you can describe your pictures in enough detail, there's a good chance the processor can locate them. But don't expect a lab to find film that was lost in January and is described merely as "Christmas scenes."

To improve your chances of getting your film back, take care in how you attach directions for returning the pictures. Film at the lab sometimes gets separated from the name and address.

■ To prevent this from happening to you, don't use gummed address labels on a mailing envelope. Kodak told us that labels with defective glue are a frequent cause of mislaid film.

■ A reader of Consumer Reports wrote us about an ingenious way to increase the odds on getting your film back: "I now have a large card printed with my name, address, and telephone number. I always photograph that card as my first exposure."

Does high quality mean a high-priced loudspeaker?

Loudspeakers need not be high-priced to be high in quality. Tests by our electronics engineers showed the many low-priced speakers performed nearly as well as speakers costing twice as much. Like receivers, amplifiers, and turntables, loudspeakers need not be at the top of the price range to be satisfactory.

Overall, the low-priced speakers we tested reproduced sound as accurately as higher-priced models. If they couldn't quite do it all, they could do enough to satisfy most music lovers. Given the price of these speakers, their deficiencies seem to be minor.

- They didn't reach quite as deep into the bass.
- They weren't quite as powerful.

Shopping for a loudspeaker

Good sound from a good stereo system depends more on the loudspeakers than on any other audio component. Choosing the right speakers is no easy task, given the wide range of prices, sizes, shapes, sounds, and sales pitches to be sorted out in the audio dealer's showroom.

In our tests, we have found high accuracy in low-priced as well as in expensive loudspeakers. But with the mid-priced models we tested, high accuracy was almost the rule, not the exception it would be with some low-priced speakers. And, in general, the mid-priced models did a better job of rendering the deep bass and in delivering lots of sound volume in a large room.

When you've narrowed your choice of speakers, try to audition them at the dealer's, preferably in a quiet room with equipment that permits switching from one speaker to another. Trust your ears—not the dealer—to tell you what you hear.

Ask for return privileges in the event the speakers don't sound right when you get them home. Check the speakers at home to be sure they sound the same as they did in the showroom. Samples of the same model may not be identical.

Choosing a loudspeaker

Accuracy of sound reproduction is the most rational basis for judging loudspeaker performance, according to our electronics engineers. A speaker should respond fully and smoothly over the entire sound spectrum.

The low-priced speakers we tested proved remarkably capable of reproducing sounds accurately, smoothly, and uniformly. Without being spectacular, they were solid performers that should be able to satisfy all but the most finicky listeners.

You should consider the following points in selecting a loudspeaker, according to our electronics engineers.

■ If the loudspeakers you select have an impedance of 4 ohms or less, it's important that your amplifier be able to drive the low impedances, as most can do. (Roughly speaking, impedance is a loudspeaker's resistance to electric current from the amplifier. Other things being equal, a speaker with low impedance draws more current, and therefore more power, than one with high impedance.)

■ If your sound system includes two sets of stereo speakers and you plan to play both at the same time, be sure that each speaker's impedance is more than 6 ohms. Otherwise, the amplifier may overheat or blow a fuse.

■ If the loudspeaker has a high-frequency level control, try the control at its maximum setting. Our tests showed that models with such a control set at maximum usually delivered the most accurate response.

■ If weak bass is a problem, check for a built-in bass boost. Speakers with that characteristic have the potential for improving the sound of music by strengthening the bass response, especially with recordings that are "bass-shy."

■ To improve bass response, you should consider changing the speaker's position in the room. Depending on room dimensions, "standing waves" can cause "dead spots" in the bass. Nonrigid room partitions may cause some bass to be lost.

■ If excessively strong bass is a problem, check for a speaker whose bass response is relatively flat. Moving the speaker, raising it off the floor, and changing your listening position are worth a try.

Speaker location

How accurately speakers render very low bass frequencies (110 Hz and below) depends more on such variables as room dimensions, speaker placement, and a listener's position than is the case with other frequencies.

■ Bass response depends in large part on the speaker's location, which affects the way sound is reflected from the walls and floor. Finding the best location was once a matter of trial and error. Nowadays some manufacturers design their speakers for a particular location. Some, we're pleased to say, even give detailed instructions on loudspeaker placement.

■ Manufacturers usually warn against putting speakers on the floor or in a corner, because those locations can make the bass too heavy. Many manufacturers recommend bringing a speaker up to ear level—putting it on a low stand, for example. Most recommend placing speakers so that the distance between them is about the same as the listener's distance from them.

■ As acoustic theory predicts, positioning most loudspeakers near a wall boosts the bass below about 150 Hz and may cause a dip at around 200 Hz. (Some speakers are supposedly designed to eliminate that dip at 200 Hz.) If the peak in loudness occurs at too high a frequency—about 100 Hz, say—it could be annoying: The peak might make the speaker sound boomy. To flatten the bass, try moving the speakers away from the wall or raising them higher from the floor.

Maintaining sound volume

You may have been perfectly satisfied with how loud your speakers sounded —until you redecorated your home. Adding furnishings to the room in which you use your sound system can change the acoustics so drastically that you may want to get a different amplifier to restore the "punch" you've been accustomed to.

If you use the chart on the facing page, you can calculate how much additional power you need from an amplifier to maintain the sound volume you had before you added wall-to-wall carpeting, say, or draperies.

Here's how to use the chart.

■ First determine the volume of your listening room. Consider adjoining rooms or hallways as part of the listening room if they are connected to it by a large doorway.

■ Next figure out the room's approximate acoustic demands—before and after the redecorating. A room with hard floors, several scatter rugs, plain wood furniture, and little or no drapery will be relatively "live." A room with thick wall-to-wall carpeting, heavy draperies, and upholstered furniture will be relatively "dead." (Consider any open doorway of ordinary size as an area equivalent to one covered by heavy draperies.) Acoustically, most rooms fall somewhere between these two extremes.

■ Then locate the room's volume on the scale at the bottom of the chart. Move up that line to the region of the chart that matches your room's former acoustics—before the redecorating. And move horizontally to the vertical scale on the left to get a "multiplier" figure.

■ Repeat the procedure, using your room's new acoustics.

■ The ratio of the two multipliers is the amount by which you need to increase your amplification.

Maintaining sound volume: A chart to help you

(Directions for using the chart below appear on the facing page.)

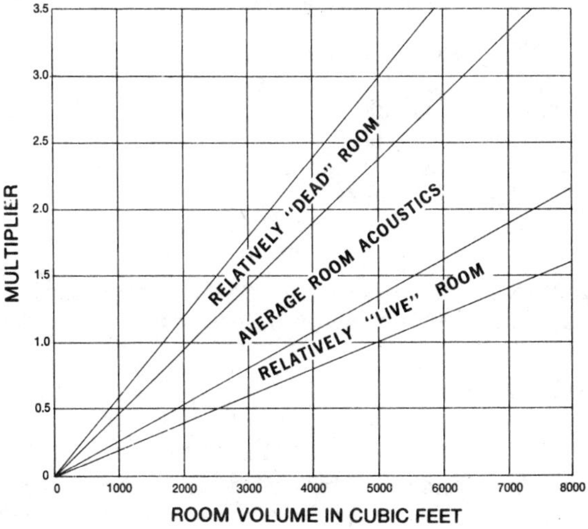

Small black-and-white TVs: What to expect

If you want a small TV set but don't want to spend a lot of money and don't want color, you should consider an inexpensive, portable, black-and-white TV. What you'll get is a compact lightweight receiver with a screen that measures 12 inches diagonally.

What can you expect from a 12-inch TV? Our electronics engineers warn that you'll probably have to do without push-button channel selectors, remote control, and other refinements available on color sets. And you'll have to tolerate a slightly lower-quality picture.

The engineers who tested small black-and-white sets found that while some 12-inch TVs provided better picture quality than others, all the sets produced a picture that was at least satisfactory.

Here are other findings from the test project.

Reception. Many of the sets did not do a satisfactory job of resisting CB signals and airplane flutter (interference that shows as rapid fluctuations in contrast and brightness).

Antenna. The sets did a generally acceptable job receiving fringe signals both with a good roof antenna and with the sets' built-in antenna. As a rule, the sets did worse when pulling in weak UHF signals with their built-in antenna.

Sound quality. The sound quality on the sets we tested was fair, at best. But given the tiny speakers in the receivers, you couldn't expect great sound.

Repairs. The relatively simple circuitry of black-and-white TV sets makes them less likely to need repair than color models, according to recent surveys of Consumer Reports readers.

If repairs are needed, the lightweight portables should be easy to tote to a service shop: Sets come with a carrying handle or handhold, and weigh no more than about 15 pounds.

Judging a TV set's picture quality

The main criterion used by our electronics engineers for rating TV receivers has always been the quality of the picture. Other things being equal, the key to picture quality is "clarity," which depends in turn on a variety of factors.

■ Good resolution is indispensable for showing fine detail such as strands of hair, textures of fabric, and the like.

■ Images should be crisp—neither harshly defined nor soft-edged and fuzzy.

■ Brightness and contrast should bring out subtle shading, giving the picture a three-dimensional look and keeping it from washing out in a brightly lit room.

■ With good interlace, the lines that compose the TV picture will be evenly spaced and invisible at a normal viewing distance. That makes for good definition of vertical detail. A TV picture that lacks good interlace may have a coarse look.

■ If black-level retention is good, all areas the TV camera "sees" as black will look black, not gray. That gives outdoor scenes shot after dark the nighttime look they should have.

■ Geometric distortion, obviously, affects picture quality. The distortion can take many forms, making people and things look fatter or thinner at the edge of the screen or causing straight lines to bend, especially at the picture's edges.

Hold off buying a turntable?

A totally new kind of record-playing system may be available in the not-too-distant future—a digital model with a laser-beam stylus. It will play a special disc less than 5 inches in diameter. The digital system promises to be so good that it will eventually replace the present one.

Should you hold off buying a conventional turntable? We say no. The revolution is coming, but it won't pay to wait.

The first digital models will probably be a lot more expensive than the conventional models. The first digital discs will also be expensive, and it will take perhaps a decade for record companies to build a full digital catalog.

Choosing a turntable

It's not hard to find a good turntable these days. Models tested by our electronics engineers were commendably free from flutter and rumble. The differences that did turn up in our tests were usually of secondary importance.

Under the circumstances, you may want to base your choice on price or on features that matter to you.

■ Fully automatic units have a control that lets you repeat one side of a record as many times as you like.

■ A sensing device on the turntable platter reads the record size and automatically adjusts the turntable. If there isn't a record on the platter and you press the start button, the sensor will stop the operation so you won't damage the stylus.

■ A cue control—a lever or button you press to slowly lower or raise the tone arm without touching it—minimizes the possibility of damaging the record. On some models, the cue control is located outside the dust cover. On others, it's inside—and that's less convenient.

■ One other point should be mentioned only because many turntable ads imply that it's important. The ads often specify whether the turntable is direct-drive or belt-drive (referring to the mechanism that turns the platter). In our view, neither has an inherent advantage.

Shopping for a cartridge

Except for loudspeakers, the cartridge is the most important determinant of the quality of the sound you get from records. Here are some suggestions from our electronics engineers to guide your shopping.

Price. Like most audio products, cartridges are heavily discounted, so list prices may be very misleading. Shop before you buy. Many models sell for less than half the suggested retail price.

Installation. If you're uncertain about how to install the cartridge, take the turntable to the store and let the dealer do it for you.

Special features. Cartridge manufacturers have come up with several handy features that you may want to consider.

■ On some models the headshell and cartridge are a single integrated unit. It can be plugged directly into a tone arm that has a fitting designed to receive it. An integrated cartridge is not only easy to install, it also keeps the overall tone-arm mass down, which helps when you're playing a record that's a bit warped.

■ Some plug-in cartridges may be *too* light for your tone arm. To get the right tracking force, you may have to add weights (supplied by the cartridge manufacturer).

■ A hinged brush that sweeps the record is useful to remove dust. The kind that also adds damping can be helpful when you're playing a warped record.

Replacing a stylus

It's hard to tell when to replace a stylus just by looking at it, even with a microscope. You should be able to use a stylus for at least 400 hours. You may be able to use it for a much longer time, if you keep it and your records very clean.

A stylus is replaceable at about half the cost of the entire cartridge. With most models you can replace the stylus yourself: Just follow the directions on the package.

Choosing a VCR

A video cassette recorder is a relatively expensive purchase. Does it pay you to buy at the high end of the price range? According to our electronics engineers, it depends on what you want from your VCR.

Our tests have shown that when you buy one of the more expensive VCRs, what you're paying for is extra convenience, not better performance. The lower-priced models generally did about as well in our tests as the higher-priced models.

It's the number and usefulness of the features that should determine whether you want to invest in a high-priced VCR. The models we tested all performed about the same. (There were some slight differences in picture quality among the machines we tested, but our engineers judged that these were due to sample-to-sample variations.) So before you spend a lot of money on a VCR, make sure the model you select will give you the group of features that best meet your needs.

The key question to answer is how much machine do you really need? Talk to some VCR owners before you select a model. Find out how they use their machines.

If you're not going to do much recording, it would make sense to select one of the less expensive models.

If you like the idea of being able to set up an extended automatic recording schedule, or if you like the convenience of a remote control, you should select one of the more expensive models with the special features you need.

Higher-priced VCRs: Special features

Below is a list of special features that can be found only on higher-priced video cassette recorders.

Automatic recording in series. Some VCRs can be set to automatically record as many as eight different programs over a period of fourteen days. (All models we tested could be set to repeatedly record programs that appear at the same time every day, until the tape runs out.) Some models will repeatedly record a weekly program until the tape runs out.

Remote control. Many VCRs are equipped with a remote unit that controls several functions. One type transmits the control signal by infrared beam. The other type transmits by a cable.

Most units will control the basic playback functions: Play, Rewind, Fast-Forward, Pause/Still, and Stop. Some will also handle such functions as recording and changing channels.

You can use the unit to switch channels on your TV set. As long as the TV set is on and tuned to the channel that links it to your VCR (3 or 4), the VCR will dictate the program to appear on the screen.

Frame advance. Like a motion-picture film, a videotape presents a series of still pictures or frames that normally appear on the screen for a split second. With a frame-advance control, you can move the tape forward one frame at a time. Every time you press the button, a new frame will appear.

Slow-speed forward is like frame advance, except the frame advances automatically at a very slow speed.

Fast-speed forward is useful for scanning a tape fairly quickly. The tape moves at roughly two or three times the normal viewing speed. The picture is visible though a little fuzzy.

Search or cue/review. With this feature, you can scan a tape very quickly, in foward or in reverse. The speed is about ten times the normal playing speed. The picture remains visible and clear enough to let you spot a particular scene.

It's especially useful when you're playing a program that was recorded automatically: You can whiz past three minutes of commericals in about eighteen seconds. It's extremely convenient to have this feature on the remote-control unit.

Auto-search is a device for electronically marking the beginning of each recorded segment on a tape. If you use the auto-search when you record, the machine can easily find the marks later. If the auto-search switch is on, the tape will automatically stop at each mark when the machine is rewinding or running fast-forward.

Audio dub lets you put a sound track on a tape you've recorded previously. You can plug a microphone in and comment on the pictures, or you can record a musical track.

Automatic rewind. With this feature, a model playing a tape or running it fast-forward automatically rewinds at the end of the tape.

Push-button tuning. With a model having a separate push button and number indicator for each channel, you push the button and the machine's tuner immediately switches to that channel and the number lights up.

Back-up batteries. Rechargeable batteries work as a back-up system for the clock. If the clock is set for later recording and the power is interrupted, the clock will keep running for several minutes. If the power comes back on before the batteries run down, your programmed recordings will start on time. But the batteries aren't strong enough to power a recording.

Beta vs VHS

When you shop for a video cassette recorder, you'll be buying a machine in one of two basic formats—Beta (as in *Betamax*) or Video Home System. In our recent tests, our electronics engineers found neither the Beta nor the VHS format superior to the other.

The most obvious difference between the two formats is in the size of the tape cassette. Both are about the size of a paperback book, but the VHS cassette is slightly larger than the Beta cassette.

When you consider either a Beta or VHS system, remember you'll be limited to tapes made to fit the format you select. If there's a chance you might want to exchange tapes with friends, you'll need a machine that's compatible with theirs. Also, make sure your local video store stocks tapes in the format you have in mind.

Of course, if you're replacing an old VCR and already have a tape library, you'll be locked into getting the same model again—unless you want to trade in your supply of tapes.

Cable TV and VCRs: A mixed match

If you receive your TV signals by cable and want to use a video cassette recorder, you may run into some obstacles when you hook up your VCR. You'll have to make some choices that may limit your viewing and recording freedom.

All VCRs can receive the standard broadcast channels, whether the signals come by cable or over the air. Some VCRs can also receive cable TV channels directly from the cable.

If your VCR is equipped to receive cable TV channels, you'll be able to view and record them. However, you won't be able to view or record any programs transmitted in scrambled form.

Some VCRs can receive cable TV channels with the help of a converter box supplied by the cable company. How you hook up the cable TV converter will to some extent determine the extent to which you can use the various features of your VCR.

The situation is further complicated if you subscribe to one of the pay-TV channels, such as Home Box Office. On these channels, the signals are usually electronically scrambled, and you'll need a special converter box to unscramble them.

None of the simpler cable hookups offers as much flexibility as you would have if you were receiving signals off the air. If you want to investigate complicated hookups that may give you more flexibility, check with your cable company.

Batteries for walkaround tape players

A walkaround player—even a relatively inexpensive model—can be expensive to feed. But you can save a little on the batteries these players require (most take four at a time).

Batteries can be a substantial expense, especially if you change batteries when the battery-condition indicators say you should. We suggest you forget the indicators and wait for your ears to tell you when you need new batteries.

Here's an example of the possible saving. When we tested walkaround players, our voltage measurements showed that the battery-condition indicator on the *Sony Walkman I* would start nagging you after only nine hours of play. Yet we found that the *Walkman* could operate satisfactorily for seven more hours.

All makers of models we tested offer an accessory power-line adapter. It's a worthwhile battery-saving investment (if you don't mind being tied to one location). So is a rechargeable battery pack, which may be offered as an accessory.

Personal care

Choosing a low-cost calculator

Even with a low-cost calculator, you can get fairly sophisticated features. A good basic calculator should have the following characteristics:

■ A liquid crystal display.

■ Keys that by touch or by tone let you know when an entry has been made. With some calculators you feel a little bump before a key is pushed all the way to the bottom. With others—particularly the very small thin ones—you hear a little beep when an entry has been made. (Some give you both kinds of feedback.)

■ Keys that are comfortable to use. Some calculators have stiff keys that require a heavy punch; others, a medium or light touch. We think it important that you try out a few different models to see which sort of key is the kind you like best.

■ A calculator should run for at least 1,000 hours on one set of batteries (which are usually included).

■ Also common with many low-cost calculators are functions such as a four-key memory and a constant capability in addition, subtraction, multiplication, and division.

Printing calculators

Printing calculators have recently dropped dramatically in price and size. There are models that are now as small as some basic calculators. The more advanced models come with keys for letters as well as numbers—a further incursion by the calculator into territory once occupied by the scratch pad.

Batteries for calculators

Most of the calculators we tested are liquid crystal display models. An LCD requires only the tiniest trickle of electricity to show segmented black numerals floating on a silvery field. And an LCD model should last a long time on one set of batteries.

We estimated that the models we tested will calculate for more than 1,000 hours, or about three hours a day for a year, before they would need new batteries. In fact, the batteries might expire from normal aging before they run down from use.

From the design of many of these calculators, it's clear that the manufacturers don't expect you to change batteries frequently. Most of the calculators we tested had no battery compartment as such: To get at the battery, you had to unscrew the back of the calculator.

Button cell batteries. The typical battery used is the 1.5-volt button cell, which comes in an alkaline or a silver oxide version. Manufacturers usually recommend the appropriate size of each type.

■ Silver oxide batteries last longer but cost two or three times as much as alkaline batteries.

■ Our calculations showed that silver oxide batteries don't outlive the alkaline batteries long enough to repay their extra expense.

Solar cells. Calculators powered by solar cells are currently popular, often sold with the slogan "never needs batteries." But the advantage of powering your calculations with the sun dims. The button cell batteries commonly used in a basic calculator cost only about $2 and last for a year or two of heavy calculating. You may well lose the calculator or want a new one before you've used up even $4 or $6 worth of batteries.

Lithium batteries. A few of the calculators we tested used a new type of battery, the longer-lived lithium battery. The shelf-life of a lithium battery is about five years, so it may never need to be changed. If it did run out, however, a new lithium battery could be hard to find in a store. You'd have to get a replacement from the manufacturer.

Shopping for disposable diapers

Choosing the right disposable diapers for your baby is by no means a cut-and-dried matter.

Finding the right fit. There are two basic styles of disposable diapers: The "elastic leg"—usually available in three sizes—and the "prefolded" style—

usually available in six sizes or absorbencies. Brands in both styles did well in our tests.

Even though most brands are sized by weight range, weight doesn't tell everything. A child's build may be just as important a factor in diaper fit.

- Don't assume you'll pick the right size for your child merely by reading labels on diaper boxes.

- You may have to try more than one size of a given brand to find the best fit.

- If you decide to switch brands, you may have to start a new trial-and-error search for the proper size.

Shopping for price. If you use diapers, you usually use a lot of them. Ordinarily, you might hope to get a significant price break if you buy in quantity.

The big mail-order houses, which packaged 120 to 216 diapers per box when we bought them for our tests, didn't give us much of a price break. In retail stores, we bought the largest boxes or cases we could find, but our shoppers didn't ask for cheaper price quotes for quantity purchases.

You should *not* follow that example. Instead, when you buy the brand of diapers you've chosen, shop for price.

- Keep an eye out for sales or discounts.

- Also ask a store manager if you can get a break on the price if you buy disposable diapers by the case.

Cleaning down jackets

Cleaning down parkas and jackets is often a complicated procedure. It's a good idea not to clean them frequently. The insulation, especially if it's down, will probably never fluff up to quite the same degree and the shell will probably never be quite as resistant to water.

But even the most carefully worn parka will need cleaning eventually. Here are our recommendations.

■ Synthetic-filled garments are generally the easiest to clean. You can usually wash and dry them in a fairly conventional way. Some materials, such as Gore-Tex (a waterproofing product), *must* be washed: Dry cleaning can ruin them.

■ Manufacturers disagree about how to clean down jackets. Some say "dry-clean only"; some give detailed washing instructions, either by hand or by machine; and some give you the choice between laundering and dry cleaning. It's best to follow the label recommendations, for that leaves you a recourse if something goes wrong.

Dry cleaning. You'll find that dry cleaning is a lot easier than washing it yourself.

■ If you have a parka dry-cleaned, find out first whether the dry cleaner has had experience cleaning similar types of garments.

■ Be sure you air out a dry-cleaned jacket. The fill can harbor fumes from the dry-cleaning solvent.

Washing. The first time you wash a down-filled parka, you may think it's been ruined.

■ Washing a down-filled parka is like drowning it. Whether you're doing it by hand or in a machine, you have to hold it under water until it is saturated. When you do that, the down shrinks alarmingly into hard little lumps, in a mass of limp fabric.

■ Most manufacturers suggest tossing a sneaker into the dryer to help beat the down back to fluffiness. That can take several hours at low heat.

■ Washing many of the garments we looked at would be extremely difficult to do in a Laundromat, where you can't control the vigor of the wash cycle or the temperature of the dryer very well. If you don't have your own washer and dryer, you might want to think twice before buying a parka or jacket that has to be gently machine washed and dried at low heat.

What our tests showed. We dry-cleaned some of the jackets we bought, and some we washed ourselves, following the label recommendations.

■ The dry-cleaned jackets came back clean and fairly new-looking. The jackets we washed were clean but lost some of their crisp new look. Seams were slightly puckered and pocket flaps no longer lay quite flat.

Rules for hand laundering

Whether or not a garment maintains its shape when you wash it has more to do with water temperature and handling than with whether you use a specialty laundering product. (An ordinary dishwashing liquid does the job just fine—see below.)

■ Before laundering any garment, it's wise to examine the fabric-care label sewn into it. Even if a garment is washable, you should check to be sure it's colorfast before laundering it the first time. Choose a small section that's not likely to show and dip it in water to see if the dyes run.

■ Soak time is important. The directions on specialty laundering products usually call for soaking; some suggest three to five minutes. The less time a garment has to spend soaking, the better.

■ Use cool water. In our tests we used 70°F.

■ Most specialty laundering products advise against rubbing. Usually they advise you to gently squeeze suds through. You may be tempted to scrub a stubborn spot, but resist that temptation. Rubbing can damage delicate fibers. So can wringing or twisting.

Dishwashing liquids for hand laundry

To launder your fine washables, you'll do well to use ordinary dishwashing liquids, according to our chemists. Resist the pitch of *Woolite* and the other less heavily advertised specialty laundry products.

There's really nothing special about *Woolite,* our tests showed. The dishwashing liquids we tested cleaned just as well or better than the specialty products—and for much less money.

So we think price should be your guide in choosing a product for hand laundering.

Ivory Snow for hand laundering?

As part of a test project on specialty laundering products, our chemists wanted to see how *Ivory Snow* worked in cold-water hand laundering.

The results were very good. In fact, *Ivory Snow* did a noteworthy job of removing red wine from polyester. And the cost per wash was cheaper than for *Woolite* or any of the other specialty products we tested.

Ivory Snow is one of the few laundry products available today that's pure soap. (Detergents, which have taken over the laundry room, are generally more efficient than soaps in hard water and in cold water.)

Because there were no cold-water hand-wash instructions on the box of *Ivory Snow,* we contacted the manufacturer, who told us to use up to 4½ teaspoons in 2 quarts of water, and a four-minute soak. We followed the same test procedure we'd used for the other products, laundering the same stains out of the same fabrics.

One suggestion: If you were using *Ivory Snow* for hand laundering at home, you might want to dissolve the soap powder in warm water before adding it to the cold-water wash.

Heating pads

Used prudently, a heating pad in good condition may safely relieve superficial muscular aches and pains, treat certain skin ailments, and even comfort cold feet.

■ If you have an aching muscle now and then, you don't necessarily need a heating pad. Consider the old-fashioned hot-water bottle, which does not present the hazards of an electric heating pad.

■ If you do need a heating pad, however, you'll probably find that a standard-sized pad will do for most purposes. But we think you should consider instead the oversized models: They are more versatile.

■ If you often need specific relief for aches in the joints, limbs, shoulders, or neck, consider a wraparound model.

■ If you already own a heating pad, we suggest you check its inner cover and line cord closely—particularly where the cord joins the pad. If you find cracks or other damage, replace the pad.

■ When testing pads, we found that a pad will heat up faster at "high" than at "low." Those who want to relieve their aches as quickly as possible should take note. As soon as the pad comes to a comfortable temperature, it should be set to a lower heat.

■ Heed the label warnings about when and where a pad should *not* be used.

Choosing an insect repellent

All insect repellents with N,N-diethyl-meta-toluamide, known as "deet," are generally safe and effective. But some products may be more convenient to use than others.

If you're shopping for an insect repellent, keep two things in mind.

■ Don't expect any brand to be effective against *stinging* insects, such as bees, wasps, and hornets. Deet works against a broad range of *biting* insects—mosquitoes, chiggers, ticks, fleas, and various biting flies.

■ Don't expect any insect repellent, no matter how effective, to survive a walk in the rain, sweating, or swimming. If you expect to go for frequent swims, don't use a high-priced product between swims. It would be a waste of money.

Concentration. For regular use, you could save a bit of money—and the bother of repeat applications—by choosing one of the products with a high concentration of deet. (Look for N,N-diethyl-meta-toluamide on the label—not deet.) The more concentrated the product, the more lasting the protection. This cuts down on the need for frequent applications.

Keep in mind, however, that a high concentration of deet would make you more aware that the insect repellent you're using is somewhat oily.

Packaging. Insect repellents are available in a wide variety of packaging.

■ Small plastic squeeze bottles and sticks are convenient to carry. Some squeeze products have been formulated into creamy lotions that can go on thinly and evenly and disappear like hand lotion when rubbed in well enough.

■ Spray containers are quick and easy to use, especially if you have to coat clothing to protect against insects that can penetrate through fabric to your skin. But the containers are bulky, and youngsters might spray into the eyes or onto sensitive skin.

■ A stick takes a bit of persistence to apply over large areas. Its slightly waxy feel shouldn't prove objectionable.

■ Towelettes make application a cinch, but each covers an area that's only about the size of an adult's face and arms. With ten towelettes to a package, you could use up a package pretty quickly. Towelettes could be worth it, though, for application to wriggling children.

Insect repellents: A safety caution

The major active ingredient in many leading insect repellents—N,N-diethyl-meta-toluamide, known as "deet"—has been widely used since the 1950s. It has been tested by many laboratories, declared effective and safe for general use by the federal government, and applied by millions of people without a hint of toxic reaction.

But a general caution is in order about deet. Don't get any type of repellent into your eyes or mouth, or on skin area with a cut or rash. Take particular care when using a spray product.

Ironing strategies

If you wear natural fabrics such as silk, linen, and cotton, chances are your clothes require the attention of someone skilled in the fine art of ironing. Even so-called "easy-care" fabrics can be improved by an occasional touch-up with an iron, often at fairly low temperatures. A good iron should offer a wide range of temperatures to meet all needs.

- Silks, woolens, and some synthetics such as acetate call for gentle handling and moderate temperatures.

- Linens and cottons call for a heavier hand and higher temperatures.

- Because most irons heat up to their maximum temperature in one to two minutes, but take a lot longer to cool down, it makes sense to iron permanent-press shirts, for example, before you do heavy cotton jeans.

Extra steam and spray. We think that the best iron is one with both extra steam and spray. You'll probably use the extra-steam function more often than the spray. But spray is handy for occasional stubborn wrinkles. Using these features requires a little practice, however.

- Irons with extra steam, properly used, can produce a billowy discharge from their steam vents. But don't pump rapid-fire on an iron's extra-steam button. Water droplets may start to appear along with the steam. That sort of uneven discharge could lead to water-spotting.

- Spray models usually have a little nozzle up front and a spray button on the top of the handle. The spray feature is, in our judgment, less useful than extra steam. It's all right for spot treatment, but it doesn't eliminate the need to predampen really hard-to-iron fabrics.

Scorching: What causes it?

If you've been scorching your cottons when you iron, the fault could lie with the iron rather than with your technique. Even though your iron is set at the "cotton" mark, it may be too hot. If you see any signs of scorching, try lowering the iron's temperature a bit. But wait before you resume ironing. Give the soleplate a chance to cool down.

The brand of starch you use could also cause scorching. Some starches are more resistant to scorching than others, so if the problem persists, switch to another product.

In very simple terms, this is what happens when you scorch a starched fabric. Starch is a carbohydrate—a compound of carbon, hydrogen, and oxygen. When you heat starch, it cooks, and its characteristics change. If you heat it too much, you drive out some of the hydrogen and oxygen as water, and you are left with a carbonized residue—scorch.

Removing scorch

Scorch is one of the problems you may have to cope with in ironing cotton with starch. But you may be able to remove scorch marks by using the following procedure.

- Soak the scorched area in a mixture of a cup of white vinegar to a quart of water.
- Let the item soak for a few minutes.
- Rinse it in clear water, then launder it.

Carry-on luggage

If you're tired of waiting around an airport for your luggage to be dumped onto the carousel in the baggage-claim area, you'll want to travel light—which means carrying your own baggage on to the plane.

■ One limit to what you can carry on is what you can carry. Hence the popularity of cases and bags with shoulder straps.

■ Practically anything that fits under an airplane seat qualifies as a carry-on bag. On some planes, you can put luggage into the overhead bins.

■ Soft and squishable bags have a clear advantage over harder suitcases when you're trying to shove your bag under the seat in front of you (or, on some airplanes, under the seat you're sitting in). A soft case that normally measures 8×15×21 inches can be punched and pummeled to fit in a 7-inch-high space. Beware of overstuffing soft cases, however. Crammed full, they can be as intractable as a hard-sided case and far too fat to fit under a seat.

■ If there's room in the airplane's storage compartments, you can count on hanging up a garment bag. Garment bags are usually accommodated on a first-come, first-served basis. When a plane's storage compartments are filled, garment bags sometimes end up stuffed into overhead bins.

Choosing and using bed sheets

When we tested representative brands of sheets and pillowcases—including polyester/cotton blends, all-cottons, and satins—we found that the most significant difference was price.

To help you get the best sheets for your money, here are some suggestions about shopping for sheets—as well as some ideas about caring for them to make them last.

■ Within the blends, we found in general that overall strength was related to polyester content: The more polyester, the stronger the sheet.

■ Our tests indicated that muslin sheets allow better air circulation than percale because of muslin's looser weave. Muslin bedding is usually slightly cheaper than percale. (For people with a sensitive touch, muslin may not feel as soft and smooth as percale.)

■ Watch for white sales. They're held in January and July or August when stores clear their stockrooms to make way for new lines. There are sales at other times of the year, but they're generally limited to just a couple of patterns or colors, or to irregulars.

■ Irregulars can be a very good buy if the flaw is cosmetic rather than functional. Inspect irregulars carefully before using them. An off-color, an oil stain, or a few thick threads won't affect a sheet's durability. Frayed edges, slight tears, or missing threads will.

■ Reverse a sheet—top to bottom or inside out if that won't affect the color or pattern—each time you put it on the bed. That distributes wear.

■ If you feel you must use bleach on white sheets, do so sparingly, and don't use it every time you wash the sheets.

■ Wash dark sheets separately, at least for the first few times. The color tends to run.

■ Even no-iron sheets can wrinkle if not properly dried. As with any no-iron product you buy, too high a temperature, too much drying time, or an overcrowded dryer can cause wrinkles. Letting sheets sit in the dryer after they've stopped tumbling will set wrinkles, too.

Buying toilet soap

Soap is a personal-care product, and personal preference usually determines which soap people buy. All soaps clean, so soap makers can hardly expect you to buy one brand over another because it will clean better—especially if the one brand is more expensive than the other.

Resist those endless commercials and advertisements for soaps. Our tests showed that all soaps clean about equally well. We recommend that you ignore the multitude of claims for various soaps and buy soap by price alone.

■ Makers of antiseptic soaps claim their products help to check the action or growth of certain microorganisms on the skin's surface, and so aid in slowing down the development of odor. But plain old soap used regularly should be effective, too.

■ Then there's pH. Soap and cosmetics ads warn you that using an alkaline high-pH soap destroys the skin's natural "acid mantle." It sounds ominous. In fact, for most people, pH doesn't matter. Skin returns to its normal acid level fairly quickly after washing.

■ Fragrance is sometimes a selling feature. In the soaps we tested, scent varied from medicinal to heavily perfumed. The fragrance was noticeable while washing and, discreetly, on the hands afterwards. If a scent with staying-power is important to you, don't rely on soap. Use perfume or after-shave lotion.

Using spray starch

Ironing cotton to perfection may require using starch. For most people these days, that means an aerosol spray starch. Here's what to expect from using spray starch.

Lubrication. In addition to providing crispness, a spray starch makes ironing easier. It typically provides some lubrication so that the iron slides more easily over the fabric.

The lubricant also helps prevent the iron from sticking to the starch. Sticking can cause the fabric to bunch up under the iron.

Starch buildup. Starch buildup on the iron is a nuisance. Built-up starch on the iron's soleplate gets cooked brown, then rubs off on the fabric, leaving dirty-looking marks. (If you're about to replace your iron, consider one with a nonstick soleplate, which should prove less prone to starch buildup and easier to clean than a plain aluminum soleplate.)

You can minimize starch buildup on the iron by using a spray starch sensibly.

■ When you're applying a lot of starch for a lot of stiffness, spray and iron several times.

■ Don't soak the fabric with spray and then try to cook the starch in. You're likely to build up a scorchable film on the iron's soleplate.

■ Wipe any film off with a damp cloth as soon as you notice it. But take care first to let the iron's heat dwindle down to warm.

Flaking. Flaking is a minor problem that sometimes crops up with spray starches. You can keep flaking to a minimum by taking these precautions.

■ Spray lightly, iron, then spray again for more stiffness.

■ If you see flakes, brush them off before continuing to iron. Don't try to iron the flakes away or blast them out with steam. There's a good chance you'll just make them cling more tightly.

■ Remember to spray-starch dark materials on the reverse side, as some manufacturers recommend. Starching on the reverse side should not only prevent flaking from showing, it will also reduce any chance of the starch discoloring the fabric.

Delivery pattern and rate. Starches vary considerably in their delivery rate—how fast the spray comes out of the can—and in the width of the spray pattern. You may have to experiment with several brands to find one that works best for you.

■ A narrow spray pattern is easier to direct to small areas, while a wide pattern makes it easier to cover a large area uniformly.

■ If you use a spray starch primarily for spot-starching small areas of a garment—just the collar and cuffs of a shirt, for instance—you may find it makes sense to use a spray with a low delivery rate. It would be easier to aim and control.

■ If you starch the whole shirt, however, a product with a high delivery rate would help you finish the job more quickly.

■ Because aerosol products spray in a typical cone-shape, you can to some extent adjust the width of the pattern by moving the can closer to or farther from the fabric.

Nozzle. If a nozzle becomes partially blocked, the spray pattern can be distorted. It's a good idea to remove and rinse out the spray nozzle in water after use.

Some products come with a "tilt" nozzle—the kind that operates with a diagonal, rather than a straight-down pressure. In our tests we found the tilt-type nozzle a bit easier on the finger than the other type.

Safety. The propellants in these products are all ignitable. So avoid using an aerosol starch near an open flame (whether the label says so or not). Don't set up the ironing board near a gas stove, for instance.

Starch: The cost of aerosol vs liquid and dry

An aerosol spray starch is expensive but convenient, when compared with old-fashioned liquid or dry starch.

If you do just a few cotton shirts or blouses a week—or if you do only the trim of the garments—then the convenience of spray starch is probably what you want, and hang the extra price.

If you do lots of cotton shirts a week—whole shirts, not just trim—a nonaerosol starch will be a lot cheaper than even the cheapest spray starches. But it's no picnic to use.

The cost of aerosol. In our tests of spray starch, we developed a rule of thumb to help you judge how stiff a price you pay for an aerosol product.

■ We used ⅝ ounce of starch per square foot of fabric. (The collar, cuffs, and placket of a medium-sized man's shirt equal about 1 square foot of fabric.) That amount of starch made cotton shirting feel smooth and crisp—moderately stiff, but not crunchy or woodlike. Using the same level of starch for the whole shirt, about 8 square feet of fabric, took 5 ounces of starch.

■ To find out how much it would cost to do the trim of a medium-sized shirt with a particular product, multiply the cost per ounce by five-eighths. Multiply by five to get the cost for the whole shirt. An inexpensive spray starch would do the whole shirt for about 17 cents, we found, while a more expensive starch came to 30 cents for a whole shirt.

■ It's possible to use our figures to estimate how many medium-sized shirts a can of starch will do. At ⅝ ounce per square foot and 1 square foot per shirt—trim only—a 20-ounce can would treat thirty-two shirts. But at the same rate, if you're starching whole shirts, a 20-ounce can would do only four shirts.

The cost of liquid or dry starch. Our calculations show clearly that you will save money with old-fashioned liquid starch, or with dry starch that mixes with water—if you do a lot of starching.

At a level of stiffness comparable to what we used in figuring costs with aerosols, a liquid starch could treat one whole medium-sized shirt for 4 cents. A dry starch could do sixteen shirts for 4 cents.

Although the old-fashioned products are much cheaper to use than aerosols, you pay a price in much less convenience. With the nonaerosol products, the typical procedure is as follows: You have to dilute or mix the starch, dip the fabric in it, dry it, sprinkle it with water, wrap it up, and perhaps let it sit for an hour or two before you iron.

If you starch just a few shirts, using a nonaerosol starch would probably seem like too much work. We agree. For small jobs, we think an aerosol's convenience far outweighs any money you might save with a liquid, especially since you might end up throwing away some of the liquid-starch mixture. (You have to make up enough to immerse the fabric being treated, so there's bound to be some left over.)

Stretching spray starch

Another approach to starching shirts was suggested by a reader of Consumer Reports. This technique would cut the cost of starch.

The reader uses a regular liquid starch in a pump-spray bottle, diluting it with water for easy spraying. To prevent clogging the sprayer, the reader rinses out the sprayer and stores the starch in a separate bottle between uses.

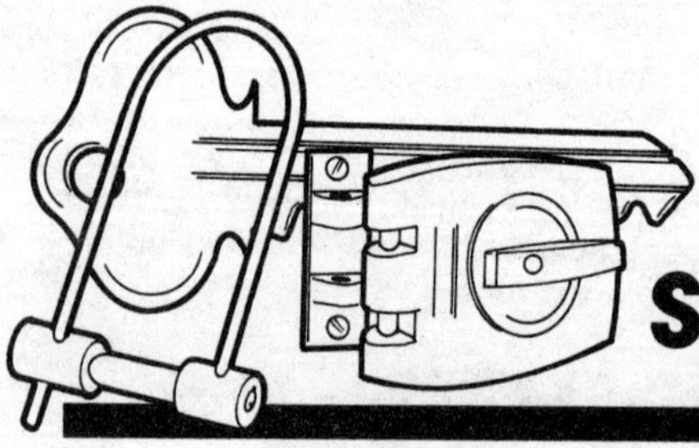

Security

Automobile antitheft devices

Any antitheft device is better than none at all. A locked car isn't much of a challenge for a determined thief. With readily available tools and hardware, an expert can unlock a car door, pull out the ignition/steering-column lock, insert a substitute lock, and start the engine—all in a few minutes.

Unfortunately, we know of no device on the market that can stop a determined and expert car thief. But fortunately, many thieves are amateurs who could be thwarted by an antitheft device. And given a choice, some thieves will pass up a protected car.

To improve security, consider installing two types of antitheft device. A system interrupter plus an alarm would probably discourage most thieves. (Antitheft devices are available from sources such as auto-parts stores, locksmiths, car dealers, and mail-order houses.)

System interrupters, as a class, provide the best antitheft protection, in our judgment.

- These devices disable the ignition, the fuel supply, or some other vital automotive system to prevent the car from being driven away.
- A thief must first guess that the car won't start or run because of an antitheft device, not a mechanical malfunction.
- Then the thief must spend time in looking for a hidden switch or in tracking wiring under the hood to disable the device.
- The hope is that the thief, feeling conspicuous, will abandon the car.

Alarms rely on a thief's unwillingness to attract attention. The presumption is that a loud siren will make the thief panic and run.

- However, noise may not be much of a deterrent in an isolated area.
- Even on a busy street, a brazen thief might simply look for a way to silence the alarm in the hope that passersby won't risk a confrontation.

In some states: A break on insurance

If you have an antitheft device on your car and you live in Illinois, Massachusetts, or New York, check with your insurance agent. These three states permit insurance companies to offer small discounts on insurance premiums to people who install certain types of antitheft devices on their car.

To qualify, the auto must also have or be fitted with an inside release for the hood lock so the thief can't open the hood without breaking into the car.

Bicycle locks

It's a shame that cyclists who've paid hundreds of dollars for a lightweight bicycle must tack on to it several pounds of deadweight to protect their investment. But that seems to be the way of the cycling world—at least for those who want to thwart the bicycle thief.

In large urban areas, where bolt cutters are by far the thief's standard tool, the first choice among bicycle locks would be one of the oversized shackle locks.

These locks do exact some penalties, however. They're relatively expensive, and their 2 to 3 pounds might be enough weight to take some of the edge off cycling performance. The oversized shackles won't fit around posts more than 3 or 4 inches wide. Fortunately, that's seldom a drawback in the city, where signposts and parking-meter posts abound. In fact, the shackle locks are the only type suitable for hitching up to parking meters, because their shackles won't pass over the meter head.

Outside bolt-cutter country, you might be able to protect your bike with a lighter less expensive lock. A lightweight cable set could offer fairly good security—unless a thief happens along with the proper tools.

Preventing bike theft

Here are a few simple rules to follow that can lessen the chance of having your bicycle stolen.

■ If you must leave your bike unattended, try to park it in a well-trafficked public area. Secure it to a tree, streetlight, signpost, or other fixed object, making sure that the chain, cable, or shackle can't be lifted over the fixture.

■ Fit both wheels and the frame within the locking device. To do that, you'll probably need a lockset with at least 4 feet of chain or cable. If you're using an oversized shackle lock to secure a bicycle with quick-release wheels, you'd be well advised to remove the front wheel and set it within the shackle.

■ If you're using a chain or cable, wrap it so there's no extra slack, and place the lock as high off the pavement as you can. That will make it hard for a thief to use the pavement as a solid base for physical assaults.

■ Record your bicycle's serial number. That may aid the police in its recovery. And if your community has a bicycle registration program, by all means take advantage of it.

Escape ladders: An essential feature

Many of the escape ladders on the market, in our judgment, don't do enough to reduce the fright or the danger of escaping from the second or third floor of a burning house.

When shopping for an escape ladder, test the footing. Don't be satisfied with a ladder that is too difficult to use. Some types are little more than glorified rope ladders, with metal rungs attached to a pair of chains.

When we tested escape ladders, we found it extremely hard to get a toehold on some because the ladders tended to swing flush against the wall of the house. "Standoffs"—horizontal extensions to hold the rungs away from the wall—would have solved the toehold problem and made the ladders easier to use. But most brands did not provide for enough rungs with standoffs.

Our recommendation: Look for an escape ladder with standoffs at least on every second rung through the middle section of the ladder. Standoffs should not be placed so far apart that they fail to provide a secure footing. Best of all would be a ladder with standoffs at *every* rung. We think it's worth the extra storage space such a ladder would require.

Plan on some practice fire drills to become accustomed to deploying the ladder. It may take some getting used to, so don't wait for a real emergency when every minute counts.

A portable security device

A reader told Consumer Reports that our tests of security devices failed to mention an offbeat system the reader has used successfully for a number of years. Here's the reader's report on home-use testing of that portable security device.

"It has five sensing devices, all controlled by a central microcomputer. The primary sensor is a very sensitive audio detector that ignores common traffic noises and distant sirens, yet goes off at the sound of footsteps, breaking and entering, or even strange voices. The secondary sensor is an optical system that quickly trains and focuses on moving objects. If the optical system detects strange people or animals, the alarm system will sound. The third system is an extremely sensitive olfactory device that can differentiate between 'friendly' and 'intruder' odors.

"The alarm mechanism is loud and persistent, but it can easily be silenced by a preprogrammed, sharply spoken oral command. The entire system is relatively inexpensive and requires virtually no installation.

"The owner doesn't need to turn it off when returning to an empty house, but should reward its wagging tail with a pat on the head."

Home burglar alarms

Police believe that many burglars are amateurs—often youngsters, who would flee if an alarm sounded or light came on. Thus, you could reduce the risk of such a burglary by installing a do-it-yourself home burglar alarm system.

Although these systems might scare off the beginner burglar, they wouldn't be much challenge to seasoned thieves who plan their jobs carefully. A sophisticated security system installed by professionals could cost a couple of thousand dollars or more—as much as ten times the cost of a do-it-yourself system. But it might be a wise investment for people with unusually valuable things to protect.

There is no ideal system that we can recommend for everyone. Your lifestyle and the size and type of your home will have a big influence on the type of system desired. So will the cost of the system and the skills and effort needed for proper installation.

The systems fall into two major categories: perimeter protectors and motion detectors. Each type has its advantages and drawbacks.

■ Perimeter protectors detect intruders in the act of entering. Simply opening a window or an outside door sets off the alarm.

■ Motion detectors generally don't operate until an intruder is in the home. They sound an alarm only after they detect movement within the area they're protecting.

Perimeter system. We think that a perimeter burglar alarm system would provide good protection. If you install such a system yourself, it can cost less than $1,000. Even with professional installation, you might get by for about $1,500.

Perimeter systems can provide protection even when you're home, without fear of constantly tripping the alarm. Unlike motion detectors, perimeter systems don't restrict the movement of people or pets in the house. They seem to produce fewer nuisance alarms than motion detectors, and they are easier to live with.

■ But the perimeter systems we tested wouldn't sound an alarm for a burglar who climbs in through a broken window instead of raising the sash.

■ And installation can be difficult because a number of the systems require extensive wiring. This can be a problem in an apartment building if the landlord objects to holes in the walls and woodwork. (The exposed wires can also be rather unattractive.)

■ Some so-called wireless perimeter systems are less conspicuous and easier to install, but even they require some wiring if you want to keep the cost reasonable.

Motion detector systems. Most of the motion detectors we tested are small self-contained boxes.

■ Because many don't have to be wired, they're easy to set up. Some need only to be plugged in.

■ Many are also easy to move around, so you can use them in different parts of the house at different times—and even take them with you when you travel.

■ But if you use them while you're home, they inhibit your movements. They're also more likely to produce nuisance alarms, as our testing showed. Unless it's carefully aimed, a motion detector can pick up anything that moves—a pet, a curtain rustled by a breeze, even an air current from a heating or air conditioning vent.

For greater protection (and, of course, at greater cost), you can use both types of systems. That way, even if intruders manage to get past the perimeter system and into your home, they can be spotted by the motion detector.

Protecting your valuables

A standard homeowners policy usually provides personal property coverage adequate to cover most things people own. But some people are collectors—of art, coins, stamps, guns, books. Others are heirs—to jewelry, silverware, antiques. Still others are hobbyists with costly paraphernalia—cameras or musical instruments, for example.

Here are some steps you can take to protect your valuables.

■ Inventory your possessions. Even if you have no unusually valuable possessions, an inventory will back up any claim you might have to make under your standard homeowners policy.

■ If you have among your possessions several possibly valuable items, you'll need to take some additional steps. Check your insurance policy for its limitations. Then talk with your broker about the possibility (or necessity) of having some of your valuables appraised and insured separately under a floater policy or an endorsement to your homeowners policy. To obtain special coverage for special things, you have to be able to prove you own them and prove their value.

Proving ownership takes a little effort on your part but is not difficult.

■A photographic inventory is one of the easiest ways to document ownership. You should take pictures in every room—wall to wall and floor to ceiling. Also, take close-ups of special items.

■Sales receipts can serve as proof of ownership, too. In a reasonably stable market, a bill-of-sale not more than three years old is usually an adequate reflection of an item's current value. But in a volatile market such as precious metals, a three-year-old receipt may be totally inadequate, and you'll almost certainly need an appraisal.

■ Estate inventories can also serve as proof of ownership. If you've inherited things, you probably received copies of the estate appraisals. Such appraisals, usually done for tax purposes, are very conservative. The prices reflect the amounts the items would bring in a forced-sale situation, not the cost of replacing them.

Proving value may require the services of an outside expert, an appraiser.

■Professional appraisers will charge a fee for their services. If you have valuables, however, such things are worth protecting properly, and the appraiser's fee should be considered part of the cost of that protection.

■Many people rely on a friend's recommendation when they're looking for a doctor, dentist, or lawyer. You will often be able to find an appraiser that way, too.

■ The world of appraisers is generally divided between specialists—in jewelry, stamps, or paintings, for example—and generalists who are able to deal with almost all categories of valuables. Decide whether you need a specialist or a generalist. Then interview several in the category you select in order to find the appraiser best suited to your needs.

■ If a substantial sum or number of pieces is involved, ask the appraiser for references and check them. Call your insurance agency, too, and let your agent know what appraiser you're considering, to find out if there is any objection.

■ It will almost always be less expensive to take your valuables to an appraiser than to have one come to your home. If you have many items, however, or if your items are difficult to transport, it would be better to have an appraiser come to you. Most generalists and some specialists are ready to do that.

■ Be sure to tell the appraiser that you want the valuation for insurance purposes. Make it clear that the item is not for sale. Appraisers who are also dealers may be looking for merchandise, and the temptation to set up a possible bargain for themselves—by appraising at a low value—could be too much for some dealers to resist.

■ Appraisals are usually written in duplicate or triplicate. One copy is for you, and one is for the insurance company. The appraiser may keep the third copy. Keep your copies of appraisals, as well as sales receipts, photos, and other records away from your house, preferably in a bank's safe-deposit box.

Steps to safeguarding your luggage

The easiest way to avoid arriving at your destination without your luggage is to use carry-on luggage. But if you do have to check a bag when you fly, here are some suggestions to help you safeguard your luggage.

Identification tags. It's extremely important to put your name and address on the outside of the bag. We would recommend adding a phone number where you can be reached at your destination.

■ Keep in mind, however, that the outside label will be visible to a lot of people, and the information could be useful to burglars. As a precaution, you might consider using your office address and phone number—or a friend's—instead of your home address and phone number.

■ Because an exterior label may be mutilated or lost, it's a good idea to put identification on the inside, too. On the inside, record not only your name, home address, and phone number but also a detailed itinerary.

Distinctive markings. Because so many bags look alike, it's easy to pick up the wrong one. You can help avoid that problem by marking your luggage with colored stickers or tape—anything that will make your bags look a little different.

Sturdy baggage. If you pack your things in a shopping bag with a rope around it, you're asking for trouble. Some airlines will put a piece of luggage in a carton if it seems vulnerable, but don't count on it. Use luggage that will withstand rough handling.

Overpacking. Don't pack too much. If you stuff your bag, it may pop open or burst its seams. But don't pack so loosely that objects will bounce around inside.

What not to pack. Don't pack anything you would consider a necessity—eyeglasses, medicines, passports, business papers, and so on. Don't pack anything fragile or valuable. *Never* pack jewelry.

Inventory. Just in case your bag does get lost, you should have a reasonably complete list of what's in it. And carry the list with you, not in the bag.

Locks. Be sure to lock your bag before you check it. That won't stop a professional thief, but it may discourage an amateur. And at least it may keep your bag from popping open.

■ Combination locks are better than key locks. Generally for any particular line of key-locked luggage made by a manufacturer, one key fits all the bags the manufacturer produces.

■ If your bag has a combination lock, don't use obvious combinations such as 000 or 111.

Check in early. If you plan to check your bags, allow plenty of time for processing. If the airline says to check in half an hour before departure time, do so.

■ If you arrive at the airport just before boarding time, you're simply increasing the odds that your baggage will be left behind.

■ Some airlines put "Late check-in" tags on bags that are checked in less than fifteen minutes before the scheduled departure (the margins vary from airport to airport). The passenger may be asked to sign the ticket, acknowledging that the bag may be sent on a later flight.

Destination tags. When you check your bag in, it will be tagged with a three-letter destination code. Of course, you should remove all old destination tags before you check in. Some of the codes are easy to decipher and some aren't. ATL means Atlanta, for example, but you'd never guess that MSY means New Orleans.

■ Make sure the baggage handler puts the right tag on your bag. If you don't know the destination code, ask the handler to confirm it.

■ You can examine the tag yourself: The full name of the destination is usually printed in small type.

Claiming your baggage. When you arrive at your destination, go directly to the baggage claim area to wait for your luggage. If you go off on an errand first, the bags may be left unattended. That's never a good idea.

Insurance. Some insurance companies may offer special coverage for baggage losses. However, airlines' excess-valuation coverage is likely to be cheaper.

■ Baggage losses may be covered by your homeowners policy. (Check coverage C in the policy form. It deals with personal property.)

■ Items detailed in floater policies may also be covered.

■ You can't collect from the airline *and* your insurance company. Because the airline has responsibility for your luggage, file your claim with the airline first.

When luggage is lost or damaged

As you wait in the baggage claim area, there's always a moment of terminal anxiety. Sometimes it's justified: Your bag never does show up—or it's damaged. Here are some suggestions about what to do then.

■ Notify the airline immediately whenever there's a problem with your luggage. If it's a lost bag, the airline may be able to make a quick check of the plane before it leaves the airport. If it's a matter of damage, the extent can be verified on the spot. Examine the contents right away if the lock is broken or if the sides of the bag have been slit.

■ Be sure to fill out a report on the damage or loss before you leave the airport. The appropriate office for reporting a baggage problem is usually located near the baggage claim area. Keep a copy and note the name of the employee you talked with. If your bag is lost, keep your claim check to prove you checked a bag in.

■ It may take months for the airline to compensate you for lost or damaged luggage. If you think you're not being treated fairly, send a letter of complaint by registered mail.

■ Direct your letter to the consumer affairs department of the airline. You can find out the address by calling the airline's local office. Your letter should be brief and typewritten. Say what happened and what you want the company to do about it. If you've been mistreated by a particular employee, mention him or her by name.

■ If you're asking for payment, attach any receipts or other evidence to back up your claim—copies only, never the originals. If you've received payment and you think it's not enough, don't cash the check. Instead, explain why you think the payment is inadequate.

Using life jackets

If you're an experienced able-bodied swimmer, you may scoff at putting on a life jacket while out on a boat. U.S. Coast Guard statistics, however, show that most drownings associated with recreational boating occur when life jackets are stowed rather than worn.

Although the Coast Guard requires all recreational boats longer than 16 feet to carry life jackets for everyone on board, it doesn't require them to be worn. And too often, they aren't worn.

Yet even when life jackets are worn, you may not be as well protected as you think. Tests by Consumer Reports engineers have shown that many models of jackets have a tendency to turn a wearer who has assumed a vertical slightly backward position in the water to a face-down position. One of the few models that proved effective in our tests had most of its buoyant material up front. That kept our testers nearly vertical or face up when they "fell" overboard.

Based on our tests of life jackets suitable for experienced swimmers out on a boat, we urge boat owners to shop as diligently as possible for jackets that are effective for emergency use and comfortable for regular wear.

Safe use. Don't assume that every life jacket manufactured is going to be effective. Buy one only with the understanding that you can test it to make sure that a conscious person who falls overboard and who has moved to a vertical slightly backward position in the water is not turned face down. The life jacket is supposed to let the wearer maintain that vertical position without effort, and without any tendency to turn the wearer face down.

If the life jacket fails your test, you should insist that you be allowed to return it for another model, again subject to use test.

Comfort. People go out on the water for pleasure and sport. They want to feel the sun and the wind and the spray. If they're crewing a sailboat, they need the freedom to move about quickly.

A life jacket can't be too restrictive—or it won't be worn. A vest type was the most comfortable for the experienced swimmers who participated in our test project. When it came to donning the vests or adjusting them in the water, our swimmers found the models with a belt in the front were by far the easiest to adjust. Vests with drawstrings at the sides were the hardest to manipulate while treading water.

Discarding old smoke detectors

Ionization detectors contain a very small amount of radioactive material. A Consumer Reports reader asked us what precautions should be taken in discarding one of the devices.

Our reply assured the reader there was no need to be concerned. We said that older types of ionization smoke detectors, sold several years ago, carried detailed disposal instructions. But the Nuclear Regulatory Commission says that special precautions are no longer necessary. It's safe to dispose of old smoke detectors with your regular trash.

Smoke detectors: The two types

In a home fire, an advance warning of minutes or even seconds can spell the difference between entrapment and escape. Any smoke detector is better than none, of course. But to get the most effective system for your home, you should consider which type of smoke detector to install.

Two kinds of detector are commonly sold for homes: ionization and photoelectric. Each type has its strengths and weaknesses.

Ionization detectors use a minute amount of radioactive material to make the air between two interior electrodes conduct a small electric current. Smoke particles that enter the detector reduce the flow of current. Electronic circuitry then sets off an alarm.

That design lets the typical ionization detector respond more rapidly to particles from a fast flaming fire than photoelectrics do.

Photoelectric detectors beam light into a chamber that contains a light-sensitive photocell. The cell "sees" the light only when smoke enters the chamber and scatters the beam. When enough light reaches the cell, an alarm goes off.

That arrangement is particularly well suited to picking up the large-particle smoke of smoldering fires, although with fires of that type warnings are rather slow—a matter of minutes, not of seconds.

There's general agreement that slow smoldering fires—the sort typically caused by a cigarette dropped on bedding or upholstered furniture—are the most common type of home fire and the most common cause of fire deaths and injury in the home.

Which is best? Our recommendations can be summarized as follows.

■ A photoelectric model represents the protection of choice against the most common fire risk in the home—slow smoldering fires started in bedding or upholstery. But a good ionization model is likely to give you an extra twenty to thirty seconds notice of a potentially deadly fast fire.

■ It would be nice to be able to predict whether a given household fire will be fast- or slow-burning. Failing clairvoyance, we think it's safest to install a system consisting of at least one photoelectric and one ionization model.

■ Because ionization models are easier to find than photoelectrics and because they're cheaper, many people choose to install just an ionization model. We think that would be a mistake. The photoelectric's relatively speedy response to smoldering fires makes one a must in any home installation. (See below for advice on how to match a system to the layout of your home.)

Placement of smoke detectors

Here's how we suggest you plan the installation of a basic two-detector system in your home.

■ Place an *ionization* detector in the hallway just outside your bedroom door. It then will be most readily heard during sleeping hours, should it ever respond to the racing smoke of a fast fire.

■ The second detector should be a *photoelectric* model. In a two-level house, put it downstairs in the general living area, where it will be positioned to detect smoke from smoldering upholstery or rugs. The best mounting would be near a stairway to the sleeping area, but not in a kitchen. In a one-level home, the second detector can be put some distance away from the bedrooms and toward the living quarters—down the hall from the bedrooms, say.

■ The detectors, photoelectric or ionization, can be mounted on a ceiling or a wall. Ideally, the detectors should be mounted in the middle of a ceiling. Less than ideally, they should be no closer than 6 inches to a corner. Wall-mounted units should be between 6 and 12 inches from the ceiling.

■ To extend your protection, you might want to locate still another detector in the basement. Either type of detector can be used, but we think a photoelectric design is the better choice. Locate the unit at some distance from your furnace.

■ An ideal installation would have a photoelectric and an ionization detector at each level of a house. Smokers should put an extra photoelectric *in* the bedroom.

Keep your bedroom door open. The instructions with most of the detectors we tested advised you to sleep with your bedroom door closed. That's debatable advice.

■ Although the closed door would slow the progress of hot gases and smoke into the bedroom, it would also mute the alarm, perhaps costing sleepers precious seconds of escape time before it woke them.

■ With the door open, the detector will respond more quickly to a fire that starts in the bedroom itself, and alert other house occupants faster.

Homemade window locks

When we tested commercial window locks, we concluded that you'd be better off making your own.

We're not the first to have noted the inadequacies of window locks on the market. Do-it-yourself experts have been hot on the trail of other means to make residential windows more secure. One of the most promising ideas we came across suggests drilling holes through the sash where they overlap and inserting nails from the inside to pin the sash together. To open the window, you merely slide out the nails. If you want to keep the window slightly open for ventilation but still secure, you can drill two sets of nail holes, one above the other, and reset the nails with the window slightly open.

The theory sounds good. An upward force on the lower sash should result in a shear stress (sort of a slicing effect) on the pinning nails, rather than a raw tearing stress on the screws implanted in the wood. Nails should be difficult to shear, and they should hold, provided they're not given room to bend first.

But our initial efforts to put theory into practice were disappointing. Although we tried using thicker and thicker nails, up to nominal ¼-inch diameter, they all bent easily when we pried the window. Apparently, the nails were too soft to resist the leverage, once we had worked some crush space in the wood around them. Then we tried hardened masonry nails. They bent too, though more reluctantly.

Finally, we decided to substitute ¼-inch-diameter cap screws for the nails. *Voilà.* The cap screws not only held firm under the mild jimmying we had been practicing, they stood up to assaults with a larger crowbar so well, we judged that only pure obstinacy would make a burglar persist.

■ One more bright idea followed before we had fully prepared our recommendations for a home-built window-security system, illustrated on the facing page. Instead of using cap screws, we suggest using 5/16-inch-diameter eyebolts, one on each side of the window. The "eyes" provide convenient handles for inserting and extracting the bolts from their holes.

■ As the illustration shows, the holes should be drilled through the inside sash and three-quarters of the way through the outside sash at a slight downward angle. The bolts should fit loosely enough in their holes so that they're easy to insert and remove.

■ Note that the same plan can be adapted to hold good for horizontal sliding windows simply by working from the same illustration—but flipped on its side.

Our recommended home-built window-security system

(Directions for using the illustration below appear on the facing page.)

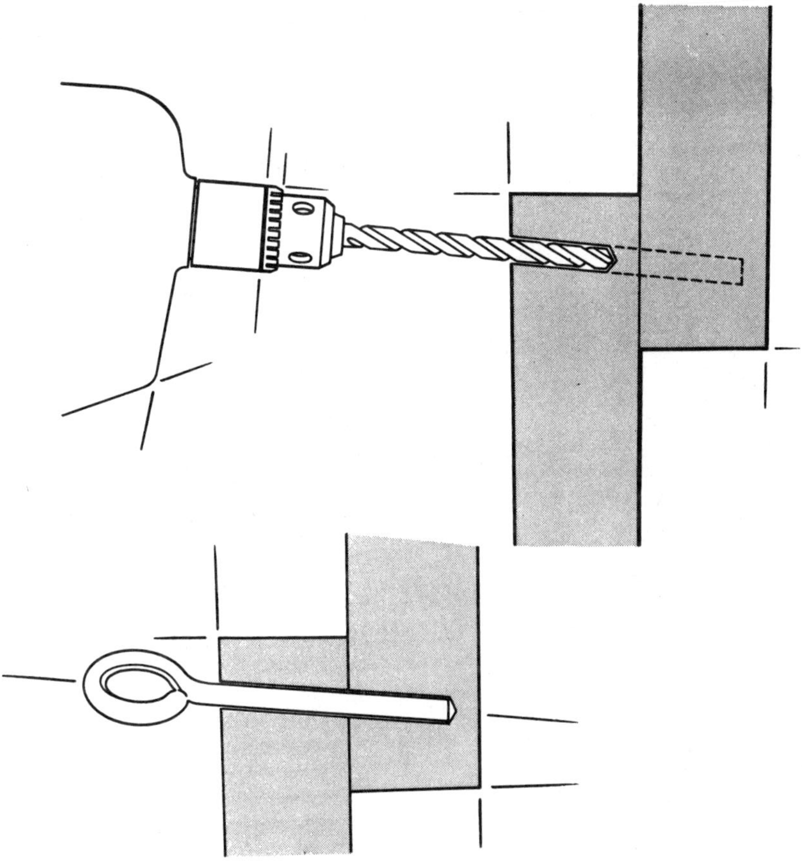

Index

A

B

C

D

G

H

I

J

K

L

M

N

O

P

R

T

Z